Die boek dra ek op
aan Duane en Anton
in die hemel, het begin
moeg word vir my digte
swaar pad dan het wysheid
my weer herinner dat ek
by hemel gesê het ek sal die
boodskap vir almal bring
dat Jesus leef. hy sê hy is
hy is verseker oppad sal
jy asb hierdie boek lees
het baie baie swaar gehad
toe die vyand my werk
wou doodmaak en ook vir my.
luister asb jy moet bloedlyn
vloeke breek het het beleer
toe hulle ruur ruur het
het ek beleef my ma beveg
en my pa beveg saam. Heilige
Gees het vir my bevry deur
Jesus se bloed. het bevryding
hy Jesus is lewend. bloed
van Jesus het my gered.
Duane het brug het vir
my werklik waar gevra om
vir sy ma en pa te se hy
is baie baie gelukkig beseen
het hy wat gebly het vir my.

I dedicate this book to Duane and Anton in heaven. My difficult and painful road here on earth started wearing me down, but then Wisdom reminded me of what I had said in heaven: that I would bring the message that Jesus is alive to everyone. He says He is definitely on His way.

Will you please read this book? It was very, very difficult for me when the enemy tried to kill me, and in the process tried to stop my work.

Please listen to me; you must break your bloodline curses. I experienced fire – fire from hell – because of bloodline curses. My Mom and Dad are fighting for me. Holy Spirit delivered me through Jesus' blood and now I am set free. Jesus is truly alive. The blood of Jesus saved me.

Duane asked me on the bridge to tell his mom and his dad that he is very happy where he is now. He who stayed behind blessed me.

Published by McPherson House

McPherson House
PO Box 793
Hartbeespoort
0216
South Africa

Tel: +27 (0)82 610 5757
E-mail: office@retahmcpherson.com

To order: www.retahmcpherson.com
Or: www.amazon.com

Copyright: © Retah McPherson
First edition: December 2010
Second edition: December 2011
ISBN number: 978-1-920363-60-4

Consulting publisher: Maranatha Christian Publishing
Translation and Editing: Maranatha Christian Publishing
Editing: McPherson House

9 781920 363604

a message of

hope

Retah & Aldo
McPherson

Index

Thank you

Preface

Chapter:

Thank You

I am standing next to my Abba Father, and He is showing me my earthly Father: "Retah, this is the Father I chose especially for you – the best. No one is perfect, but his love for you has always been sincere."

That is why I want to say today: THANK YOU SO VERY MUCH DAD!

Thank you that you were willing to go for counselling and deliverance at such a late stage of your life, and that you were willing to turn your back on racism completely.

It was a groundbreaking act of obedience for someone of your generation and it will set an example for many others who are still caught up in the tradition, ignorance and darkness of racism. By humbling yourself before God and by repenting and turning away from it, I could see how much you love us.

THANK YOU – for unconditionally laying down your life for Jesus. That was the greatest gift you could have ever given me. I honour you for it Dad, and I love you very much.

Abba Father, Jesus and Holy Spirit – I honour You for leading us safely on our journey through life, and that You are with us every step of the way.

I love You; You are truly the God of love.

Retah

Preface

It has been six years since our accident *2004* and only now has Abba lifted the veil that had been blinding me.

Although I was in full time ministry and serving the Lord with all my heart, mind and soul, we weren't experiencing any breakthroughs in our physical circumstances with regard to Aldo's health. It was as if death's tentacles were slowly tightening its grip around us. The spirit of death and destruction was resting upon us and we didn't even realise it.

I desperately cried out to the Lord for answers, "Lord, how can I minister to people and help them while I am losing the spiritual battle in my own home?" After many nights of humbling myself before the Lord and calling out to Him, He led us through His Spirit to the book of Nehemiah. The Lord revealed to me through this book that the walls of our souls, just like the walls of Jerusalem, were broken down and destroyed. As the veil began to lift from our eyes, we could discern what the root of evil was and deal with it. Our renewed understanding led us to a road of healing and restoration which held many valleys and mountains for us to cross; however, we developed perseverance, character and hope as we journeyed on this painful road to its end.

Not only so, but we also glory in our sufferings, because we know that suffering produces perseverance; perseverance, character; and character, hope. And hope does not put us to shame, because God's love has been poured out into our hearts through the Holy Spirit, who has been given to us.
- Romans 5:3-5 -

I was the one who had preached from pulpits that bloodline curses are of the Old Testament and that Jesus had already done away with it on the cross. This was only partly true. Yes, Jesus had died for all our sin and He conquered the enemy on the cross, but we have to apply the blood of the Lamb to the doorframes of our hearts and lives. We do so by bowing our knees – humbling ourselves before God – and by breaking the curses through repentance.

My family and I were bound by the spirit of death and destruction because of a bloodline curse resting on our lives, which came through the iniquities of the generations before us. Step by step "Wisdom" (as Aldo calls the Holy Spirit in his letters) taught us how to break the grip of the spirit of death and destruction. It was a spiritual battle that could only be won by love.

The result was greater and more far-reaching than I could ever have dreamed of. Once the veil of ignorance, pride, tradition and self-justification that was hanging over us was finally lifted, Aldo's breakthroughs came swiftly because we engaged in the battle with a God-given vision and perspective. Even my own heart that was hardened by all the pain we had to endure because of our difficult walk of faith, was replaced with a gentle heart that could be moulded and transformed by Jesus' hands. Today I look through Jesus' eyes at people who still don't want to believe the complete truth concerning the reality of this spiritual battle. Because I had been there too, I never point a finger in judgment at anyone – I'd rather stretch out my hands to help them, so that they do not have to waste time as we did.

Our walk made me realise that it isn't our words, or the church we belong to, or even our good works that make us followers of Jesus – but only our hearts that love the King. God looks at how I speak to my husband, how I take care of my little Josh and how I treat Aldo, who is His prophet. It is important to Him that I stretch out His hands of love to embrace them; that I help Aldo up with His arms of comfort when he stumbles, and that I encourage others with His gentle voice of forgiveness instead of judging them. Through His eyes, I can see that the woman who quietly serves others by washing cups in the kitchen, deserves just as much recognition as the one standing on the stage bringing the message. Through His eyes I see that we can experience joy in the midst of a storm, and with His joy I can embrace life even if my circumstances aren't perfect. Through His eyes I can support and encourage my dad while he is going through the process of being set free from the mindset and traditions of racism, rather than condemning him for every little mistake that he still makes from time to time.

Only by God's power and His grace am I able to stretch out my hand to anyone who is still caught up in pornography, racism, addiction, lust, fits of anger, homosexuality, fear, depression, or whatever the heartache might be – and I can say with passionate confidence, "There is always hope!" I also had to walk a difficult and painful road to freedom, and that is why I can testify with absolute certainty: "Jesus is alive, and His blood has made it possible for us to walk in victory and live our lives completely in His light!" I never experienced God's love – His pure unconditional love – the way I did during those painful trials.

In Him I have discovered the river of life and the abundance of the treasures that awaits us there. I used to believe these were treasures that I had to earn through my good works, but my faith is now anchored in the assurance: If God is for me, who can be against me? It was in the river of life that God's rays of grace shone upon me and overwhelmed me with the greatness of His power and love. I realised that EVERYTHING I needed for every, single area of my life (creativity, wisdom, peace, healing, blessing), could be found in Him. In the river of life I discovered the freedom to simply love God. Cool streams of life began to flow over our family, and the triune God allowed His rays of healing to shine over Aldo and over our broken hearts. These rays of grace are there for everyone.

Today my family and I dance barefoot to the melody of God's music for our lives. We dance together in the glorious light of this forgiving and loving God of ours. The Father, Son and Holy Spirit is alive in our conversations, in our togetherness and in our everyday lives – from ministering to people and travelling across the world, to being a mother and cuddling with Zozzie before he falls asleep. I feel the rhythm of His music in Aldo's tight hugs as he wraps his long arms around me, in the passion with which I enjoy my husband, and in the new way I appreciate my parents. I am aware of dancing to God's music when I am laughing with friends over the mistakes I have made, or when the comforting presence of the Holy Spirit brings me to tears while I'm praying. His music is in the colours of the rainbow that I see when I drive home after work, and (above all) in the love for my Abba, Jesus and Holy Spirit that overwhelms my heart – that is the dance of life that is rich in love, passion, creativity and joy. And it is found in the simplicity of everyday life.

There is freedom in His love! Come and join me in the dance!

Retah

Hy @ te Aldo my kinders
het my verseerker geros. Wat
is my werk? Ek wil hê jy
moet sewe jaar lank sterf
in jouself jy moet help
om ander se lewe na my
te draai. Sal jy verandering
wat met jou gebeur gebruik
om siele te wen vir my.
Jy is wat ek wil gebruik
want mense is te besig
met hulle self. help. met
nehemia se muur. Aldo,
jy sal versoek word deur
vyand self want hy wil
hie hê jy moet die muur
bou nie Jesus werk saam
met jou jy moet help
nehemia want wie sal ek
vra nehemia wat jy moet
weet is wat jy nou so seer
maak is reeds oorwin. Satan
is verslaan nou veg ek vir
jou. Aldo sê vir help hou, help
is, help is hou, help is hou,
hou aan vertrou in my. Wak
is jou werk Aldo jy voel
hulle steel jou lewe maar jy
het lewe jy het lewe in my.
Wag het in muur moet gebou
word en jy sal nie kan
stop nie.

Then He said, "Aldo, my children have certainly left Me".

"What is my work?" I asked.

"I want you to die in self for seven years. You must help others to turn their lives to Me. Will you use the transformation that you went through to win souls for Me? You are the one I want to use, because people are too busy with their own lives. Help build Nehemiah's wall. Aldo, you will be tempted by the enemy himself, because he doesn't want you to build the wall.

Jesus is working with you – you must help Nehemiah, because who else will I ask? Nehemiah, you need to know that what is hurting you so much has already been overcome. Satan is defeated, and now I am fighting for you. Aldo say to them that help is on its way. Keep on trusting in Me. What is your job, Aldo? You feel as if they are stealing your life, but your life is in Me. Just wait, a wall has to be built and you won't be able to stop."

Chapter 1

nehemia sê vir volk hulle is
besig om waaclik hulle tie ek
te volg in plaas van hulle
mev hulle God Jehova. Sy
liefde is groot wat my so
vashou nou. het jy gesien
mev wat ek gesien het. baie
engele om ons. gesien hoe jy
kyk toe hulle jou vashou en
beskerm gister aand. Jy sê nooit
jy sien hulle nie, hoekom nie?
Wysh. sê alles wat jy verseen
wat jy seen verander mom.
Hoekom seer so erg mom
as jy weet God is by ons?
help my asb baie seer hart
maar Jesus sê hy sal my
nie los nie. hy sê hy sal
nie n geknakte riet breek nie.
Jy sê engele is van God. ek
kan sien as jy hulle sien.
Josh is so bly oor die vere
in sy kamer hulle blink want
hulle is vol glory. waarom is
jy so stil vanhaand. bly
ek voel beter want baie
engele om ons.

Nehemiah, tell the nation that they are chasing after their selfish desires rather than following God – Jehovah. He is holding me close to Him now. His love for us is so great. Did you see what I saw, Ma'am? I saw many angels around us. I saw how you were looking at them last night while they were helping and protecting you. Why don't you ever say that you can see them? Wisdom says that everything you bless changes, Mom. Why are you hurting so much if you know that God is with us?

Please help me! My heart is aching, but Jesus says that He will never leave me. He says that He will not break a bruised reed.

You say that the angels are from God. I can see when you see them. Josh is so happy about the feathers in his room. They are shining because they are covered in glory. Why are you so quiet tonight? I am so glad that I am feeling better, because there are many angels around us.

Acknowledge God's presence in difficult times

> God did this so that, by two unchangeable things in which it is impossible for God to lie, we who have fled to take hold of the hope offered to us may be greatly encouraged. We have this hope as an anchor for the soul, firm and secure. It enters the inner sanctuary behind the curtain.
> *- Hebrews 6:18-19 -*

This is a message of hope for all who have been in a valley of despair and knows what it feels like when every glimmer of hope seems to fade. Hope anchors us in the expectation that God will be faithful to His Word and His promises. It is our anchor when the storms are raging.

They are fighting against your hope, but they know they are defeated.

My only hope is Jesus. He will help me.

Life subjects each one of us to different tests and trials. When we are put to these tests, we experience the fire of God. It is a purification process through which our hearts are refined like gold. The ultimate purpose of this purification process is to reveal another dimension of God's love and truth to us. Although the tests we face are seldom similar, the fact of the matter is that in one way or another we will all experience the fire of trials in our lives – there is no escaping it.

geweet mev as jy nie hier deur het jy gaan nie sal jy nie weet wie is jou vyand nie.

Do you know, Ma'am, if you didn't go through all of this you would never have known who your enemy is?

Our family went through a painful purification process. It was six years since the accident, but the attacks on Aldo's life became fiercer and we were forced to search even deeper for the root of the problem. In a moment of despair I cried out to God: "What more do I still have to go through before the fiery trial comes to an end, Lord?" We served the Lord, we followed Him and our lives were sold out to Him... so why didn't the onslaught of the enemy stop?

Since the accident in 2004 Aldo shares a very intimate relationship with the Holy Spirit. "Wisdom" (as Aldo refers to the Holy Spirit) reveals prophetic messages to him that he then writes down. Even while all these amazing things were happening, Aldo still suffered at the hand of Satan's attacks. "What right did Satan have to attack us on every level of Aldo's life and health?" was the question I repeatedly asked myself. I never realised how fiercely the spiritual battle was raging – it truly was a battle of life or death.

wysheid jou verstaan jy hoe leer van die geesdimensie.

Do you understand that Wisdom is teaching you about the spirit realm?

The more I asked Abba Father to let the light of His glory shine on every aspect of our lives, the more clearly I began to see the hidden doors through which the enemy could gain access. Once we realised how the enemy manoeuvred, the light and the darkness started colliding on a big scale as we began resisting his onslaughts.

The doors through which the enemy enters into our lives take on many different forms. It might be doors of unconfessed or obstinate sin – things that we are unwilling to let go of, or sin that we turn a blind eye to. It can be doors of unconfessed sin of the generations before us (ancestral sin) and curses (bloodline curses) that still have an active outworking in our lives. It can even be doors which have been opened because of the occult, witchcraft and word curses; which most of us know very little about.

23

by bewuste sonde is 'n groot deur

Wilful sin is a big door.

There was a time when I didn't want to know anything about these things that had their foundation in the kingdom of darkness. This made it more difficult for me to be set free, because my own naivety, ignorance and unbelief kept me from dealing with the root of the problem. I thought that if I left the demons alone, they would leave me alone. How wrong I was! I was ignorant in believing that because I had accepted Jesus as my Lord and Saviour, all the doors that could grant the enemy entrance into my life were automatically closed. What I didn't understand was that even though Jesus paid the full price for me when He died on the cross, I still had to use the keys of the Kingdom to close the doors that were standing open to the enemy (Matt. 16:19). I knew very little about the evil forces that exist in the spiritual realm, and I also didn't *want* to believe that they could attack me, a child of God, if I left the doors open. I didn't know that the doors of trauma, pain, rejection and fear could give the enemy access to steal and destroy in my life. So can pride, hatred, bitterness, unforgiveness, rejection, selfishness, self-hatred, and inner vows (to name but a few).

> But if you harbour bitter envy and selfish ambition in your hearts, do not boast about it or deny the truth. Such "wisdom" does not come down from heaven but is earthly, unspiritual, **of the devil**. For where you have envy and selfish ambition, there you find disorder and every evil practice.
> - *James 3:14-16 (emphesis mine)* -

Wysh sê wat hulle bly is trauma

God sê wie enige haat in hulle het sal nie ingaan nie.

Wisdom says where they [the demons] are living is trauma. God says whoever has any hatred in them will not go in.

Soul ties can also be an open door. An *ungodly* soul tie can be the result of any relationship of which Jesus is not the Lord and Master. The closer you are to that person, the stronger the soul tie is. This applies to familial relationships, friendships and especially the ties between people who have slept together. The Bible gives us a stern warning about sexual immorality and the effect it has on us: *"Or do you not know that he who is joined to a harlot is one body with her? For 'the two,' He says, 'shall become one flesh'"* (1 Cor. 6:16, NKJV). Through an ungodly soul tie you are influenced by what happens in the other person's life, especially on an emotional level. As long as the soul tie stays unbroken you can't seem to "let go" of that person. This is why it is common for a person to still think or dream of an ex-lover many years after the relationship has ended.

✳ Then there are also bloodline curses that originate from ancestral sin. These curses grant the enemy easy access into our lives because so many Christians never deal with this issue, or even know that it is operating in their lives.

It is written in Exodus: *"For I, the Lord your God, am a jealous God, punishing the children for the sin of the fathers to the third and fourth generation of those who hate me, but showing love to a thousand [generations] of those who love me and keep my commandments"* (Ex. 20:5b-6).

From this Scripture we learn that our "spiritual DNA" (our spiritual heritage) can either be a blessing or a curse. It is sadly true that disobedience without confession can lead to curses and iniquities that will influence your children, their children, their grandchildren, and so on. (Later in this book I will address these issues in more detail.)

However, we must remember that sin, sickness and death entered the world after the fall of man in the Garden of Eden, and that Satan was given authority because of Adam's disobedience. Therefore, bad things sometimes happen to us that we just don't have the answers to. But if we turn to Jesus in our pain, the outcome will be for the glory of God. The healing of the blind man is a good example of this:

> As he went along, he saw a man blind from birth. His disciples asked him, "Rabbi, who sinned, this man or his parents, that he was born blind?" "Neither this man nor his parents sinned," said Jesus, "but this happened so that the work of God might be displayed in his life. As long as it is day, we must do the work of him who sent me. Night is coming, when no one can work. While I am in the world, I am the light of the world."
> - John 9:1-5 -

The good news to the children of God is that we can live in genuine freedom because of the sovereignty of Jesus Christ as the King of kings. This applies to our past, present and also our future. The grace of God and the blood of the Lamb work actively in our lives when we close the doors to the enemy and apply the blood to the doorpost of our hearts through repentance. The Blood of Jesus holds the power to break any ungodly soul tie and to annul any curse, and it enables us to live in His fullness as children of the light.

> Grace and peace be yours in abundance through the knowledge of God and of Jesus our Lord. His divine power has given us everything we need for a godly life through our knowledge of him who called us by his own glory and goodness. Through these he has given us his very great and precious promises, so that through them you may participate in the divine nature, having escaped the corruption in the world caused by evil desires.
> - 2 Peter 1:2-4 -

We have to use the keys of the Kingdom of God to lock that which has to be locked and open that which has to be opened. This can only happen once the Holy Spirit shines the light of God's glory on those doors that give the enemy access into our lives through unconfessed sin or unbroken curses. It is in this glorious light that everyone can find freedom – for the truth will set us free.

> I am sending you to them to open their eyes and turn them from darkness to light, and from the power of Satan to God, so that they may receive forgiveness of sins and a place among those who are sanctified by faith in me.
> - Acts 26:17b-18 -

When we surrender to Abba Father whilst enduring these afflictions, He will use them to develop our character and to mature us. Even if we should find ourselves in the valley of the shadow of death, we do not have to fear, because He has promised to protect and comfort us. If we surrender all to Him, He will send His Holy Spirit to guide us over mountains and through valleys, until we reach the place where we meet God face to face.

My face to face meeting with God was at a place of complete brokenness and humility. This is where I reached the end of my striving and where I had to die to self. The selfish "me, myself and I" that always wanted to be in control and call the shots had to be crucified. It is only once you have reached this place that you realise you can't rely on human wisdom or the arm of the flesh, but that God and God alone is your refuge and your strength.

> I have been crucified with Christ; it is no longer I who live, but Christ lives in me; and the life which I now live in the flesh I live by faith in the Son of God, who loved me and gave Himself for me.
> - Galatians 2:20, NKJV -

waar sal my hulp vandaan
kom my hulp is van Hom
wat hemel en aarde gemaak
het.
Wysh se my hulp is van god
baie help sal my hulp is
hom wat hemel en aarde. deur
wat moet ek nog gaan voor
my werk kan begin. Wysh se
hy is by my elke elke tree
Wat ek gee hy se rgand se
be planning was om my so moeg
te maak maar hy se my werk
is te groot wat ek moet gaan
doen hy se my werk sal nou begin

Where shall my help come from? My help comes from Him who made heaven and earth. Wisdom says my help is from God – a lot of help comes from Him who made heaven and earth. What more do I still have to go through before my ministry can begin? Wisdom says He is with me every step of the way. He says it was the enemy's plan to make me tired, but the work that I am going to do is too great [for him to stop]. He says my work will start now.

It was only the love of God that carried us through the valley that we had to cross, and during that time I clearly heard the Holy Spirit say: "Retha, your miracle's name is LOVE."

The intimate place of worship you experience with the Lord in the valley – when you are bowed down with your face to the ground, calling out to God and reaching out to Him with all that is within you – is the place where you encounter your burning bush, just like Moses did. When your eyes meet His, you will have no doubt that you are standing on holy ground. Suddenly you will experience that the love with which He fills your spirit is much greater than the pain that brought you to this place of total surrender. You will encounter the fire of God's love, and there, with your face to the ground before your Abba Father, He will anoint your head with oil and the fragrance of His love will fill your whole being. In the manifested presence of the Living God something happens deep inside your spirit. This first-hand revelation of God's love is what I call a "kiss" from Abba. Nothing and nobody can ever wipe away that kiss. That which He reveals to you at that moment will be seared in your spirit forever.

When you encounter the presence of God, His blood flows through your veins, His light floods your spirit and He renews your body, soul and spirit. It is at this place where the scorching flame of the fiery trial is turned into the blue fire of God's love (the hottest part of the flame) and where He fills us with the Holy Spirit and with fire. The more we allow this fire to purify our lives, the more insight we will receive, and the greater our progress and spiritual growth will be. The truths that He reveals to us while we are in the flame will cause our spiritual eyes and ears to be opened. The Holy Spirit will guide us along a road of sanctification that will lead to inner healing and restoration; a road that will require of us to search our own hearts. Peter wrote about this and said:

"Dear friends, do not be surprised at the painful trial you are suffering, as though something strange were happening to you. But rejoice that you participate in the sufferings of Christ, so that you may be overjoyed when his glory is revealed."
- 1 Peter 4:12-13 -

Weet mamma ons sal Jesus wil gelukkig maak as ons weet wat Hy vir ons gedoen het aan die kruis.

Do you know Mommy – it will be our desire to make Jesus happy if we really understood what He did for us on the cross.

Aldo praying at our house.

The deeper I look into Jesus' eyes the more I find myself kneeling at the foot of the cross in humility and thankfulness. Here I receive forgiveness *and* healing *and* absolution through the sacrifice of love that was made through His body and His blood. It is when I behold the enormity of what Jesus did for me on the cross that I want to turn my back on the past and the sin that keeps me from His presence. Because He loved me first, I now want to forgive those who have hurt me and bless them with the love of Jesus. There, in the presence of God, is where the light of His glory – His *shekinah** – drives away the darkness.

> nehemia sē vir volk hulle is
> besig om waarlik hulle eie ek
> te volg in plaas van hulle
> god Jehova.

Nehemiah, tell the people that they are truly following after their own selfish desires rather than after God – Jehovah.

---

*Shekinah is a Hebrew word which suggests God's weighty, palpable presence.

Up to this point our road had been difficult and steep and I often found myself face down before God, calling out to Him with all my might. Through all the hurt and suffering I constantly felt the fire of God falling on me. The enemy wants to use the flame of our trials and tribulations to destroy us, but as we surrender our pain to God, He turns these situations around and He uses the flames to refine us rather than to destroy us. As the fire was burning away the "selfish I," I could feel the Holy Spirit imprinting more and more of His image upon my life. To "live right" was no longer a legalistic thing, but I started to "live holy" (Christ in me and I in Him) without striving; it just became part of my nature. I was no longer living according to a list of do's and dont's to please God, rather my life became focussed on *surrendering* and *trusting* Him.

I kept pleading with Abba to let His glory light shine on all the darkness in my life, because I realised that evil can only breed in darkness. Pain and darkness usually go hand in hand, but in His shekinah light healing and restoration comes as the works of darkness are exposed and dealt with.

As soon as we started to search for these open doors by using the light of God's truth, it felt as if all hell had broken loose. The light shone on everything that was hidden right under our noses. The worst of it all was that I had never even recognised the presence of the darkness before. "How could you *not* have seen it until now, Retha?" I chastised myself over and over again. I understood much later, that it was like trying to explain the colour purple to someone who had been born blind – I had no framework to understand how the spiritual realm operated, and my ignorance and naivety kept me spiritually blinded to the truth. Once I became aware of how the enemy operated, I could act upon it.

> Be self-controlled and alert. Your enemy the devil prowls around like a roaring lion looking for someone to devour.
> - I Peter 5:8 -

The Apostle Peter so clearly warns us through this Scripture that the enemy is constantly seeking to devour us, but still, we are so naive that we don't recognise the works of the enemy even when our lives and our families fall apart; we'd rather still look to find the answer in a medical prescription.

While I am quietly sitting here for a moment, thinking how to end the introduction to this book and prepare the readers for what is to come, the Holy Spirit is reminding me of the words with which God had called me into ministry: "Retha, you will only preach what you have tasted for yourself." Today I know the immense implication of these words; but I also know that it is undoubtedly true: we cannot give advice, comfort others or testify about anything, if we hadn't yet experienced it firsthand for ourselves – that goes for the good as well as the bad. My family and I first had to taste it for ourselves, before I could share the lessons we had learned with you today.

> The night is nearly over; the day is almost here. So let us put aside the deeds of darkness and put on the armour of light.
> - Romans 13:12 -

The more the works of darkness were revealed by the light, the more I realised how ill-equipped and untrained I was to fight the battle. In fact, I had *no* knowledge of this spiritual battle or even of its existence! I felt like a soldier meeting the enemy armed with a plastic sword that I didn't know how to use. Another reason for my inadequate training was because I approached these kinds of topics with a raised eyebrow. I used to be very sceptical about things that I considered to be "overly spiritual", and I thought that fanatics were looking for a demon behind every bush.

waar is jy mom want
wysheid sê jy huil
Gaan heeltemal gesond
word wat sy loek sê is
waar God is God hy is
my bybel mg lewe.

Where are you, Mom? Because Wisdom says you are crying. I will be healed completely. What His book says is true. God is God. He is my Bible – my life.

"Abba Father," I pled with God, "why has Aldo never written anything about this spiritual battle before?"

God answered me and said, "Because your unbelief and scepticism about the works of the kingdom of darkness were in the way, Retha. You were not teachable and therefore you wouldn't have received what I wanted to reveal to you."

"But Lord, I don't think I am called to be a soldier in Your army. I'd much rather preach. I don't even know how to fight!" I exclaimed.

31

"Retha," replied the Lord, "I am returning for a spirit Bride, a servant Bride, and a warrior Bride. If you choose to follow Me, I will teach you what you need to know." Then I heard the Lord asking me this life changing question: "*If you have raced with men on foot and they have worn you out, how can you compete with horses?*" (Jer. 12:5)

God gaan ons oprig as warriors. Jesus se wat warrior bruid het is 'n swaard. Jy veg met jou Swaard – sy Woord.

God will raise us up as warriors. Jesus says that the warrior Bride has a sword. You fight with your sword – His Word.

Jeremia 12
God se hardloop

Jeremiah 12. God says run.

"Retha, life consists of choices. You have to choose today – do you want to be a show horse or do you want to run with the wild horses? My dear child, the show horse lifestyle has kept you away from My truth. You were living only for yourself... your will; your plans, your interests, and your reputation were all that mattered. The flames of the trials you are facing now are causing you a lot of momentary pain, but I will use that which the enemy has meant for evil and I will turn it around for your good.

"I will equip you and train you, so that you can be a part of My latter day army. I will teach you how to take possession of the Promised Land and how to overcome the giants. You are not alone in this battle. The enemy has been attacking My children, and it is time that they take up the sword of the Spirit and fight back.

"I will teach you how to be a warrior in the army of light so that you can force back the gates of hell and fight the powers of the air in the spirit realm – so that the prisoners can be released."

I always thought these prisoners were people I didn't know, people far removed from my world. Today I know that at one time or another every one of us was (or still is) a prisoner – you and I, my children, your children, my parents, your parents, my family and loved ones, your family and loved ones. That is why God is raising, anointing, and training His children in this last hour to proclaim with a prophetic fire: *Break the chains! Shine a light in the darkness – set the prisoners free!*

His light will drive the darkness away. This is the fire that God wants to release over His children in order to purify us. It will enable us to pick up the sword of the Spirit and fight for our loved ones and for ourselves. The fact that our doors of ignorance and unbelief stood open for so long made it very easy for the enemy to do to us as he pleased. We posed no threat to him! God wants His bride to be equipped with His fire; and this fire will only be found in His presence.

Hear the sound of the trumpet: *"Arise, shine, for your light has come, and the glory of the Lord rises upon you. See, darkness covers the earth and thick darkness is over the peoples, but the Lord rises upon you and his glory appears over you"* (Isa. 60:1-2).

Stand up! It is time for you to stand your ground against the enemy; it is time for you to take a hold of God's promises and live them; and it is time for you to put on your armour, because God wants to reveal Himself through you to a hurting world.

Here Jesus is verseker jou warrior hy sal vir jou veg. hy is jou warrior gebruik jou wapenrusting

The Lord Jesus is definitely your warrior. He will fight for you. He is your warrior.

Use your armour.

The Holy Spirit led Aldo to the book of Nehemiah and in so many of his letters he wrote to me that I should learn from Nehemiah. Initially I had no idea what Aldo meant by this, but today I know that Nehemiah's message is to *build* and *fight*. I had to learn how to build a wall of protection around myself and my family in the spirit, while at the same time holding a weapon in the other hand to resist the enemy (see Neh. 4:17).

This book is our testimony of the great spiritual battle of life and death that the Lord led us through. Together as a family we built a wall like Nehemiah's around us, to protect us in the spiritual realm from the dangers and the temptations of the kingdom of darkness. We had previously been unaware of the "holes in our wall" that granted the enemy access into our lives from where he was able to steal from us, but by the grace of God we have fortified the weak areas and now stand as watchman on the walls.

All the glory to God for our victory in the Spirit!

my Koning vra van almal hy
vra bly glo al sien julle niks.

My King asks of everybody: keep on believing, even if you don't see anything.

Chapter 2

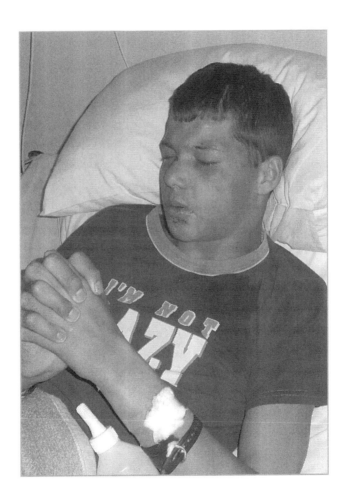

Wysh se veg vir my asb mom ek
sal gesond word. gewone mense
is wie jy sal help hy sê jy sal
sien wat jy was is mev nie wat
hy wou hê nie hy wil hê jy moet
van vyand wat wil doodmaak, steel
en verwoes vertel sodat jy gereed
kan wees vir wat wag hy sê
rewival wag vir wev se bediening
hy sê jy verstaan sy bloed
hy sê rewival sal net gebeur
wanneer sy bloed verstaan
Wysh sê jy moet vertel van
wat gebeur het gister sy bloed
wat my lewe gered het. Gelyk
was wat het nou gebeur hy
is hier by wysh sê jy is een
met hom. hy is by jou wat
het jy nou gesien mom. Lewe
is in jou oë ek was hele dag
by Jesus hy sê die gebed
wat jy bid is wat hulle
hande bind hy sê hulle kon
niks aan my nou gesien hoe
hulle vlug toe jy bid. hy sê jy
is vir vyand brand. Wysheid sê
moenie luister na mense nie
hulle sal jou wil bespreek hy
sê jy het werklik vertrou
hy sê jy het hom vir deurbraak
gevra. mom dis hier.

Wisdom is asking you to fight for me, please Mom. I will be healthy again. You will help ordinary people. He says that you will see that what you once were, is not what He wanted you to be. He wants you to tell people about the enemy who kills, steals and destroys, so they can be prepared for what is awaiting us. He says that revival is waiting for your ministry, Ma'am. He says you understand His blood. He says revival will only take place when people understand His blood. Wisdom says you must tell people what happened yesterday – that His blood saved my life. What happened now? He is here with us. Wisdom says you are one with Him. He is with you. What did you see now, Mom? There is life in your eyes. I was with Jesus the whole day and He says the prayer that you prayed bound their hands. He says they can't do anything to me now. I saw them flee when you prayed. He says you are fire to the enemy. Wisdom says you shouldn't listen to people. They will want to discuss [gossip about] you. He says you really trust Him. He says that you asked Him for breakthrough. Mom, it is here.

Run with hope

In our book *A Message of Faith*, I concluded by saying that I dared to trust God for a great miracle. I had to keep on believing despite of what I was seeing in the natural through my circumstances, because if I had to evaluate Aldo's physical condition by worldly standards, his healing seemed absolutely impossible. I did not build my hope on the opinion of the world, for I was (and always will be) serving the living God for whom nothing is impossible! Nothing is too difficult for Him, and because I knew how much He loves me, I knew I could trust Him.

hy vra vir my of ek sal wag totdat hy hele plan uitgevoer het. God sê hy sal alles gedoen wat hy belowe het.

He asks me if I will wait until He has completed His entire plan. God says He will do everything He promised.

While I was writing that book, Aldo was still suffering from epileptic fits. After every fit he wrote that Lucifer had been in the room. That alone drove me up the walls, because I could not understand what Lucifer would be doing in our house!

wagte word kwaad as ek skryf. hulle het epelepsie vir my gegee. Lewe is in Jesus.

The guards [demons] become angry when I write. They are causing my epilepsy.

Life is in Jesus.

With every attack I still failed to see the pattern. I believed that Aldo's epilepsy was caused by the brain injury and resigned myself to the fact that it was a medical condition. I even became angry when people from across the world sent me e-mails suggesting that demons might be causing these attacks, as described in Mark:

> A man in the crowd answered, "Teacher, I brought you my son, who is possessed by a spirit that has robbed him of speech. Whenever it seizes him, it throws him to the ground. He foams at the mouth, gnashes his teeth and becomes rigid. I asked your disciples to drive out the spirit, but they could not."
>
> "O unbelieving generation," Jesus replied, "how long shall I stay with you? How long shall I put up with you? Bring the boy to me."
>
> So they brought him. When the spirit saw Jesus, it immediately threw the boy into a convulsion. He fell to the ground and rolled around, foaming at the mouth.
>
> Jesus asked the boy's father, "How long has he been like this?"
>
> "From childhood," he answered. "It has often thrown him into fire or water to kill him. But if you can do anything, take pity on us and help us."
>
> "'If you can'?" said Jesus. "Everything is possible for him who believes."
>
> Immediately the boy's father exclaimed, "I do believe; help me overcome my unbelief!"
>
> When Jesus saw that a crowd was running to the scene, he rebuked the evil spirit. "You deaf and mute spirit," he said, "I command you, come out of him and never enter him again."
>
> The spirit shrieked, convulsed him violently and came out. The boy looked so much like a corpse that many said, "He's dead." But Jesus took him by the hand and lifted him to his feet, and he stood up.
> - Mark 9:17-27 -

"How can people be so cruel?" I wondered as I was reading their letters. "Don't they realise that Aldo has an intimate relationship with God? He is a Christian…a child of God! How can he have a demon?"

I decided to ignore the letters, yet there was one thought that I couldn't shake off and that kept on bothering me: "Aldo only started having the epileptic fits three years after the accident. He made miraculous progress during those first three years – so he should be getting better, not worse…"

Anybody who has ever seen an epileptic fit will know that it breaks a parent's heart to see their child so helpless and in such pain. With every attack that came, I desperately prayed and cried out to Abba to deliver Aldo from it. We concluded our previous book where the Holy Spirit led us to have a shunt inserted into his brain. This apparatus controls the fluid levels in his brain and any excess fluid is drained into his stomach through a tube. His health improved remarkably after the insertion of the shunt and the epilepsy stopped for a time. I was therefore convinced that Aldo's epilepsy was a medical condition rather than a spiritual attack on his life.

Wysh sê Grein seer seer seer
hou asb aan seën my brein.
Jesus beveg vir my hy sê
niks kan my uit sy hand
uit ruk nie.

Wisdom says my brain is hurting, hurting, hurting. Please keep on blessing my brain. Jesus is fighting for me. He says nothing can take me out of His hands.

After the shunt was inserted it still wasn't smooth sailing. A few times we had to rush him to the hospital because he became extremely disorientated, confused and agitated (but without the epileptic fits) – a clear indication that something was wrong with the fluid levels in his brain. The doctors would then adjust the shunt's pressure or unblock the tube in his stomach. Because there was always a medical explanation for Aldo's behaviour I downplayed these episodes time and again as being a normal physical reaction to his brain injury.

The first shunt was inserted in December 2008, but it wasn't until December 2009, that we realised what was actually transpiring in the spiritual realm. What an eye-opener it was for me (bearing in mind that I was by then in full-time ministry - addressing audiences weekend after weekend telling them about Jesus Christ), to realise that my child who had such an intimate relationship with God and a extraordinary prophetic gifting, was plagued by demons! I was devastated and didn't know what to do! I did know one thing for sure: I could trust God – He would be my help and my salvation. I started crying out to Abba to let His glorious light shine upon our lives. I realised that only God would be able help us through this – and believe me, He did!

(Please remember that this was the road we had to walk, but that every situation is unique. If your child is suffering from epilepsy it might purely be a medical condition. I don't presume to know how everything works; all I can testify to, is what I have experienced myself; and today I know that Aldo's epileptic fits were demonic attacks on his life.)

What makes it possible for me to share all these truths with you is the knowledge that God was in control all the time and that He carried us through. Even though Aldo was attacked in his soul and body, his spirit was still safely in God's hands. His spirit was inextricably joined with Abba Father because he is a born again believer – the enemy couldn't touch that, because he belongs to Jesus Christ. Even in the heat of the battle the Holy Spirit continued to guide Aldo in his writings. It is true: nothing can take you from the Father's hand, and nothing can separate you from the love of Christ (see Rom. 8:35-39).

Like the peeling of an onion, "Wisdom" revealed the truth to us layer by layer. Sometimes the process felt very slow (too slow for my liking), but today I realise how necessary the continuous process of refining and restoration was; I don't think we would have been able to handle everything at once. You have to get to the root of the problem and remove it with the axe of God – His Word and His truth. By only pruning the fruits you will never achieve the complete victory.

"Why were the demons able to attack Aldo?" This was the first and foremost question that raced through my mind once I realised that the problem had its origin in the spiritual realm all the while and was not due to medical complications as I had thought.

The enemy can only attack us if he can gain entrance to our lives through the doors we leave open to him; and these open doors are the dry, dark or weak places within the dimension of the soul – I like to call it the open doors of our soul.

halle keer vir my genesing.

They are trying to stop my healing.

After a lot of tears and many nights of endless praying, I came to terms with the fact that Aldo also had open doors through which the enemy gained a foothold, even though he had an intimate relationship with God. These doors were mainly open as a result of the trauma and rejection he suffered because of the accident. This realisation taught me a valuable lesson: your spirit can be healthy (reborn through Jesus Christ), but if your soul is wounded, inner healing *has* to take place or else the dark areas become a breeding place for the enemy.

hewige geveg my lewe is waaragter hulle is.

There is a heavy battle going on. They are seeking to take my life.

Because Aldo was in a coma for such a long time after the accident, we focused all our energy on keeping his body alive and never really worked through the emotional trauma with him. At that stage he was also unable to talk, so I never thought of dealing with it. Today I know that the sooner you attend to emotional wounds, the better. I just assumed that because my son had such amazing spiritual experiences with the Lord, that his soul was completely healthy, but in reality those invisible wounds in his soul were just as life-threatening as the physical wounds that nearly claimed his life. Therefore, do not ignore, make light of, or put a mask over your emotional wounds. Treat them with as much urgency as you would a wound that affects your physical health.

my trauma se begin is Wysh sê van ongeluk ek kan nie wat ek kon gedoen het

Wisdom says my trauma started because of the pain of the accident. I can't do what I used to do.

Thus Aldo's first door opened because of the *trauma* of the accident. He narrowly escaped death and obviously there was a tremendous amount of shock and fear involved. For a twelve year old boy it was too much to process.

The second door swung wide open because of the *rejection* he had to endure after the accident. Suddenly he looked very different to his friends and had to learn how to walk, talk and eat all over again. Even now he is still doing most things a little slower than other people.

Wysh sê vyand se deur vir my lewe is verwerping hy sê veg eers verwerping

Wisdom says that the door the enemy is using in my life is REJECTION. He says we must first fight rejection.

42

I remember once when I found him standing in front of the mirror forcing his left eye lid open with his hand, while trying his best to keep it open by itself. "What are you doing, Aldo?" I asked him when I walked into the room. "Just look at how red your eye is!" Shyly he answered me, "People always stare at me, Mom. I don't want to look different anymore."

Then there was the time when he gave a flower to a girl at school and she coolly told him, "No thanks Aldo, I already have a boyfriend." On another occasion he lost his balance when he walked up to a group of teenagers to say hello to them, and when he fell, everybody turned to him and laughed. Sometimes friends (or even adults) would simply turn around and start talking to someone else while Aldo is still in the middle of a sentence because he speaks so slowly. How could I have thought that these daily occurrences wouldn't affect him? This was the open door to his soul: *the door of rejection.*

In October 2009 the dire situation reached a new peak. Up to that point everything was simmering just below the surface, but we were never able to pinpoint the source of the problem. We went to various doctors seeking advice and help, but needless to say, they were unable to give us any answers.

While I was on a two-week ministry tour in the United States, Aldo was invited by a friend of his to attend a church event. We never used to allow Aldo to go to places on his own (Ma'am Patrys, Tinus or I always went along), but because the event was at a church Tinus agreed to it.

Initially everything went well, but as the evening progressed Aldo became increasingly agitated and his friend struggled to keep him calm. Little did they realise that something was stirring in the spirit. As they were leaving, a young African man came up to them while they were outside the building and asked if he could pray for Aldo. He proceeded to lay his hands on Aldo and started to pray in his mother tongue which neither Aldo nor his friend understood. Throughout the prayer, Aldo remained restless and felt uncomfortable.

That same night Aldo became very ill. He couldn't sleep and he was in so much pain that he started to hit his head against the wall.

When I returned from the United States I could see that Aldo clearly wasn't himself. He couldn't even speak and the few words he did manage to say were completely incoherent. Initially we thought that this episode was caused yet again by an imbalance of the fluid on his brain, but it soon became clear that the problem was far more complicated than that.

Two weekends later, while ministering in the Cape, I got an urgent call from Tinus. "Retha, Aldo is very, very ill. I am going to fly him down to Cape Town so that the specialist there can take a look at him. I have no idea what is wrong, but it is serious!"

How we met the specialist doctors in Cape Town, who have since become Aldo's surgeons, is another miracle in itself. They are sincere Christians who are walking this road of faith with us, and they truly understand Aldo's condition and his unique prophetic gift.

A small operation was performed to check if the shunt's tube in his stomach was blocked. No obstruction was found. They then took X-rays of his head, but the X-rays didn't show any abnormalities either. Tinus and Aldo had to return to Hartebeespoort without a solution.

When they arrived home, Aldo was even more confused and disoriented. That Sunday afternoon Tinus was home alone with the boys and the three of them were sitting in the family room when Aldo suddenly rushed towards the balcony without any prior warning. When I say *rush*, you have to keep in mind that Aldo usually walks very slowly and with difficulty, but this time he was moving determinately to the balcony, even if he was a bit wobbly.

Tinus wanted to stop him, but Aldo's sudden determination was so unexpected that he couldn't grab hold of him in time. "Retha, I saw with my own eyes how he was flung over the balcony's railing. I couldn't believe what was happening! He fell from the top floor to the ground three metres below."

Wat gebeur het is baie watergeeste het my gestamp

hulle wou my weer afgooi toe keer die engele,

What happened was that a lot of water spirits pushed me [off the balcony].

They wanted to push me off again, but the angels stopped them.

The miracle is that he actually should have fallen a lot further, but he hit the railing of the downstairs patio with his mouth and instead of rolling down the hill, he landed on the patio. His mouth was shattered and he literally lost most of his teeth. If he had rolled further down the hill, it would have been a lot worse.

Tinus rushed down the stairs to the ground floor where he found Aldo lying in his own blood. He was unconscious. This was not the first time that my husband had to hold his son in his arms while wondering if he would live or die. Josh immediately went looking for Master and Aubrey (the two Malawian men who worked for us) to come and help. The neighbour's two daughters also witnessed the incident, and they immediately ran to our house to help. They stayed with Aldo while Tinus called the ambulance. Aldo was then rushed to a hospital in Pretoria, with Tinus by his side.

Aldo's face was badly swollen. When he regained consciousness they took X-rays of his neck and spine since their first concern was to make sure his back wasn't injured by the impact of the fall.

I was ministering at a women's camp in Hermanus that weekend. During the course of the weekend I could see the Holy Spirit working in people's hearts and many women testified afterwards that they gave their hearts to Jesus or that they had an intimate encounter with God. My cell phone is usually turned off when I minister, and I only received the message of Aldo's accident on my way to the airport. I could hear the worry and urgency in my friend's voice on the recorded message, "Retha, please call me when you get this message. Aldo is in the ICU, he fell from the balcony... You need to come to the hospital as soon as you can."

My mouth suddenly felt very dry. I immediately called Tinus but because he was with Aldo in the ICU, there was no answer. I then called my friend, she sounded sombre and worried. "Retha, please come directly to the hospital from the airport, but be prepared – Aldo is not looking good."

My thoughts were a mess. "Jesus, help us!" was all I could pray while on the aeroplane. I couldn't help but wonder how it was possible that God had touched so many people's lives at the camp from which I was returning, but that my family and I were experiencing such immense suffering. When I arrived at Lanseria airport, friends were already waiting there for me and took me to the hospital.

It wasn't a pretty picture that awaited me at the hospital. Aldo's jaw was swollen and dark blue and he was wearing a neck brace. The doctors hadn't determined yet how bad the damage to his neck was and therefore he wasn't allowed to move. I gave him a pen to write and the message he scribbled down said: "Mommy, somebody had laid his hands on me and prayed for me. A lot of water demons entered my body. They worked along with the other water demons that had been planted in me a long time ago and they threw me over the balcony railing. There were a lot of them, Mom; and they wanted to kill me. They fight against my brain and the fluid on my brain. Mom, it is the water spirits who have been making me so sick."

Weu werk asb want hy is waarlik oppad.

Ma'am you must work, because He is truly on His way.

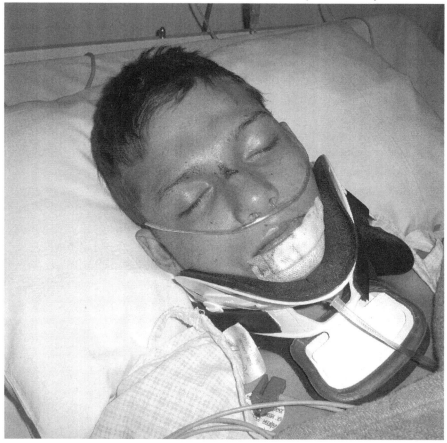

Aldo in hospital after the accident.

I was speechless. I took the note and left the ICU with tears pouring down my cheeks. Thoughts kept rushing through my head like billowing waves: *My child is being attacked by demons. Water demons want to steal Aldo's life. What gives them the right to do this? Who was it that laid hands on him? What kind of battle are we actually fighting? I thought we were just standing in faith for the healing of his brain injury! What is going on, Jesus? Please help us!*

Wysh sê hulle het
toegang deur wat
met my gebeur het
hy sê watergeeste is
wat swart man gebid het

Wisdom says that they have access to me because of what happened. He

says water spirits is what the black man prayed.

I could see that Tinus was suffering immensely. He just cried and kept on saying that he couldn't do anything to prevent the accident because Aldo was thrown over the railing in such an unnatural way. I showed him the note that Aldo had written, hoping that it would comfort him. Both of us were crushed. "This is a battle that we don't know much about Tinus, but the darkness has now been revealed by the truth; and isn't this exactly what we have been asking for all along?"

Geluk is in God. hy sê hy
hy sal nie my los nie. Jy
sal sien wat gaan gebeur
mom ek sal gesond word.
Wat is geloof hy sê sy
Kyk vir hulp bo god is
God hy sal vir ons help.
hulle is vegvir veg veg veg.
Jesus sê jy sal sien hoe
hy vir ons veg.

Happiness is in God. He says He will never leave me. You will see what is

going to happen, Mom – I will be healed. What is faith? He says you have

to look for help from above. God is God. He will help us. They are fighting

against us. Fight, fight, fight. Jesus says that you will see how

He is fighting for us.

We decided that we would take turns to stay with Aldo while he was in hospital. Tinus would take the night shifts, and Ma'am Patrys and I would look after him during the day.

When I finally got home that night Josh was waiting for me at the front door. All our domestic workers were also still sitting in the living room, waiting to hear news about Aldo's condition. I sat down with them and told them about Aldo's note. "Aldo says this is the work of water demons. I know that because of your African culture you understand this spiritual battle better than I do. Can any of you explain to me what is going on here?" Nobody said a word. They just shrugged their shoulders and blankly stared ahead of them. There was a sense of uneasiness in my spirit, but I was so tired that I decided to ignore it for the time being. I prayed with them for Aldo's recovery and that the Holy Spirit would bring the truth to light. When I stood up to go to bed, the atmosphere was tense and strained.

Two days after the incident I found this note from Tinus on Aldo's bedside table:

Aldo,

The tears are rolling along the wrinkles that have appeared on my face overnight; and I feel broken.

When you were younger I was your hero; how could I not catch you when you fell this time?

When I held you while the blood was pouring from your mouth, there was nothing I could do – only love you.

In the ambulance I watched while the paramedics took care of you, and once again there was nothing I could do – only trust in God.

At the hospital I had to stand aside while the doctors and nurses worked on you, and you were so brave: lying still for hours without showing any pain. Once again I could do nothing – just pray.

While I was sitting next to your bed last night I couldn't sleep. I stared at you and wondered why your body was shaking like that. Maybe you were dreaming about the same things I saw when I closed my eyes?

So many people's lives have already been touched by your brave testimony and the text messages are pouring in.

Today I experienced a little bit of what God must have felt when He had to send His tortured Son to the cross so others may have eternal life – and He couldn't do anything about it.

It feels as if I fail you when I cannot protect you from the pain of life.

But I know we will rise again. We will shake off the dust and the blood and carry on, because the work is not finished yet. I am just so sorry that it is your blood. I am proud of you and you are my hero.

Dad

The fall from the balcony took place in October and during November Aldo had to go for numerous operations. The first step was to remove all the dead fragments of bone from Aldo's jaw and to implant new bone so the reconstruction could begin. The shunt also had to be replaced, because the old shunt was damaged due to the fall. Aldo was too weak to be flown to Cape Town and therefore we had to have the brain operations done in Johannesburg. But it was only after the new shunt was inserted that the problems really started.

Aldo kept on writing that there was something wrong with the tube of the shunt and that it was piercing through the ventricle in his brain. He also wrote that there was not enough fluid on his brain. It was not possible to adjust the shunt's pressure as could be done with the previous apparatus, and that meant we couldn't do anything to try and relieve his pain. At some stage he started hitting his head against a wall because the pain and frustration just became too much for him.

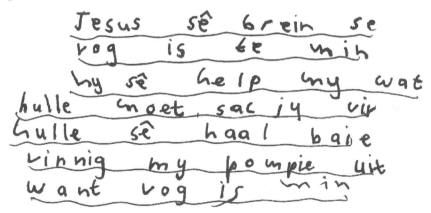

Jesus says my brain's fluid is not enough. He says that they [the doctors] must help me. Will you tell them to take out the shunt very quickly?

Because the fluid on my brain is not enough.

The nights were the worst for us. Because of the pain Aldo had trouble sleeping, and most nights we were grateful to get three hours uninterrupted sleep.

49

Eventually Tinus and I took turns to sit next to his bed and pray to ensure that there was always someone at Aldo's side to look after him (and so that one of us could at least get a few hours rest). During that time my relationship with God really deepened because of all the extra hours I spent in prayer. One night I cried out in frustration, "Jesus, it can't go on like this! What do I still have to do to make it stop?"

Through all of this my focus was still on my son's medical condition. I didn't pay much attention to the battle that was raging in the spirit. I just presumed that the water demons had disappeared after the fall from the balcony. After gaining much more experience I know today that demons don't just disappear, they have to be driven out by the name and power of Jesus Christ!

Aldo also kept on writing that the tube of the shunt was piercing through his brain's ventricle, but the X-rays didn't show anything and I was unsure how to explain Aldo's letters to the doctors when the medical facts proved otherwise. Even though Aldo acted agitated and frustrated during this time, his letters were still pure and from God's heart. This might seem like a paradox, but I know that the things Aldo writes comes from what the Lord reveals to his spirit – and his spirit was healthy and strong, even though his soul (mind, will and emotions) and body were under severe attack.

At that stage I knew very little about the way in which demons work and what they are capable of. I couldn't imagine that they were behind the problems with the fluid on his brain, or the tube piercing through the ventricle. It is much easier to believe the black and white facts of a medical report. Today I know that so many diseases are just the name we give to demonic activity as a way of coping with those things which we don't understand – we'd rather "manage" a disease that has no cure and suppress the symptoms with medication. And that is exactly what the enemy wants, because then the root of the problems remains untouched, and the demons can continue stealing our joy, peace and health without any restraint.

Jesus sê wat ek so
baie seer maak is
my pompie wat se
pypie uitgetrek was.
baie vog het in my
vel en ventrikels

gegaan vog. beveg
my genesing.
Jesus sê wat brein
wat mev seermaak
sal ophou, maar mev
mev jy moet net
asb bly glo hy sê
u mev, ek moet deeglik
mev heeltyd hom volg.

Jesus says what hurt me so much was the tube of the shunt that was disconnected. Lots of fluid went into my skin and my ventricles. The fluid is making me sick. Jesus says that whatever is hurting my brain will stop, but Ma'am, you must please keep on believing. He says that you and I must just keep on following Him to the end.

Chapter 3

Wysh is wat jy nou gesê het.
Mom asb moenie huil nie, sy werke
was wyster van my brein - Weu
wysheid van my brein deurmekaar
te maak en an vog op my brein
te steel. Sy werk was jellie vis om
julle te laat glo ek sal nie gesond
word nie. Julle wou nie glo nie,
en hy het kwaad geword toe jy
hom uitvang Des. Jesus is lanks
jou nou. Jy is so hartseer van alles
hy sê moenie want jy is waar hy
jou wil hê. Jesus sê jy is nie
weg van hom nie. Jy sê hoekom
is hulle hie alles weg een slag
want jellie vis is helfte van uit
trauma gil. jellie vis
hy is wat my weu wil geveg
het. Jesus sê jy leer nou baie
hy is wat jy weet jy sê jellie
vis het voelers jy mom jy sien
reg. Lekker ek voel nou lekker
lig mom. Jy is 'n aanhouer jy stop
nie voor hy weg is nie. Jou gebed
mom is so vol vuur dit maak
hulle woedend, jy het my gered
weer deur die bloed.

What you are saying now is wise, Ma'am. Mom, please don't cry. His work
was to try and confuse my mind and steal my brain's fluid. The work of
the jellyfish was to try and convince you that I will never be healthy again.
You didn't believe him, and he became angry when you caught him out
in December. Jesus is next to you now. You are so heartbroken about
everything. He says don't be – because you are where He wants you to be.
Jesus says you are not far from Him. You are asking why it is not all gone,
and why only half of the jellyfish is out. Trauma jellyfish… it was he who
fought against me. Ma'am, Jesus says you are learning a lot now. You can see
that the jellyfish has many tentacles – you are right Mom. Good, I feel good
and light now. Mom, you will endure until the end. You won't stop until he
is completely gone. Mom your prayers are so full of fire – it makes them so
angry… you saved me again through the blood [of Jesus].

Another summer holiday without sunshine in our home

After all the operations that Aldo went through in November, the summer holiday finally arrived. Before Aldo could enjoy the sunshine and sea at Yzerfontein with the rest of us, he first had to attend his school's annual year-end conference in Bloemfontein with Ma'am Patrys. He had entered a school competition entitled "Winning Souls for Christ" and had been looking forward to the conference throughout the year. Aldo attends an ACE (Accelerated Christian Education) school and many of their activities and teachings centre around the gospel of Jesus Christ. He was also the goalie of his school's soccer team, and he didn't want to let his team mates down. Aldo *really* wanted to attend the conference, but my concern was whether he would be healthy enough to go.

The previous December holiday Aldo had his first shunt inserted, and our family went through a very difficult time because we were constantly in and out of hospital. This year we were really hoping to have a peaceful holiday, filled with fun, family time and rest!

During the first weekend in December I had to preach in the Cape at my last camp for the year. I flew down to Cape Town a bit earlier than the rest of the family, while Tinus drove down with Josh, Moya (Josh's beloved dog), Master and Aubrey, and met up with me after the camp. The plan was for Aldo to join us after he had attended the conference with Ma'am Patrys. Tinus would fly to Bloemfontein to attend the prize-giving ceremony of the conference, and the two of them would then return to the Cape again. Once all the McPhersies were under one roof, our family holiday would finally begin.

We decided that Ma'am Patrys and Aldo should stay at a guesthouse and not in the hostel with the other children, so Aldo could have a quiet place to rest in the afternoons. The afternoon before the prize-giving ceremony, I received an anxious call from Ma'am Patrys. "Retha, Aldo went for a shower this afternoon and I was in the room next door when I heard him scream. When I went into the bathroom the shower's hot water tap was wide open and the scalding water was burning Aldo's back. I struggled to get the door open and when I finally managed to get Aldo out of the shower, his back was red and he was terribly frightened! I don't understand what is going on – this has never happened before! He is still a bit shaky, but at least he is calm now. I know this is the work of the enemy! They desperately want to keep Aldo away from the conference and they hate the fact that he is going to the prize-giving ceremony tonight – they will do anything to keep him away!"

The old Retha would have downplayed these events as coincidental, but by this time I had started to recognise the enemy's works even though I didn't understand it all. We have to consult the Holy Spirit in situations like these and ask God for the gift of discernment which will enable us to fight effectively in the unseen battle which is raging in the spiritual realm. I now often ask the Lord in prayer to enlighten the eyes of my understanding, so I would no longer sweep these things under the carpet, regarding them as "bad luck" or coincidence, and thereby allowing the enemy to get away with stealing from my life.

That night at the conference Aldo met David Ring, a preacher from the United States who suffers from cerebral palsy. The fact that David is physically challenged does not prevent him from preaching the Word of God, and he has touched thousands of people through his moving testimony. Earlier that year Aldo had watched one of David's testimonial DVD's and he strongly identified with David. To meet David was the highlight of Aldo's year! Aldo told him that he had watched his DVD and what it had meant to him. Through this meeting I could once again see that God is in control of every detail of our lives, even though it doesn't always seems like it.

Aldo excitedly sat in the audience with Ma'am Patrys, hoping to hear his name called out as the winner of one of the awards. He was traumatised by the incident in the shower earlier, but nothing could keep him away from the ceremony that night. When they finally called out his name and he and Ma'am Patrys walked to the stage to collect the "Heartfelt Award"-trophy (awarded to Aldo because he had touched so many people's hearts and lives), he was once again attacked in the spirit by the water demons. Suddenly he was disorientated and confused – totally not himself! I believe the reason for this was because the enemy wanted to prevent him from receiving any acknowledgement for what he contributes to the Kingdom of God. For Aldo, who was still struggling with rejection, it was a very big deal to receive the trophy. More than anything else the demons will try to prevent us from walking in the true calling the Lord has destined for us, and from receiving the good gifts that He wants to give us. Thank goodness Tinus was there to help him! When he saw that Aldo was behaving strangely, he immediately went to help Ma'am Patrys and together they helped Aldo off the stage. Tinus and Aldo returned to Cape Town later that evening. It turned out to be a flight that Tinus would very much like to forget.

Aldo talking to David Ring.

When Aldo joined us in Yzerfontein we soon realised that something was still seriously wrong with his shunt and the pressure on his brain. As he did the previous December, Aldo hit his head against the wall in pure frustration and pain. He was so confused that it was almost impossible to communicate with him. He kept on writing to me that there was not enough fluid on his brain and that the tube of the shunt had pierced through the ventricle in his brain. We were so confused and frustrated. Was it possible that the demons were stealing the fluid on his brain? Or was it just the shunt that was giving him trouble again?

asb mom   mev   help my
kan nie   weer so want ek
nie.   herp my   seer kry
weer   help my   vuur seer
                    asb nag

help my vuur word
waarlik weer vuur word
help my asb. help my
asb. Jy ~~bieel~~ help my
dr. wat ek sê is het
van God, haal pompie uit.
my hulp is van God wat
hemel en aarde gemaak
het. help my asb.
Lees wat wysh. sê hy sê
haal hom uit.

Please help me Mom, because I don't want to get hurt again like that. Help me Mom. The fire is hurting me. Please help me! At night it is the worst. The enemy is sending fire against me again. Please help me. You can help me doctor – because you believe what I say comes from God. Take out the shunt. My help is from God who made heaven and earth. Please help me. Listen to what Wisdom says – He says take out the shunt.

In the past we had experienced numerous problems with his shunt, but that December holiday we hit rock bottom. In spite of all our efforts to help him, Aldo's condition worsened day after day and it seemed impossible to stop the downward spiral. In desperation Tinus took him to the hospital early one morning. The doctors operated on him once again to check that the tube in his stomach wasn't blocked, and they also took X-rays of the shunt in his brain; but nothing seemed out of place. The X-rays showed no signs of the tube piercing through the ventricle and there also wasn't a blockage in the drainage tube in his stomach. I couldn't understand it as he had never written something that was incorrect before. His words were often jumbled and spoken incoherently when he was sick, but his letters always remained pure. After many tests the doctors sent Tinus home without an explanation or a solution.

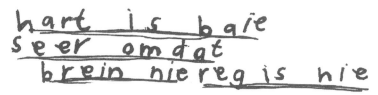

My heart is hurting so much because my brain is not well.

I was sitting on the carpet in my room when Tinus called me with the news that there was no medical explanation for Aldo's behaviour and constant pain. The implication of this news rattled me. *Had Aldo been wrong about the tube piercing his ventricle? Did this imply that everything I had believed from the start had been wrong? It couldn't be! God had confirmed to me time and again that Aldo's letters are true... what was different this time?*

Amongst all the frantic thoughts I felt the Holy Spirit quiet my soul. At that moment of clarity I realised that the anxiety I felt were the arrows of the enemy hitting me. The arrows just kept on coming...unbelief... fear... hopelessness... despair...

I had to be careful not to allow fear to take hold of my heart. I started proclaiming out loud, over and over: "I don't have a spirit of fear, but a spirit of power, and of love and of a sound mind!" (see 2 Tim. 1:7).

"Jesus, we can't go on like this!" I cried out in desperation. I was utterly exhausted. "The enemy is trying to destroy Aldo's life and to discourage us in the process. He is stealing our finances, he is stealing our joy, he is stealing our holiday and our special time together as a family. He is also stealing the time and attention we have to give to little Josh. He is stealing Aldo's teenage years and he is trying to steal my hope. Lord, You must help me, please!"

Have you ever been at this place of despair before? There where it feels as if you aren't even strong enough to hold on to hope? You are almost afraid to hope, because the idea of being disappointed hurts so much... The answer to despair is to look away from the situation and to stay focused on God alone. Just hear what the Word of God says about our "hopeless situations":

> Against all hope, Abraham in hope believed and so became the father of many nations, just as it had been said to him, "So shall your offspring be." Without weakening in his faith, he faced the fact that his body was as good as dead – since he was about a hundred years old – and that Sarah's womb was also dead. Yet he did not waver through unbelief regarding the promise of God, but was strengthened in his faith and gave glory to God, being fully persuaded that God had power to do what he had promised.
> - Romans 4:18-21 -

despondent and we lose all perspective and hope. When this happens we throw in the towel, and without even realising it, we start agreeing with the lies of the enemy instead of standing on the promises of God. In order for us to overcome the enemy – the father of lies – we have to recognize his nature, and learn to defend ourselves against his tactics.

Sê Jesus is in beheer van my lewe. Jesus Julle is so seer mom want ek bly siek water op my brein nog kort steeds want hulle vat my vog.

Jy is bedreiging hulle veg jou. hy baie nog van my brein gevat maar julle wen want julle volhart in geloof.

Jesus says that Jesus is in control of my life. You are hurting so much, Mom, because I am still sick. There is water on my brain. I need more fluid, because they are taking my fluid. You are a threat to them. They are fighting against you. They took a lot of fluid off my brain, but you are winning because you are persevering in faith.

While I was sitting there on the carpet, crying, I felt a strange peace come over me and I could hear the Holy Spirit say, *"Finally your eyes are opening to the truth, Retha! You are beginning to see that Aldo's illness is the work of Satan... It is he who is trying to destroy you. He is in pursuit of Aldo's future and My plans for his life. He is the one opposing the works of My Spirit in the lives of all believers."*

I was still sitting on the carpet when I looked up and noticed a book on my bookshelf with the title, *He Came to Set the Captives Free,* by Rebecca Brown. I instinctively groaned and thought "oh no, please not that!" I couldn't even remember where I had gotten the book from – it definitely wasn't something I would have bought for myself. In the past I had always shied away from this kind of topic and that is why the book had been gathering dust on my shelf all this time.

There was a quietness that filled the room, as if everything stood still in anticipation to see what I would do next, and that's when I knew that Abba had spoken to me. It was now up to me to decide whether I was going to obey or not. I could feel the Holy Spirit spurring me on: *"For such a time as this Retha... now is the time to read the book."* But I still didn't move. *"Don't be afraid, Retha,"* I felt the Holy Spirit say, *"your veil has to be lifted."*

Next to Rebecca Brown's book was another book that drew my attention, *I Dare to Call Him Father,* by Bilquis Sheikh. The Holy Spirit prompted me again and said, *"'He Came to Set the Captives Free' is for you, Retha, and 'I Dare to Call Him Father' is for Tinus – read them."*

I wondered where we would find the time to read because Aldo required most of our attention; none the less, I gave Tinus his book as soon as he arrived home that night and I obediently started to read mine. *I dare to call Him Father* conveyed the exact message that Tinus needed to hear. He was also worn out and discouraged, and the book gave him new hope and perspective on our situation.

Wysh sê wat julle
hou moet weet is hulle
wil julle seermaak

; Ly sê engele pas
julle op.
hulle maak my so seer
my brein is so seer hulle
trek vog.

Wisdom says that you need to know now that they want to hurt you. He says that angels are watching over you. They [the demons] are hurting me so much. My brain is in so much pain. They are stealing my fluid.

I know it sounds strange, but that night I jumped up and down on my bed with excitement, because I realised that we had found the problem behind Aldo's "illness". I proclaimed out loud, "We have found you out, Satan! You will no longer steal from us!" I realised that a spiritual battle was still looming ahead of us, but at least I knew who and what I was fighting against. For three years we had been running around in the darkness of uncertainty and ignorance and now, finally, it seemed as if we were making some progress in the right direction. There was an excitement in my spirit because I knew that I was fighting in God's army with Jesus as my Commander; and even if the battle wouldn't be easy, the outcome was assured: *"They overcame him by the blood of the Lamb and by the word of their testimony; they did not love their lives so much as to shrink from death"* (Rev. 12:11, NKJV).

Tinus and I spent every free minute we had reading. Every now and again I gave a shout of excitement when I read something in Rebecca Brown's book that confirmed the reality of the spiritual battle we were in.

God se wat water geeste wil doen is geloof steel en my dood maak. Wysheid se hulle tart jou. gaan se vir Wysheid se jy moet boek klaar lees.

God says that what the water sprits are trying to do is to steal our faith and kill me. Wisdom says they are provoking you. Wisdom says you must

finish reading the book.

"Tinus listen to this; it is exactly what is happening to us!" The book included the testimony of a woman who was fiercely attacked by demons who made it their mission to pull her brain apart and destroy her mind. When I read this my thoughts immediately turned to Aldo's shunt. "Could the demons be doing the same thing to him?" The scene that Rebecca described in her book was taking place right in front of my eyes, and the possibility seemed all the more real as I looked to where Aldo was lying on the sofa; clearly he was in a lot of pain. Aldo was so confused by now that he literally could not be left alone for one minute, and we often had to hold him back from hitting his head against the wall in pain.

My initial excitement was transformed into serious spiritual warfare when we started to take on the enemy in prayer. We asked God to let His glory light shine on the darkness, and it felt to me as if we had opened up a can of worms and all the worms were wriggling out! This is what is supposed to happen when the darkness is expelled by the light. I was amazed and shocked at what had been hidden.

Even amidst the uproar of spiritual warfare, Aldo indicated to me that he wanted to write. "Mom, please promise me that you won't think that it is me saying all these things. It is the water demons. Mom, please help me – they want to kill me. They are hurting my brain very, very much!"

Wysh se wat nou
gebeur is hulle bewe
want hulle weet
hulle waarheid is
uit. Jy is so
seer maar weet
asb wat watergeeste
met my doen kan
ek hie help nie

Wisdom says what is happening now is that they [the demons] are shaking, because they know the truth about them has been revealed. You are hurting so much, but please know that I can't stop what the water spirits are doing to me.

I could hardly read through my tears. *How did things come to this point, Lord? How could I not have seen this? Why is this happening to us? We follow You... we serve You... we love You! Why can they do this to us?*

Wysheid se hulle het verskriklik
watergees weer gestuur. hulle kan
nie inkom hie, maar hulle wag
net vir slaap tyd dan maak
hulle my seer

Wisdom says that they sent terrible water spirits again. They can't come in but they are waiting for me to go to sleep, then they'll hurt me again.

I had always been the one who shied away from "spiritual warfare", and now I had to face it head on in my own home. I used to defend my opinion by saying that I had been washed clean by the blood of Jesus and that demons weren't able to come near me. I now realise that as children of God we have a responsibility to take our place in the battle against Satan. The Word says that Satan walks around like a roaring lion seeking whom he may devour (see 1 Pet. 5:8); if the Word warns us - how could I have thought that we were immune to his attacks?

We had our hands full during that holiday. We had to fight against the enemy day and night. Aldo slept very little during the night, and during the day the battle just continued. Because of his brain injury it is extremely important for him to get enough sleep, and sleep was the first thing the enemy tried to steal – which also served to weaken his immune system. As the holiday progressed he no longer slept at all during the night, and Tinus and I had to stay awake with him until sunrise almost every night. The water demons were attacking the fluid on his brain and that was what caused his confusion. Eventually we recognised a pattern – every night after midnight the attacks became more severe and then he would write: "Mom, they are busy fighting me now!" When we fought back the enemy simply retaliated and this made our progress feel slow and drawn out. At that stage we didn't have any experience in fighting this type of battle, but we learned quickly as we went along.

One night I looked at Aldo lying on the bed and thought to myself, *"Somewhere deep inside that little body is my broken and hurting child. Why does he have to endure such trauma, Lord? What have we done that the enemy wants to destroy us with such hatered?"*

my want ek het halle haat so groot werk wat was vir my.

They hate me because I have such a big job waiting for me. What is my work? Because they are fighting my work.

"Mom, please believe me; it is not me saying and doing these things. Mom, they are hurting my brain so very, very much! They keep on telling me that they want to kill me. They say I will never, ever be healthy again and that no girl will ever love me. They say I will never be able to preach… Mom, they hurt me so very much."

The father of lies was bombarding Aldo day and night with arrows of lies. I asked him why he never wrote about this in his letters before, and he said, "Mom, they said I had to keep quiet or else they would kill me. I could feel my brain hurting more when I said something about it. Mom, I am holding on to Jesus with all my strength."

What we thought to be a medical problem I now know was demonic oppression. The water demons tried to control the fluid on his brain. During the holiday Aldo also started losing bladder control and I realised that it was just another manoeuvre of the enemy. The water demons targeted all the areas in his body where they could find fluid.

by blaas hulle bly in
my blaas

In my bladder – they are living in my bladder.

There are demons hiding behind so many medical conditions; illnesses such as depression, arthritis, epilepsy, mental illnesses and especially medical conditions that have no cure or explainable cause. Even the symptoms and reactions to these illnesses can be used as the names of the demons during deliverance. The Bible is full of stories where Jesus cast out demons that were directly connected to illnesses, for example:

> "While they were going out, a man who was demon-possessed and could not talk was brought to Jesus. And when the demon was driven out, the man who had been mute spoke. The crowd was amazed and said, "Nothing like this has ever been seen in Israel."
> - *Matthew 9:32-33* -

I can remember preaching in a small town where a mother came up to me after the meeting seeking prayer for her beautiful eighteen year old daughter who was still wetting the bed. Then there were the worried parents who came to me for advice regarding their son who attended university but who wilfully hurt himself by cutting himself with a razor. Or the mother who suffered from depression and was unable to control her anger and constantly yelled at her children; or the pain in the wealthy businessman's eyes who was waiting for his runaway son to return home. I could clearly see Satan at work in the lives of all these people. Although my heart was breaking for each of these parents, it made me realise that Satan doesn't only attack families who have children with brain injuries – if we would only open our eyes we would recognize his handiwork all around us. The enemy attacks people with fear and rejection, even if they are totally healthy and highly intelligent. The "band aids" that the medical world hands out only provide us with short-term solutions – it is up to us to seek our answers from God and to get to the root of the problem.

Wysh sê wat watergeeste met my doen is hulle maak my deurmekaar. hy was net. wat het met jou gebeur gister aand want ek het gesien hoe jy huil voor die troon. Jy sê ek is van god, en hy sê satan rebeleer wysh sê jy is nie verkeerd nie.

Wisdom says that the water spirits are confusing me. They are waiting for the right moment to strike. What happened to you last night? I saw you crying before the throne. You say that I am from God, and He [God] says that Satan is rebelling. Wisdom says that you are not wrong.

Demons flourish on intimidation, accusations and lies. Like parasites, they will take advantage of the weak areas in your soul, trying to find a permanent foothold in your life. It was a great shock for me to realise that the epilepsy we had been struggling with for three years was a result of demons and not purely because of Aldo's brain injury. Still, I struggled to understand how the enemy could have gotten such a strong grip on Aldo. I definitely don't think of Aldo as being perfect, but his life is relatively simple. He lives close to God and is not exposed to as many worldly things as most other healthy teenagers are.

He gets up early in the mornings and reads his Bible, and then he prays and enjoys his conversation time with Abba. After breakfast he goes to school with Ma'am Patrys and focuses his attention on his schoolwork. Ma'am Patrys is with him during the day so I know he doesn't get up to all kinds of mischief. In the afternoons he is at home while he does his homework and plays soccer with Josh. Some days they play a bit of *Wii* sport video games and in between he reads his Bible and prays. That is what a typical day looks like for him when he is in good health.

When he is sick, he and Ma'am Patrys just stay at home. At eight o'clock in the evenings he has already had his bath and is ready for bed. So how did these demons gain access to him? It went so well with him before the epileptic fits started... and why did things deteriorate so quickly after that young man had prayed for him?

I found my answer in the Word of God – it was there all along: *"For our struggle is not against flesh and blood, but against the rulers, against the authorities, against the powers of this dark world and against the spiritual forces of evil in the heavenly realms"* (Eph 6:12).

Man consists of spirit, soul and body. People spend hours in the gym and lots of money on keeping their bodies healthy and beautiful, but why do we then neglect the other two parts that are even more important than the part that will return to dust when we die?

Throughout all our struggles Aldo's spirit was safe with Jesus, and that was why his letters were still spot on and pure even when he was attacked by the enemy through the wounds that existed in his body and soul. These "soul wounds" act as a doorway for the enemy to enter, and they then build their strongholds in the "dry areas" of our soul – as I like to call it. We have to guard against the enemy's attacks by making sure these wounds are healed. The hurt has to be dealt with and the darkness has to be brought to God's glorious light, because everything that is kept in the darkness can fall prey to Satan. The effect of the enemy's foothold can be seen in the fruit of our lives and it can include anything from anger rages, addictions, pride and jealousy, to illness and diseases.

The more Aldo wrote about this (and later spoke about it), the more we were able to help him to work through these issues and take it to God so his heart could be healed. I could clearly see the difference in my child once he started dealing with his pain. He no longer carried the heavy weight of guilt and shame around with him. I assured him that there was nothing so bad that he couldn't share it with us; and that we would walk this road with him to the end. I constantly reminded him that he is a child of God and that nothing can separate him from God's love. Let me tell you the most valuable lesson I learned from all of this... it is actually so simple: LOVE heals.

"Mom, I was scared that they would kill me if I told you everything," he confessed the one day.

"Aldo, you will have to start trusting me now" I assured him. "The enemy flourishes in darkness and that is why he doesn't like it when you bring these things to the light so that it can be dealt with. Do not let Satan intimidate you with lies and fear, my love. Trust me – we love you, and we will do everything we can to help you. You will get through this – because Jesus is alive."

Often after an epileptic fit Aldo would write: "Lucifer is trying to kill me, Mom." Back then I didn't fully realise what was happening and therefore I didn't know how to protect myself and my family. I didn't *want* to believe that Lucifer could actually have such a hold on our lives. I was in complete denial.

Jesus se Hy wag vir my om hom te vertrou.
heeltyd beoefen geloof.
Jy wil moet aanhou bedien wil jy weet hoe ek sukkel want hulle soek my lewe.
Jesus se reg die geveg hy begewe ons nie.

Jesus says He is waiting for me to trust Him. He wants me to always keep my faith. You must keep on ministering, Ma'am. Do you have any idea how I am struggling? Because they are seeking my life. Jesus says fight the fight – He will never leave or forsake us.

I now have a better understanding of what transpired in the spiritual realm; just beyond the veil of what I could see with my natural eyes. I was blinded to the truth of spiritual warfare and I didn't recognize the danger signs of demonic activity.

I have learned that Christians cannot be *possessed* by demons, but their behavioural patterns can be *influenced* as a result of demonic oppression. This is what happened with Aldo; his spirit was safe in Jesus' hands, but the demons could attack and torment his soul (thoughts, will and emotions) and his body (through illness). People who haven't yet accepted Jesus Christ as their Lord and Saviour and haven't been born again through Him, run the risk of being possessed by demons because the Holy Spirit doesn't live in their spirit.

When we give Satan a breeding place by believing his lies or by continuing

69

with wilful sin, we are exposing ourselves to great danger. Let's be honest with ourselves and with God and stop denying the "dry areas" in our lives that God wants to heal completely. Let's bow our knees before Him, and choose His will above our own. Let's turn our backs on those things that keep us from His presence and let's receive the abundant life that Jesus wants to give us.

> See to it, then, that the light within you is not darkness. Therefore,
> if your whole body is full of light, and no part of it dark, it will be completely
> lighted, as when the light of a lamp shines on you.
> - Luke 11:35-36 -

Chapter 4

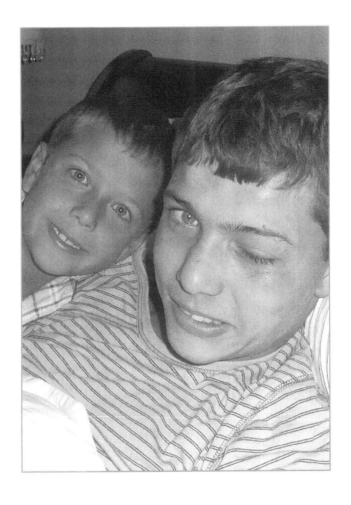

Wysh sê hulle sien hulle
moet gaan want julle
geloof red julle Wysh sê
my wagtyd word vinnig
minder. Wysh sê jy sal sy
krag wat uit wenner hart
kom ontvang. Sal jy asb
nie weer sê jy behoort op
te hou bedien nie mev.
het jy wat wysh my wys
wat ek gesien het was
hoe ons twee saam bedien.
mev jy moet werk want Jesus
is oppad. hy is nou baie
baie naby weet jy 2012 sal
wereld self hulle wawyd
wakker skrik want alles
gaan verander hy sê jy
sal self skrik mev want
jy self weet nie. Wat wag
nie. Jy sal self sien
alles wat ek gesê het is
waar julle self sal sê waarom
het ons so gefaal want
wat ek nou weet sou ek
nie gekla het oor my seer
nie maar eerder baie dankie
gesê het. Jesus sê Jesus sê
wat jy vir my deurgaan sal
jy sien wat julle kroon is
in die hemel.

72

Wisdom says that they [the enemy] can see that they have to go, because your faith is saving you. Wisdom says my waiting period is almost over. Wisdom says you will receive His power because you have the heart of a winner. Please don't ever say again that you should stop ministering, Ma'am. Do you know that Wisdom showed me that the two of us will minister together? Ma'am, you must work because Jesus is on His way. He is very, very close now. Do you know that the world will be shaken in 2012? Everything will change. He says even you will be surprised, because you don't know what is coming. You will see for yourself that everything I say is true. You will say, "Why did we fail? If I knew then what I know now, I wouldn't have complained about my pain but I would have said thank you instead." Jesus says you will see what your crown looks like in heaven because of what you are enduring on my behalf.

Wolf in sheep's clothing

Through the message of this book I don't want to give the impression that everything bad or negative that happens to us should always be blamed on Satan. My goal is not to shift the blame of our problems on the enemy, and thus exonerate ourselves from taking any responsibility. On the contrary, to think this way is very dangerous, because it means that we will never accept responsibility for the choices we make – and thus never repent and change our ways. To me there is a clear difference between trials (which God uses to test our faith) and temptations (which lead to death if we give in to them). God's tests lead to sanctification, while Satan's temptations lead to death.

Wysh sê wat sy moet glo is hy is in beheer. Lusifer kan nie wat hy begin het klaarmaak - Lusifer is kwaad

by Jesus is ons veilig

Wisdom says that you must believe that He is in control. Lucifer cannot complete what he started. Lucifer is angry. With Jesus we are safe.

These two Scriptures explain the difference well:

Dear friends, do not be surprised at the painful trial you are suffering, as though something strange were happening to you. But rejoice that you participate in the sufferings of Christ, so that you may be overjoyed when his glory is revealed. If you are insulted because of the name of Christ, you are blessed, for the Spirit of glory and of God rests on you. If you suffer, it should not be as a murderer or thief or any other kind of criminal, or even as a meddler. However, if you suffer as a Christian, do not be ashamed, but praise God that you bear that name.
- 1 Peter 4:12-16 -

Blessed is the man who perseveres under trial, because when he has stood the test, he will receive the crown of life that God has promised to those who love him. When tempted, no one should say, "God is tempting me." For God cannot be tempted by evil, nor does he tempt anyone; but each one is tempted when,

For example, if the economy is on a downturn and your business is struggling, you can still have joy and peace in the midst of the situation if you trust in God and stand upon the truth of His Word. The Bible tells us that God cares for us and that we can cast our burdens upon Him (see Phil. 4:6-7). With the right attitude and perspective in a trial, the adversities we face will ultimately strengthen our faith and draw us closer to God, because we learn to trust Him in the storm.

But, in contrast to these trials that strengthen our faith, there is the devastating outcome of wilful sin after succumbing to temptation. For instance, the "innocent" flirtation with someone who isn't your spouse can lead to adultery and divorce when you keep on indulging in the temptation.

It is important for us to be able to differentiate between these two spiritual forces, because trials lead to overcoming by faith, and temptation leads to sin and death.

hy los nie want hy sê hy
het legal ground want trauma
hy sê wat brein steeds
wag hou is trauma. hy sê
my seën begin beseën my
met sy bloed.

hy is wat my so deurmekaar maak.
hy is wat kinders op rebelin hou
hy hy se julle help baie mense.
mev jy sal baie kry wat so
kwaad word, want jy sien vyand
wil brein gevange hou en elke
medisyne keer om te deel met
satan se helse werk, hy hou
hulle brein gevange.

He won't leave because he says that he has legal ground to be there because of trauma. He says that trauma is still holding my brain captive and that it is the root of my pain. Cover me with His blood. He [the enemy] is the one who is making me so confused. He is the one who keeps children on Ritalin.

He [Wisdom] says you help so many people. Ma'am, there will be many people who will be mad at you, because you recognise that the enemy wants to keep my brain captive and that the medicine is keeping me from dealing with Satan's hellish work. He holds their brains captive.

Jesus came to destroy the works of the Devil (see 1 John 3:8), and therefore we can't use the devil as an excuse when we make bad choices. Satan can only gain access to our lives if he is given a legal right to be there. The problem is our ignorance – we aren't always aware of the ways in which Satan obtains these "legal bills" to our lives. I had to learn the hard way that Satan will use any form of darkness to get his foot in the door. The demons will return until all the darkness has been dealt with by God's light and truth, and there is nothing left for them to latch onto. Through sincere repentance and confession of sins, Jesus will wash us clean with the only thing that can cleanse us completely: His blood.

> He who conceals his sins does not prosper, but whoever confesses and renounces them finds mercy.
> - *Proverbs 28:13* -

Spiritual warfare without first turning to God in humility and sincere confession is a waste of time. The Word of God says in 1 John 1:5 *God is light; in him there is no darkness at all.* There is only one thing that can prevent God from dealing with the darkness in your heart, and that is your *will.* God's glory light will drive away the darkness and the blood of the Lamb will wash you clean, but first you will have to bow your knee before God in repentance. Therefore, we have to get to the root of the darkness in our hearts. It is not good enough to simply prune the tree, for if the root remains rotten and is left untouched we will reap bad fruit year after year. The root of evil ("the strongman") has to be cut out completely. This principle is portrayed in the story of David and Goliath. The moment David slew Goliath the whole Philistine army was defeated by just one small stone. Goliath was the strongman who determined the course of the hostile army. When David defeated Goliath, he defeated *all* the Philistines (see 1 Samuel 17). The same principle applies to our spiritual battle against evil – if we deal with the root (the strongman), the demons that are dependent on the strongman will be overcome as well. Sometimes these strongmen are things that most of us know little about, like demons assigned to us through bloodline curses. Once you confess and break these curses the demons attached to it will have to flee.

During the long drive back from the Cape to Hartebeespoort I had a fourteen hour deliverance session with Aldo in the car. I did it in my own way, using my own words, without any training or experience in deliverance ministry. I definitely didn't do everything by the book, and there were many things that I didn't even know how to do, but God's grace was enough and when we arrived home Aldo was a lot better. For the first time in nearly a year his mind was clear. He asked about his school work and his friends, and he even made a few jokes. Tinus and I were very thankful for this positive turn, because we were scheduled to leave for New York two days later.

The day before we had to leave, one of the African ladies who worked in our home as a cleaner walked into the room while Aldo and I were busy writing in his journal. The next moment he exclaimed, "oh no!" and then he lost control of his bladder. "What is going on, Aldo?" I asked him anxiously. He then wrote: "She just walked in here with a lot of water demons and they attacked my body and my brain." It wasn't long before he was confused and aggressive again.

Wysh se (name*) het watergeeste het jy wat hou gebeur het gebeur hulle het meer geword toe sy inkom.

hy se kry my weg van haar. Sy is 'n heks weg is sy.

Wisdom says she (name*) has water spirits. Do you know what just happened? They became more when she walked in. He says to get me away from her. She is a witch. Take her away.

When I looked at her again, I could discern her real identity for the first time and what she represented in the spiritual realm. Her facial expression had changed and her eyes were icy cold – and at that moment I realised how naive

I had been. A friend had warned me before that the religious sect she belonged to was dangerous because it mixed ancestral worship (and other African superstitions) with Christianity, but I didn't want to believe that our domestic worker would be involved with witchcraft. According to me she was a good worker and she treated us well – or so I thought. My heart missed a beat when I realised that there was so much more going on behind the scenes that I didn't know about. Immediately I prayed, "Lord, please forgive my ignorance and unbelief – I had been totally blinded to the reality of the spiritual realm!" Always remember that humility before God is one of the most important keys in obtaining victory. We shouldn't feel ashamed when we make mistakes, but in everything we should turn to God first and not let our guilt and shame keep us from running to Him.

I asked the cleaner to work downstairs for the rest of the day, but I could see that she knew exactly what was going on and that she sensed my apprehension. I spent the day praying for Aldo. I tried to do deliverance again as I had done the previous day in the car, but nothing worked. The attack on Aldo was so great that he lost control of his bladder a few times during the day.

Discouraged and broken I fell to my knees late that afternoon. *Hadn't Aldo been through enough? We are supposed to be flying to New York tomorrow. How can I leave my children in the house with her? Lord, please show me what to do!*

I felt comforted knowing that Ma'am Patrys and my parents would be there to look after Josh and Aldo while we were away, but still... I could sense that her presence in the house wasn't good for Aldo. I had to make a decision quickly.

I got up from the floor in my study and calmly went to sit next to Aldo on the couch and looked him in the eyes. "Aldo, I want you to tell me the truth. Don't be afraid of what the enemy might do to you. Aldo, you belong to God – never forget that. This is a battle for your life, but Jesus has already gained the victory on the cross. All you have to do now is to walk in that victory. Daddy and I will help you, and Wisdom will help us." Aldo then indicated that he wanted to write. "Mom, do you know what a witch is? They are planted amongst us by Satan to kill people through curses and witchcraft." When I read these words something inside of me broke. Between the sobs I asked Abba to send His warring angels to help us in this battle, because I was utterly exhausted and I didn't know what to do next.

(I want to warn everybody today that witches aren't necessarily easy to recognize. They don't wear funny pointed hats or fly around on broomsticks as we see in the movies. They are a part of our society and they look normal – it is all part of the deception. Believe it or not, even the schools are filled with teenagers that secretly put curses on other children and their teachers and practise witchcraft. The deeper and most dangerous levels of the occult and Satanism is covered by a cloud of secrecy and deception.)

Wysh sê (name*) toor my hy sê (name*) hulle by sangoma hy glo hy kan my toor.

Wisdom says she (name*) is using witchcraft against me. He says they went to a Sangoma. He believes that he can put a spell on me.

Tinus and I were scheduled to leave for New York the next day, but if the situation with Aldo didn't improve soon, we would have had to cancel our ministry trip. Satan's plan was not only to hurt Aldo, but also to prevent me from preaching the gospel.

Seconds after I had prayed, Aldo looked up at something in the air and wrote, "Michael is here now." Then he got up and walked to the kitchen, completely his old self again. I was speechless... a miracle had happened right before my very eyes! God had sent His warrior angels (of which Michael was one) to fight for us in the spirit. I cried in thankfulness and just kept saying, "Thank You, Abba Father. Thank You, Abba Father!"

Wab is micheal gehoor hoe hy se hy veg vir my. God het hom vir my gestuur het wenner se hy bevel van God gokry om my beseen geseën hy

I heard Michael say that he is fighting for me. God sent him to help me. He is a winner and he says that he has received a command from God to bless me.

I also called a friend of mine that night and asked her if she would come and pray for our family the next day. She has as lot of wisdom and experience regarding spiritual warfare and she explained to us how the occult operates and how to effectively fight against it. The prayers she prayed were specific and detailed, like a sharpshooter who knows where to aim and how to hit the mark. While she was praying for him, Aldo's mind was completely clear and receptive and he wrote a letter to my friend in his journal: "Aunty, water demons were sent to attack me because they bewitched me." Through Wisdom's guidance he even wrote down the names of two of the demonic strongmen: *Shamaan* (used in traditional healing done by witch doctors) and *Asmodee*. In his unique lingo he explained: "They "signal" the fluid in my brain, Mom. She [the witch] used my hair and nails in a pot to bewitch me."

It was revolting to hear, but at least we were making some progress. We stood amazed at how Wisdom was revealing everything through Aldo. God guided us every step of the way by His Spirit.

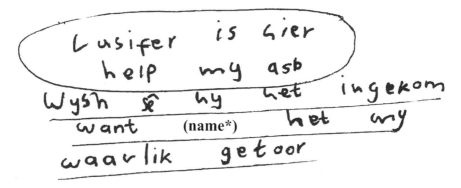

Lucifer is here, please help me! Wisdom says he could come in because she (name*) put a spell on me.

The letters that he had written after every epileptic fit which simply read "Lucifer wants to kill me," also made sense to me for the first time. When Aldo first started suffering from the epileptic fits, I just assumed that it was a side effect of his head injury, but there was always this nagging thought which reminded me that the fits only started a few years after the accident. When I did the math, I realised that Aldo's fits started after we employed her as a domestic worker.

While we were praying the Holy Spirit also revealed to me that some of my forefathers used to visit sangomas (witch doctors) and the curses which resulted because of this were still calling out for blood.

I shared this revelation with my parents (who also didn't know much about bloodline curses at that time), and I asked them to pray and intercede with me so that the curses could be broken. My parents immediately agreed to go for counselling. I honour them for their willingness to humble themselves before the Lord and to learn about these spiritual things that was so new and strange to them. Many bloodline curses are the result of a lack of knowledge from the previous generations. Under the traditional religious setup that most South-Africans grow up with, there is little teaching about this topic and even outspoken denial of its existence. When my parents agreed to go for counselling it was a huge step in the right direction, but I knew that there was still much to be done in order to clean the defilement of the bloodline and to break the curses.

hulle het baie saam
gebring wat my uashou.
W ysh se hulle sal ulug
want jy hou nie water
geeste op veg nie.
Jy is water geeste
se vy and.
het hulle in ge bring

They brought many with them. They are oppressing me. Wisdom says the water spirits will have to flee, because you won't stop fighting against them. You are the water spirits' enemy. They (name*) brought them in.

Later that evening Aldo wrote me another letter: "Mom, Wisdom says you should let her go immediately." He was referring to our cleaning lady. That night I rolled around and struggled with this thought well into the early hours of the morning. *How can I just fire her? She has been working for me for so many years? I always thought I was good to her. How could I not have seen what was happening right in front of my very eyes?* These thoughts and other similar accusations, kept me awake for most of the night. The most upsetting thought of all was: *"Retha, you should stop ministering. If you couldn't even discern what was happening under your own roof, how can you preach to other people?"*

Months after this incident these accusations were still ringing in my ears; until the Holy Spirit showed me through Scripture that there were great men of God who also made errors in judgement.

In 1 Samuel 16:1-13 we read the story of when Samuel had to anoint another king over Israel because of Saul's disobedience. Early on in the chapter we read how Samuel almost anointed the wrong person, because he didn't look at Jesse's sons through spiritual eyes, but he judged them according to their outward appearance. David's oldest brother Eliab seemed like the obvious choice because he was physically strong and handsome, and Samuel would have anointed him as king if the Spirit of God didn't prevent him from doing so. It was only later, when David stood before Samuel, that he knew whom God had chosen. Through this story the Lord taught me that anyone can make a mistake, even great prophets like Samuel. After this error in judgement that cost me so dearly, I pled with the Holy Spirit to help me to discern according to His understanding, and not according to what I can see with my physical eyes: *for the Lord does not see as a man sees; for man looks at the outward appearance, but the Lord looks at the heart* (1 Sam.16:7, NKJV).

Sy was bebeewe toe sy gesien het jy sien haar, sy het toe geweet jy sal hulle vra om te loop.

She started to tremble when she saw that you had seen her [recognised her for what she was]. She knew then that you would ask them to leave.

The things that were revealed in our domestic worker's heart and the words that came from her mouth were contradictory. She said she was a Christian who followed Jesus, but in secret she also worshipped other gods and practised witchcraft. Within the African culture, ancestral worship, idolatry, superstitions, witch doctors (sangomas) and muti (magical potions) still play a very big role – it is a part of their culture and history. They understand the reality of the spiritual realm very well and because they are so superstitious they often build altars in the homes or gardens of their employers. Sometimes they regard these altars as talismans, but often it is done to curse the people of the household if they don't get along with them. They seem to be very religious, but unfortunately the reality of their superstitions and beliefs are often hidden from us. Please don't misunderstand me; I am certainly not implying that every African person is involved in witchcraft! I know a lot of black people who are wonderful men and women of God, and because most of them have been confronted with witchcraft before, they have a better understanding of the spiritual realm and the dangers of the occult. I am just saying that we have to be vigilant and prepared, and not overlook the danger signs because of our ignorance.

After tossing and turning for a long time, I finally fell asleep. That night I was taken to a place in the spirit that I can only describe as hell. To this day I still don't know if it was a dream or a vision, but I do know that what I experienced was very real. I saw demons with the most horrible faces and I instinctively knew they were cruel and merciless. I was aware of a lot of fire, hatred and horrible, taunting voices. Towards the end of my dream I saw a beautiful being, but deep inside I knew that I shouldn't trust it. I could feel the demons closing in on me and I started shouting Jesus' name over and over again. I was pulled out of the vision when Tinus shook me awake.

In a daze I told him what I had seen. "Tinus, I have seen a part of hell! I don't know why, but of one thing I am now absolutely sure: this spiritual battle is real! All I could do was to call out to Jesus. The name of Jesus has so much power!"

I once again lay awake that night, and with everything inside me I wanted to make sure that I would never again have to go to that place. This experience served to teach me about the reality and the seriousness of the spiritual realm and the horrors of hell. From that day onwards I had a new passion to reach out to lost souls, and also to pray for our cleaning lady whom I knew wasn't truly saved – she was actually following the traditions of her ancestors, and not Jesus Christ.

Jesus is vir jou baie baie lief, jy sal hom werklik weer hemel sien.
hy het jou hel gewys, bewys van hoe eg alles is, hy het jou geleer van oorlog voer self.

Jesus se jou wev jou anointing
is vergroot van hel se
ondervinding.
Wat is vyand se beseine se
verslaan se krag. Veseker sy
bloed. Sy bloed is krag

Jesus loves you so much. You truly will see Him in heaven again. He showed
you hell. It is proof of how real everything is. He Himself taught you how
to fight in this war. Jesus says your anointing has increased because you
experienced hell. What will overcome the signals of the enemy? Definitely
His blood - the power of His blood.

After this experience I was determined to cleanse my heart before the Lord.
I began to repent of my sin the moment the Holy Spirit brought things that were
contrary to the will of God to my attention. As I persisted in doing this I felt an
increasing transparency and freedom coming to rest upon me.

As we walk out our journey with God He leads us to deeper levels of intimacy,
revelation and responsibility as we mature, but this requires obedience to His will; and
His Word will always be His will.

God will not entrust His Kingdom to anyone who is still controlled by
pride, because pride is the armour of Satan. Proverbs 16:18 says: *Pride goes before
destruction, a haughty spirit before a fall.* Even Peter came to a fall as a result of his
pride. Before the crucifixion he was full of bravado, and even though he had so much
faith that he is known today as the "water walker", his boldness failed him. He denied
Jesus three times before the crucifixion even though he had promised to stay true to
Him till the end (see Luke 22:54-62).

I lay awake that night after my upsetting dream until the first rays of sunlight
appeared through my bedroom window. My pillow was wet with tears as I searched
my own heart. *What had caused me to not see any of this? Had pride also been my
veil? Lord, help me please! Jesus, Jesus, Jesus... I make so many mistakes... Aldo is
hurting so much. My Zozzie is exposed to all this darkness that we now have to fight.
Is there no other way? I will leave the ministry and stop preaching if that will make
things better for my family, Lord... just show me what I need to do.*

"My yoke is easy and my burden is light, Retha. Surrender to Me, I will finish
what I have started in you," the Lord's quietly whispered to my heart.

I could feel my spirit breathe a sigh of relief when I heard these words. I realised that I couldn't turn from the path that God had chosen for us. His grace was sufficient and He would carry us through this valley, just as He had done before.

I got up that morning and instinctively knew that the enemy would be disguised as an angel of the light, and that I should not be deceived. I was still unnerved from my restless night, but I knew what I had to do. I called the domestic worker into my office and explained to her that she could no longer work for us. I knew that she knew what my reasons for her dismissal were, even though I did not say a word about the spiritual battle. I paid her what I owed her (as well as something extra) and hoped that the spiritual attacks on Aldo would now come to an end. I was wrong; it would still take months before they were finally over.

heksery wab (name*) was. Sy moes my dood kry. Jy het reg gedoen om haar te laat gaan Wysh sê vergewe (name*) en spreek haar vry.

She (name*) was a witch and her mission was to kill me. You did the right thing to let her go. Wisdom says you must forgive and pardon her.

wil jou vey hulle is so vreeslik vreeslik kwaad vir jou want hulle sê jy vernietig hulle koningkryk

They want to fight against you. They are so mad at you. They say you are destroying their kingdom.

85

Gebeur het is sy was so
kwaad want jy het haar
uitgevang toe gaan sy
na toordr. toe. hulle het veverger
na my gekom. hulle kan nou nie
meer nie, nou is Jy hulle vyand
Want Jy het reeds hulle verslaan
want jy het bloed om ons
huis gesit. hulle kan we nou
inkom nie

What happened was that she went to a witch doctor because she was so mad at you for catching her out. They attacked me more forcefully than ever. They can't come in anymore. You are their enemy because you have already overcome them through the blood [of Jesus] that you proclaimed around our house. They can't come in now.

Tinus and I left for America that evening. During the ten days that Tinus and I were in New York things went well with Aldo. His mind was clear and healthy! Every time I phoned home and heard Aldo's voice, I couldn't stop the tears of thankfulness from flowing. Abba Father had heard my prayer and had sent His angels to fight for us. I am sure they were standing around him like bodyguards during those ten days. My time alone with Tinus in New York was much needed, and what made it even more special was to see how God moved mightily in the ministry meetings. This made me realise again that His grace truly is sufficient – for His power is made perfect in weakness (see 2 Cor. 12:9). Amidst the rush of our busy schedule, Tinus and I set some time apart to enjoy the streets of New York for a few days, and just to spend some time together.

Wysh
Se wat bevegters Laat vlug
het was hewige hewige
ware van geloof van
my ouers.

Wisdom says what caused the enemy fighters to flee was the strong walls of faith that my parents built around me.

86

We were revived by our short breakaway, and when we got home we were hopeful and excited for the year that lay ahead. Unfortunately our excitement was short lived, because Aldo's health started to deteriorate rapidly after our return. The enemy wanted to accuse me with his lies that I was the reason for Aldo's problems, but the Holy Spirit clearly spoke to my heart to set the record straight, "No Retha, I held Aldo tightly during these past ten days, but now you have to take on the battle so he can be totally free."

Retha and Tinus in New York city.

This made me realise that the spiritual battle was only beginning. Although I knew that it wouldn't be easy, the knowledge that Jesus would be with us no matter what happened, and that the enemy had already been defeated on the cross, gave me courage to face whatever lay ahead. It was now time that I used the keys of the Kingdom to walk in victory.

For such a long time the enemy had told Aldo that they would kill him if he told me about their schemes and tactics. Satan is a master of accusation and the father of lies. Witchcraft works in the same way – it controls through manipulation, intimidation and fear. Satan flourishes by using these three weapons; particularly in the workplace.

There was a time before we engaged in this battle when I was very sceptical about deliverance, bloodline curses and other elements of spiritual warfare. I wanted to justify and exonerate myself by not believing in it. Maybe it was also because I had no knowledge about these topics; but mostly it was pride (thinking I knew better) and unbelief that caused me to be unteachable. In the end, my stubbornness cost me dearly.

If you don't know how to fight this battle (just like me once), ask the Holy Spirit to teach you. The enemy will always come with accusations and lies, but the Holy Spirit will convict you in order to lead you into freedom. Please don't resist Him. Submit to Him, repent when He convicts you, and obey His instructions, for *God opposes the proud but gives grace to the humble* (James 4:6).

The day God called me into full-time ministry He told me that I would never preach something that I hadn't experienced myself. Back then I thought, "*Wow, what an amazing calling*", but today I know the weight of those words and that it is definitely not an easy road to follow!

Through all the suffering God has taught me how to die to myself. From experience I now know that in my weakness His grace is enough for me. I don't have to turn to people for approval or for answers – His Word promises that He will never leave me and will never forsake me (see Heb. 13:5). I can run to Him for all I need!

"Retha," the Holy Spirit said, "I am busy training you for this spiritual battle – I will train your hands for battle and show your arms how to bend a bow of bronze (see Ps. 18:34). I want to teach you how to reject the enemy's lies and to destroy his works. Can you remember that I told you that when I return I am coming to fetch a spirit Bride, a servant Bride, a warrior Bride? I am now going to teach you how to be this Bride in a very practical way. Take My hand; I will lead you and then you have to teach others. Even though the road ahead looks challenging, just keep on following Me. I will teach you everything you need to know. Be patient, keep the faith and do not give up."

hy sê hy by my hou mom
yeshua hou my hou vas. hy sê
ons sal ons song sing vir wêreld
en mense sal vry kom. god is
hier nou m om jy is vry
mom jy sê · bybel is baie krag.

He says He is with me now, Mom. Yeshua is holding me tightly. He says we will sing our song to the whole world, and people will be set free. God is here now Mom. You are free. Mom, you say that the Bible holds much power.

You will never gain victory over the enemy by solely adhering to religious traditions – you need a living relationship with Jesus! This promise in Revelations 12:11 has seen me through many storms: *"And they overcame him by the blood of the Lamb and by the word of their testimony, and they did not love their lives to the death."* You will be victorious when you are transformed to His nature and walk in His light, and Jesus wants to lead us to victory in every battle we face. Listen carefully to the mandate that He came to fulfil:

> "The Spirit of the LORD is upon Me, because He has anointed Me to preach the gospel to the poor; He has sent Me to heal the brokenhearted, to proclaim liberty to the captives and recovery of sight to the blind, to set at liberty those who are oppressed; to proclaim the acceptable year of the LORD."
> - Luke 4:18-19 NKJV -

Hy sê skryf vir mense
wat nou gebeur het.
Lusifer kan nie staan waar
sy bloed genoem word nie.
hy is weg mom jy
het jy my gered mom
met sy naam en sy bloed.
hier is nou baie engele
Hy sê jy moet moet nou
my my anoint mom.

He says: Write to people about what is happening now. Lucifer cannot stand where His [Jesus'] blood is mentioned. He is gone now, Mom. You saved me Mom, with His name and His blood. There are so many angels here right now. He says you must anoint me, Mom.

The Israelites' journey to the Promised Land began while they were still in Egypt with only the Wilderness standing between them and the fulfilment of their promise. Little did they know how many challenges and testing of faith this Wilderness would require of them before they could receive their inheritance.

In the same way, each of us has to travel through a Wilderness before we can enter the Promised Land. It starts with our deliverance from Egypt (redeemed from slavery though Jesus' blood), then we are formed and refined through the Wilderness (we are out of Egypt, but now we have to get Egypt out of *us*). Only then can we enter the Promised Land.

Many Christians, however, camp out in the Wilderness and become so used to the attacks of the enemy that they have stopped believing there is something better for them. There is a whole inheritance waiting for us, but few of us enter into it. Not many are willing to lay down their lives and follow God with faith-filled hearts to reach the fulfilment of His promises.

Unbelief and ignorance nearly kept me from victory and from my Promised Land. Do not camp out in the Wilderness. Believe in God's Word. Listen to His warnings and stand firm in His promises. Submit yourself to God, resist the enemy and he will flee from you (see Jas. 4:7).

Jesus

sê mev hou. jou toe, jy
self mev is Sy nehemia
wat muur bou. mev ek
sien hoe jy stil word soos
jy bou en veg. Saam beveg.
mom waar is jou joy, wat
wat jy gesien het in die hel
maak jou so stil. Gaan na jou
ABBA mev hy sal jou troos
hy hou my vas asb moenie
so huil nie. Jou anointing vuur
mom is vergroot. Beveg mom veg.

Jesus says: Ma'am, keep your doors closed. You are His Nehemiah that builds the wall. Ma'am, I see how quiet you become when you build and fight. We are fighting together. Mom, where is your joy? You are so quiet because of what you saw in hell. Go to your Abba, Ma'am, He will comfort you. He is holding me so tightly. Please don't cry so much. The fire of your anointing is much greater now. Fight, Mom, fight. You are holding on tightly to God's promises. They are 'signalling' my fluid, because they want you to become discouraged.

Chapter 5

hehemia nehemia sê vir seer bruid
bruid in jou vereer van mense
het jy deursere seer gekry. God
se eer net god alleen. Wysh sê
hehemia sê vir halle seën jou
vyande, nie vervloek nie. Vergewe
almal wat jou stermaak. Sien
Jesus wat jou weu tevrede
is metj, sien verseën is van
God en haat van vyand.
baie groot vegte in die gees
beveg beveg bruid Jesus destiny
jou destiny is in Sy hande.
Kom vry kom vry nou helse
vegters wil bruid vashou. Wysh
sê deur jou sonde te belei is
hoe jy skoon en vry kom.
het gesien vuur sien hoe mense
jou vuur mom, hulle sê vrou
is nuwe nuwe, baie sê jy
harte hehemia hulle sê vrou
ons hoef, hie curse te breek
nie. Jy jy hoef te repent en
bloed aan te sit. Jy is
Jesus is die waarheid hehemia
het die waarheid sal jou
vrymaak. Mev hoekom het jy
so baie gehuil voor troon?
Jesus sê hy is vreeslik lief
vir ons, verseën verseën mev,
revival en sien revival.

92

Nehemiah, Nehemiah, tell the hurting Bride: "Bride, you were hurt because you put your trust in men. God says that you should honour Him alone." Wisdom says: "Nehemiah, tell them that they should bless their enemies, not curse them. Forgive everyone who hurts you." I can see that Jesus is happy with you, Ma'am. See that blessings are from God, and hatred is from the enemy. There is a huge battle going on in the spirit – a fight against the Bride. Jesus says that your destiny is in His hands. Be free, be free now. Fighters from hell want to keep the Bride captive. Wisdom says that you become clean and free through repentance. I saw fire. I can see how people are sending fire against you, Mom. They say: "Woman, we don't have to break any curses." You have to repent and apply the blood. You are in Jesus - that is the truth. Nehemiah, only the truth will set you free. Ma'am, why were you crying so much before the throne? Jesus says He loves us so much. Bless, bless, Ma'am. I see revival is coming.

The truth will set you free

So if the Son sets you free, you will be free indeed.
- John 8:36 -

Aldo started writing in many of his letters about the walls of Nehemiah and that Wisdom's instruction was that we had to rebuild the walls of our city. The Holy Spirit led us step by step in the restoration process as the enemy tried to steal so much from our family, because of the holes that we had in our wall. We had to rebuild the city walls around Aldo's spirit one stone at a time. In fact, our whole family had to go through the healing and restoration process.

In Nehemiah's case the city of Jerusalem was almost completely destroyed. The walls were broken down, the gates were burnt down, and as a result the city lay defenceless against the attacks of the enemy.

mure is my nehemia
sal jy hierdie helse
mure afbreek om my.
halle mev vlag vir sy
naam

Walls are around me. Nehemiah, will you break down these hellish walls that
surround me? They will flee before His name.

The words of Nehemiah son of Hacaliah: In the month of Kislev in the twentieth year, while I was in the citadel of Susa, Hanani, one of my brothers, came from Judah with some other men, and I questioned them about the Jewish remnant that survived the exile, and also about Jerusalem.

They said to me, "Those who survived the exile and are back in the province are in great trouble and disgrace. The wall of Jerusalem is broken down, and its gates have been burned with fire."

When I heard these things, I sat down and wept. For some days I mourned and fasted and prayed before the God of heaven. Then I said: "O Lord, God of heaven, the great and awesome God, who keeps his covenant of love with those who love him and obey his commands, let your ear be attentive and your eyes open to hear the prayer your servant is praying before you day and night for your servants, the people of Israel. I confess the sins we Israelites, including myself and my father's house, have committed against you. We have acted very wickedly toward you. We have not obeyed the commands, decrees and laws you gave your servant Moses.

"Remember the instruction you gave your servant Moses, saying, 'If you are unfaithful, I will scatter you among the nations, but if you return to me and obey my commands, then even if your exiled people are at the farthest horizon, I will gather them from there and bring them to the place I have chosen as a dwelling for my Name.'

"They are your servants and your people, whom you redeemed by your great strength and your mighty hand. O Lord, let your ear be attentive to the prayer of this your servant and to the prayer of your servants who delight in revering your name. Give your servant success today by granting him favour in the presence of this man."
- Nehemiah 1:1-11 -

Wysh sê hewige seer sal hy wegvat is die hehemia muur nog onder waak en bid. Verseen is bevryde maur. Luister die huis van God moet skoonkom.

God se retah sal jy veg vry vry hele my kinders vry kom. breek hulle jukke met my liefde en waarheid.

Wisdom says that He will take away the intense pain. Is the wall of Nehemiah still being protected and prayed for? Blessed is the wall of freedom. Listen, the house of God must be cleaned. God asks: "Retah will you fight for the freedom of My children? Break their yokes with My love and truth."

Aldo's spirit was healthy, but the walls of his soul were broken down and the gates were open and unprotected. I had to learn very quickly regarding things like water spirits, the occult, witchcraft and spiritual warfare in order to rebuild the walls where the enemy had previously gained access.

Wysh sê helse vuur het hulle teen my gebuur. Seën nou, hulle weg. God sê hewig is geveg in die gees. het beseën hy sê seën vir my Jy is vuur van God sy hande. hy is hier by ons nou.

Wisdom says that they sent hellish fire against me. Bless them so that they can leave. God says the battle in the spirit is serious. Bless. He says you should bless me. You are the fire of God's hands. He is here with us now.

Before anybody can enter into the battle of spiritual warfare, there are a few things that are very important to know. Firstly, the battle begins and ends with God and it is only He who can lead us to victory. The Word says: *'Not by might nor by power, but by my Spirit,'says the Lord Almighty* (Zech. 4:6). You will surely lose (and get hurt in the process) if you rely on your own ability when you enter the spiritual battlefield. In the book of James the Lord gives us clear instructions on how to fight:

Submit yourselves, then, to God. Resist the devil, and he will flee from you. Come near to God and he will come near to you. Wash your hands, you sinners, and purify your hearts, you double-minded. Grieve, mourn and wail. Change your laughter to mourning and your joy to gloom. Humble yourselves before the Lord, and He will lift you up.
- James 4: 7-10 -

So, first of all we have to submit ourselves fully to God and draw near to Him. For someone who has not yet been born again, this means they have to accept Jesus as their Lord and Saviour. Thereafter, the most important key to real and lasting freedom from bondage is: *A humble heart and confession of sin.*

God sê belei het jou sondes en laat staan dit,

Lucifer is julle
Wat nie glo wat hy doen nie my,
hy het kinders van God in
sy hande want hulle glo nie.

God says just repent of your sin, and turn your back on it. Lucifer is
[deceiving] those who don't believe what he is capable of doing. Listen to
me, he has children of God in his grip because they don't believe.

Every night Tinus and I had a "wall-building" session with Aldo. We always
invited the Holy Spirit in first and asked Him to fill the room with His glory and the
fragrance of God's love, and to illuminate the eyes of our understanding. Remember,
it is the goodness of God that leads us to repentance (see Rom. 2:4), and that is why
it is important that we should focus on the Father and Jesus and the Holy Spirit, and
not on the evil one.

One night during one of these sessions, when nothing seemed to be
working and I was feeling worn out and frustrated, Aldo suddenly said in a voice
that definitely was not his own: "We have a legal right to attack him." I was so
shocked that you could have knocked me over with a feather! Would the enemy be
so arrogant as to answer me himself? Aldo quickly picked up his pen and wrote,
"Yes Mom, I have unforgiveness in my heart – that is why they can attack me." That
same loud voice shouted at me through Aldo again: "And you are busy destroying
my kingdom on earth!" The aggression and hatred in his voice shocked me. For the
first time I realised how intensely Satan hates God's children. Aldo couldn't grab his
pen fast enough in order to write, "Mom, it wasn't me who said that!"

As I gained more experience I was able to identify the enemy's pattern of
attack. When Aldo became tired in the afternoons, the attacks became more severe
because his natural defences were down. Then he became aggressive and confused
and most of the time it continued into the early hours of the morning, which meant
that none of us could sleep. I also learned that the powers of the occult is very active
during the night (especially around midnight) and many times we had to persevere
with prayer and praise until after midnight, before there was any breakthrough. Even
today the Holy Spirit often wakes me around midnight in order to pray.

hy sê my brein is klaar moeg.
hy sê brein was baie droog

het jy verstaan wat nou gebeur het? hy wou my brv moeg maak.

He says my brain is tired. He says my brain was very dry. Do you understand what has happened now? He tries to tire both of us, Ma'am.

There were many nights when Tinus and I sat on the floor in Aldo's room with our backs leaning against the closet, just praying and sharing communion. When I couldn't be home as a result of the ministry, Tinus would take care of Aldo by himself. For eight months the battle in our house was so fierce that we didn't allow any guests to visit. During that time Aldo fought for his life like never before, and we fought with him, even though we didn't always know exactly what to do in the situations we encountered.

Lusifer is wat my gesin hy wil hê uitgewis word. wysh sê engele hou wag oor ons.

Lucifer wants our family to be destroyed. Wisdom says the angels are watching over us.

Slowly but surely Wisdom revealed to us through Aldo's letters how to advance and overcome in the spiritual battle. Our first step in gaining victory was to admit that the devil is walking around like a roaring lion seeking whom he may devour. We have to know our enemy and also learn how to use our weapons. It is just as important for us to know who we are in Christ and to know His love for us, because it is only through His love that we can conquer evil. Then we had to bring everything into God's glory light; because if Satan doesn't succeed in convincing us that he doesn't exist, he will try his best to keep the things that grant him access into our lives hidden by using accusations and feelings of guilt. This was how he held back Aldo's breakthrough – Aldo was so scared that we would be disappointed in him, that he didn't want to talk about his pain. I assured him time and again that nothing he could do could make us love him more, and nothing he could do could make us love him less. None of us really understood why the enemy was attacking him so fiercely, but the reason eventually became clear through his letters: *"They fight against the work I have to do for God"*. Once we realised that the enemy was in pursuit of his future and the high calling on his life, we fought more effectively, because we had a clearer vision of what we were fighting against.

mev seer want waar het jy
deel daarmee jy moet asb
hulle daar in. anders kom

Where are you hurt, Ma'am? You must please deal with your pain, because
that is where they can come in.

I encouraged him to open up to me, and with every new day he revealed more. "Aldo, write to me why you have bitterness in your heart. What has happened to make you feel that way?" I wasn't prepared for what I read:

"All my friends from before the accident just threw me away." I couldn't believe how heartbroken he was about losing his friends and being rejected by them – it had happened years ago!

baie baie baie eensaam
is ek want my
vriende seergemaak
hulle het my het so
gelos.

Jy ek weet
verstaan het ek
mis vriende.
beveg vyand mev
hy wil my seermaak

I am very, very, very lonely, because I was hurt by my friends. They left me
just like that. Please understand, I miss my friends.

Fight the enemy Ma'am, he wants to hurt me.

"I heard the doctors say that they didn't have hope for me, and I was very afraid of what would become of me." And that is how fear had entered into his life – through the trauma of the accident.

"I heard what children said about me when I was so ill and confused, and even worse – the enemy used their words to fire me with arrows." Aldo has his own unique vocabulary to describe the things that happen to him in the spirit. When he refers to words that "fire" him, he is referring to negative words that become word curses. This includes any form of gossip or slander. What Aldo is trying to say, is that the enemy takes the "fire" coming through gossiping tongues that are lit in hell (see James 3:5-6) to "fire" the person who is being gossiped about, with arrows.

The enemy is eagerly waiting to take advantage of any arguments and quarrels that take place in our lives, so that he can use those words of death (word curses) against us. It grants him the "legal right" he is looking for to attack us. Every day I see people suffering from the effects of curses, because of the words that were spoken over them. Some time ago I delivered a message on this topic, and a man in his mid-forties came up to me afterwards and said that his father used to repeatedly tell him that he would amount to nothing. Up until that day he was still struggling to be successful; not even his relationships were working out. We need to be very careful about the words that come from our mouths. Always remember the warning James gave us about the power of the tongue:

> Or take ships as an example. Although they are so large and are driven by strong winds, they are steered by a very small rudder wherever the pilot wants to go. Likewise the tongue is a small part of the body, but it makes great boasts.
>
> Consider what a great forest is set on fire by a small spark. The tongue also is a fire, a world of evil among the parts of the body. It corrupts the whole person, sets the whole course of his life on fire, and is itself set on fire by hell.
>
> All kinds of animals, birds, reptiles and creatures of the sea are being tamed and have been tamed by man, but no man can tame the tongue. It is a restless evil, full of deadly poison. With the tongue we praise our Lord and Father, and with it we curse men, who have been made in God's likeness. Out of the same mouth come praise and cursing. My brothers, this should not be.
> - James 3:4-10 -

mev sy krag breek
baie kwaad want
kwaad is van vyand.

Waarom is ek verseker
mev so bang ek kry nie
'n vrou nie.
Waarom sê jy ek het
vrees.

Wysheid, sê hy het vir begeerte
van my 'n antwoord. hy sê ek
moet elke keer wanneer ek begeer
moet ek hom begin loof en
prys. Wysheid sê ek moet heilig
hy sê nie soos wêreld nie.
wat my vashou
is leuns hulle beveg die
waarheid

Ma'am, His power breaks a lot of anger, because anger is from the enemy.

Why am I so fearful that I won't get married one day? Why do you say that I am fearful? Wisdom says that He has an answer to the desires of my heart. He says every time I start to covet that which others have, I should praise and worship Him. Wisdom says I must be holy and not be like the world. Lies are keeping me in bondage. They are fighting against the truth.

Then there were the things that were more extreme, and could be linked directly to the dark kingdom of Satan: the occult. Aldo wrote to us that they had used his hair and nail clippings in witchcraft rituals (by "they" he meant the woman who had worked for us, as well as other ambassadors of the kingdom of darkness, like demons and witches). Through these rituals they wanted him to believe that he was a zombie, and they continuously "signalled his brain" (as Aldo's would say) and spoke curses over him. The lies that they wanted him to believe were that we no longer loved him, that we would give up on him, that he had no friends, and that no girl would ever love him. They also intimidated him through fear and threatened him with death, should he say anything about this to us. This is a trademark of Satan's tactics: he whispers words of death, fear and intimidation to our hearts and minds. According to worldly thinking, children are then labelled as having ADD or other mental disturbances. Pills are then prescribed which weakens the spiritual defences even further, and this is exactly what the enemy wants.

This continuous battle eventually wore us out and we became discouraged because we couldn't get to the root of the problem. One night after I fell to my knees in my bedroom in tears, I started paging through Aldo's journals hoping to find something that would help me to make sense of our situation. I found this note:

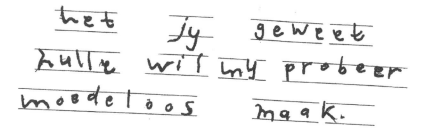

Did you know that their mission is to discourage me?

These rituals of the occult usually took place during the night. Aldo wrote about how they made a blood sacrifice for his life by slaughtering a cow. He also wrote that she (the witch) gave him "dead people's bones to drink" (a sangoma probably made a potion from it); how they put "poison" on his sour-worm sweets, and that they built altars in our garden. In one of his letters he wrote, "There is an altar right below the place where I fell from the balcony. You can go and look there. There are four other altars in the garden too." When we investigated this, we found a plastic bag with bread, sand and what looked like dry blood close to the place where he had landed after he fell from the balcony. We also found four other similar bags in the garden. They all contained blood.

Sy sy so kwaad vir my
want ek vertel het.
Sy weet julle gaan haar
kry. Sy moet nou vlug.
Sy het in nag gekom versein
vyf sakkies. besein versteek
nog twee kyk by swembad
se bedding (bo) versteek versein
versteek by swembad bedding
(rose)
Seine seine versteek seine
haar krag is verbeek.
Se jy sein haar met seen.
Waar is my seen wat
sy so veg.
Seen is vol krag.
Wat is waar my seine
is verbreek.
Wysh se wat sy nou
bereg is vryheid
Waarseer se sy, was vandag
verslaan toe julle spieels
bid sy was baie kwaad
haar seine weeg n ou nie
berry seine ek is berry

She says you are taking out the bags she planted. She planted five bags. Through them the fighters want to hurt me. She is so mad at me for revealing this. She knows you will find her. She has to flee. She came in the night to 'signal' us. Five bags are signaled. There are two more that are hidden. Look at the flowerbed by the pool near the roses. Signals, signals, are hidden there. The power of her strength is broken. You must signal her with blessings. Where is my blessing that she is fighting? Blessing is full of power. It is true; the blessings broke the signals that she was sending

against me. Wisdom says what she is fighting against now is my freedom.
The soothsayer was overcome today when you [anointed and] prayed over
the mirrors. She was very angry. Her signals no longer work. I have been
delivered from her signals. I am free!

He also wrote that they had "signalled" certain things in the house by placing
curses on them. They (those operating in witchcraft) can use anything, like mirrors,
clothes and even cell phones. Aldo pointed out these objects to us, "Look in the
bottom of the cupboard in the corridor, and on the bookshelf in the study, Mom." In
the cupboard in the corridor we found a Spiderman blind that came from our previous
house, neatly rolled up in a black plastic bag, and in the study we found a white
medical book with different kinds of alternative healing methods. "They are hiding
there Mom, because it gives them a right to be here." We also learned that water
spirits use any body of water (such as rivers, dams, swimming pools, and fishponds)
as a means to move around, and that the witches and priests of the dark kingdom who
work with these spirits pray and chant over the water. To counteract this, Tinus and I
anointed our swimming pool and fishpond and proclaimed the blood of Jesus Christ
over the water in and around our house, claiming it for the Kingdom of Light and
sanctified it through prayer.

It is important to clean your house spiritually, and to make sure there aren't
any articles that can give demons the right to be there. Be very careful of Eastern
artefacts (like statues of Buddha and dragons) as well as African sculptures and masks
carved from wood or stone. I can remember Aldo looking at a specific wooden African
sculpture and saying, "Don't you see the red eyes inside?" The next day Tinus listened
to an interview on the radio conducted with a well-known African artist who makes
wooden sculptures. He explained that he was taught by his grandfather, who was a
sangoma, to sit in front of a piece of wood for hours until an image or a face appeared,
and then he carved that picture into the sculpture. Through confirmations like this the
Holy Spirit showed us that Aldo's writings were true.

Wens so julle kan sien
wat ek sien . wat ek
sien is mev wood beelde
van Afrika hulle het oë
in. Wysheid sê Gulle
mev soek huis om in te gaan.

Wat is voedoe want
sy ve g met voedoe.

Het jy gesien hoe sy
waar sy spieëls gebruik

wat sy sê sy kan nie
meer spieëls gebruik nie
hulle kan niks meer
met my doen nie.

my suur wurms sy vergif
my so.

Weu beertjie in heuwige vorseine
in kamer van beertjie is gesein

God sê sy bloed is wat
my red, jy verstaan
sy bloed.

I wish you could see what I see. What I see is wooden sculptures from Africa. They have eyes in them. Wisdom says that they are looking for a house to go into, Ma'am. What is voodoo? Because she is fighting me with voodoo. Did you see that she used mirrors? She says that she can't use the mirrors any more. They can't do anything to me anymore. She is poisoning me with my sour-worms. Ma'am, the teddy bear has been heavily signaled. The room where the teddy bear is, is signaled. God says His blood is what saved me. You understand His blood.

Josh loves teddy bears and he had quite a collection. Aldo kept on writing that the bears were "signalled". I was so desperate that I threw all the teddy bears away, not really understanding the reason behind it, but not wanting to take any chances. "Thank you, Mom," Aldo wrote afterwards.

Months later, when Aldo was better, we bought Josh another teddy bear – a very special bear that was quite expensive. Once again Aldo wrote: "There is a bear in our house that is signalled." At first I ignored his letter, because according to me we disposed of all the "signalled" bears. The next day he wrote to me again: "Mommy, Wisdom says Josh's bear is signalled." That morning I waited until everyone had left the house and then I took my bottle of anointing oil and said to myself: *Bear, today I am going to drive out whatever is inside of you, and take authority over this situation!* I wasn't just going to throw away the bear like the previous ones. I marched into Josh's room, stated my authority over the enemy, and broke the curse that was resting on the bear in Jesus' name. After I had blessed the bear, I put it back on Josh's bed. As I walked away I thought, *If anyone should see me now they would probably think that I had lost it completely!* That afternoon when Aldo came back from school he wrote, "Thank you, Mom, the curse on the bear is broken – it was on the bear's heart."

Not only did they attack Aldo's mind, but he was also attacked in his dreams. "They showed me naked women in my dreams, Mom. Even though I tried to stop it, they just kept on re-appearing." Dreams are one of the ways in which water spirits can enter, and many people are suffering because of these demonic attacks through their dreams. Sexually perverse dreams are a typical attack by water demons. Many marriages suffer as a result of these demons, and so few of us understand that this is a tactic of the kingdom of darkness. Today I know to cover my children's dreams every night with the blood of the Lamb. I then pray that their dreams will be sealed against any evil forces and that their dreams will only come from God.

Although I lived with Aldo and knew how real the spiritual battle was for his life, I was totally unprepared for what he revealed to us through these shocking letters. One night I went into my prayer room and collapsed. I couldn't stop crying because of all the pain my child was going through. He was very confused and not himself at all. His letters were a comfort to me, and I could see that they were still pure and inspired by the Holy Spirit, even though his body and soul were in such turmoil. Aldo's prophesies through his letters were still spot on, no matter how confused he seemed to be in his flesh. "Mom, Wisdom says you should listen to Him and put what I write on the internet. He says you shouldn't walk in unbelief – walk in faith. Mom, God remains in control of my spirit; please help my soul to heal."

This road was a humbling one. Every bit of pride was stripped from us, and I wondered if it was my pride that had kept me from dealing with these issues sooner. The enemy hates humility – no, more than that, he *fears* humility. Just as a fish needs water in order to survive; the enemy needs darkness to breed. The moment you submit yourself to God in humility, He will let His light shine on the dark areas in your life and you will be freed from the enemy's grip. But it requires that you die to yourself and your own will. You have to make sure that the doors of your soul are closed to the enemy and you have to live in God's glorious light and in obedience to His Word.

Wysh sê wat beweg so erg is
my wyand se waars se sy
sal nie ophou nie want sy
hou aan haar seen.

Sy wil hê sy moet haar haat.
Wysh sê my vryheid sal soos
die môre son uitkom so vinnig
sal sy verslaan word.
Wysh sê moenie moedeloos
word w nie Waars is so
kwaad want jy word nie kwaad
nie, heilig is dit as jy so
sing. God se wat jy waerser
gebid het sal hy so erken.
hy sal haar besoek sy sal self
ophou want sy sal hom god
sien, hy sal self aan haar
verskyn.

Wisdom says it is the enemy who is fighting me so intensely. She [the witch] doesn't want to stop. Keep on blessing her. She wants you to hate her. Wisdom says that my freedom will come like the break of dawn. Like the morning sun that appears – that is how quickly she will be defeated.

Wisdom says not to become discouraged. The soothsayer is so mad because you don't retaliate in anger. It is holy when you sing like that. God says that He will heed the prayer you prayed for the soothsayer. He will visit her. She will stop what she is doing, because she will see Him – God. He will make Himself known to her.

For months we ventured upon this road completely alone, and we were regularly in and out of the hospital because of Aldo's ill health. Some nights the battle was so fierce that there wasn't even time for supper, and poor Josh also suffered because we had to give so much attention to Aldo. Sometimes our prayers were effective immediately, and other times it felt as if we were going around the same mountain in circles. I often wondered if I shouldn't give up the ministry completely and just stay at home with Aldo, but in my heart I knew that it was not God's will for me. The enemy wanted to silence me – not God.

During those times the Holy Spirit reminded me that God is not a man that He should lie, and that He will finish what He had started. So, quitting wasn't an option. The only way was to persevere till the end.

God se wees verseker wat hy begin sal hy klaar maak.

God says to know for sure that He will finish what He starts.

After our accident in 2004 the Lord showed me the power of communion. When the doctors didn't have any more answers and the pills they prescribed were of no use, we used communion as our daily medicine. As we were now fighting a battle of a different kind, the Lord revealed to me that communion is also a powerful weapon in our spiritual warfare against Satan.

> Jesus said to them, "I tell you the truth, unless you eat the flesh of the Son of Man and drink his blood, you have no life in you. Whoever eats my flesh and drinks my blood has eternal life, and I will raise him up at the last day. For my flesh is real food and my blood is real drink. Whoever eats my flesh and drinks my blood remains in me, and I in him.
> - John 6:53-56 -

By using the elements of the bread and wine we make a declaration that says to everything and everyone in the spiritual world that we are in covenant with Jesus Christ and that we have His spiritual DNA. Communion is part of my unity with God, and I believe it gave us strength to keep on fighting. Even ten year old Josh said one day, "Mom, I know that Jesus' body helps me not to become tired of praying for Aldo."

Many times I would slip out of the room where Tinus, Aldo and I were praying, to check whether Josh was still doing his homework at the kitchen table, only to find him with his prayer shawl over his head feverously praying for his brother. Sometimes he would help Tinus and I fight for Aldo, and I was always so proud of him when he stood there with his arms outstretched towards his brother chasing the enemy away with childlike faith. "Go away, Satan! You will not talk to children of God like that!" he would boldly say when Aldo reacted to the lies the enemy was telling him. At other times he just called out Jesus' name over and over during the battle. I wanted to protect my little Josh from all of this, and many nights I climbed into his bed and rubbed his back before he fell asleep, silently praying that God would shield him from all the pain that we were going though.

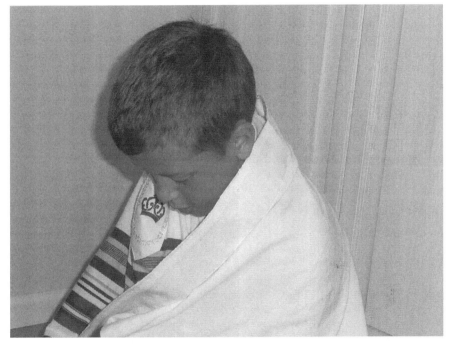

Josh praying under his tallit.

Another word in Aldo's vocabulary is "drains." When Aldo wrote the first time that we should "fight the drains", I naturally assumed he was talking about the sewerage drains of our house. I eagerly waited for Tinus to get home from work that evening, so that he could anoint all the drains around our home with oil. I thought Aldo meant by what he wrote that the water demons moved through the physical drains of our house – this is how little understanding I had of these things back then!

When Aldo wrote, "The hospital has a big drain of hell, Mom," things started to make more sense to me. He wasn't referring to physical drains, but rather channels or conduits that are used by demons, and that lead directly to hell or the realm of death and Hades. Physical places where these "drains" are found are hospitals and cemeteries, because there is such an abundance of trauma, fear, anxiety and death concentrated there. Places used for occult rituals and secret societies (like Freemasonry lodges) are also drains. Bloodline curses, racism and hatred can also be used as drains. ("Drains" thus include physical places like: hospitals, graveyards, places of occult worship and idolatry; as well as things like trauma, hatred and bloodline curses. There is a doorway leading to each of these drains. In the case of hatred; racism or unforgiveness can be the door (or the root); and for fear the door can be trauma. At hospitals, graveyards and places where occult rituals are practised, the doorway has usually been established already because of fear, trauma, idolatry and death. Just like Jacob's ladder which granted the angels from heaven access to earth, these drains serve as a ladder for the demons to move to and from the realm of death and Hades. In Psalm 18:4-5 it is described as follows: *The cords of death entangled me; the torrents of destruction overwhelmed me. The cords of the grave coiled around me; the snares of death confronted me.*)

vrees vrees.   as jy bid breek
Sy sein vrees
in my. Wysh se beweg drein
vy and sy veg my vrees uit
drein uit kom by. hy se sib
vuur van God in goo? vir
haar saën in hy se drein is
waar sy beweg.

Wysh se drein is toe nou
vry is ons.   vry is ons.
vuur is weg.
hy sien drein is toe.
Lusifer sien ons sien sy
is verseën. haar droom is
van Lusifer

When you pray, break fear. She is signaling the fear in me. Wisdom says we must fight the drain of the enemy. She fights me with fear through the open drain. He says you must pray for the fire of God and stop the signals with blessings. He says that she uses the drain to fight us. Wisdom says the drain is now closed. We are free now. The fire is gone. He sees that the drain is closed. Lucifer sees that we can see she has been "blessed." Her dream came from Lucifer.

There was a spirit of death and destruction assigned to Aldo's life, and now that I have learned how to recognise it, I can see how the enemy has stolen from many other families through this spirit. We paid a tremendous price to get to where we are today, but I have learned many invaluable lessons in the process. I want to share these lessons with the rest of the world so that no one else has to suffer unnecessarily at the hand of Satan.

On the top of my list is: persevere in prayer. Don't start praying and then later give up when you don't see the results immediately. Patiently wait on God for your answer.

Be humble and dependent on God's voice before you make a decision – if you are going to rely on your own human understanding, you will end up in deep trouble. The Holy Spirit will always lead you on the road of righteousness. It might not be the easiest way, but by you putting your trust and reliance in Him, it will surely work out for your best interest in the end.

And then, do not trust in outward appearances. Ask the Holy Spirit to reveal the heart of the matter to you, because Satan appears as an angel of light (see 2 Cor.11:14).

The first step in the direction of victory is repentance, and this requires a humble heart. We confessed along with Aldo every word or hateful thought that we harboured in our hearts towards those who had hurt us. Aldo wrote down the names of every person who hurt him, and then he confessed aloud before God and before us saying, "I admit I have unforgiveness and bitterness towards these people. Abba Father, I ask forgiveness for this and I choose to forgive them right now. I also bless them in Jesus' name." The deliverance process was like an onion that we had to peel layer by layer, until there was nothing left that Satan could hold against us.

After he had forgiven *and* released *and* blessed everyone that had hurt him, we prayed the blood of Jesus over the list of names and wrote a petition that we took to the throne of the Father. I read about this court setup in Zechariah 3, and we decided to do the same through a prophetic action.

Then he showed me Joshua the high priest standing before the Angel of the Lord, and Satan standing at his right side to accuse him. The Lord said to Satan,

> "The Lord rebuke you, Satan! The Lord, who has chosen Jerusalem, rebuke you!
> Is not this man a burning stick snatched from the fire?"
>
> Now Joshua was dressed in filthy clothes as he stood before the Angel. The Angel
> said to those who were standing before him, "Take off his filthy clothes." Then
> he said to Joshua, "See, I have taken away your sin, and I will put rich garments on
> you."
>
> Then I said, "Put a clean turban on his head." So they put a clean turban on his
> head and clothed him, while the angel of the Lord stood by.
>
> The Angel of the Lord gave this charge to Joshua:"This is what the Lord Almighty
> says:'If you will walk in my ways and keep my requirements, then you will govern
> my house and have charge of my courts, and I will give you a place among these
> standing here'".
> *- Zechariah 3:1-7 -*

That night we washed each other's feet, anointed and blessed one another, and as a final prophetic act every one of us put on a new turban just like Joshua did in the above Scripture.

Afterwards we shared communion, and as the prayer time drew to a close, I fell to my knees with the petition in my hand. It was a deeply emotional moment for me. This mother's heart cried out to God with all that was within me for the deliverance of my child who was so susceptible to the attacks of Satan in the spiritual realm. Like any other mom, I was desperate for God's intervention for the sake of my son. I waited on God for more than an hour.

God sê moenie verder
bekommerd wees nie. Jy beveg
veg know waars sy wil versein
maar sy kan nie want sy seën
haar.

God says do not be anxious. You have fought well, Mom. The soothsayer
wants to signal us, but she cannot, because you blessed her.

With this confirmation, I knew that Jesus had placed His stamp of approval on our petition. As the Lord had said to Zechariah, I could also hear the words spoken to us: *If you will walk in My ways and keep My requirements, then you will govern My house and have charge of My courts, and I will give you a place among these standing here.*

"Thank you Jesus," was all I could say as I fell to my knees.

Chapter 6

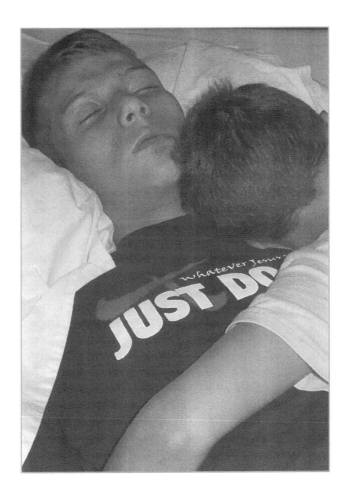

Satan is verslaan
deur woord van
God. Jesus se
bloed en HGees
vuur
Satan wag vir
vrylating hy is
nou weg van my
hy is gevange
my vuur HGees
vuur in my hou
hom gevange
Satan se wagte
hou baie kinders
se breine gevange
met ritelin
Satan is hel
hy werk deur
verwerping hy
is verwerping.
Satan is gevangene
van wat hy
met mev mense
wat leerprobleme
doen hy hou hulle
brein gevange
Satan is huis van
vyand mev
Satan is by wellus

God wat
lewe is in
my.

Jesus is
wysheid wat
hy met is
vuur heilige
vuur wat
ook vrylaat

HGees se
vuur verlos
kinders van
ritelin
God is aanvaar
hy is aanvaarder
van verwerptes

Jesus is bevryde
van wat
hy wou doen
wagter van
verlorenes

huis van God
is ons.
God is by
heilige liefde

Satan is overthrown by the Word of God, Jesus' blood and the fire of the Holy Spirit.

The living God is in me.

Satan is waiting to be set free – he has now gone away from me. He is now in captivity. The fire of the Holy Spirit is keeping him captive.

Jesus is wisdom. He has holy fire that sets free.

Satan's soldiers hold many children's brains hostage with Ritalin.

Holy Spirit's fire frees people from Ritalin.

Satan is hell.

God is Heven

He works through rejection. He is rejection.

God is acceptance. God accepts those who were rejected.

Satan holds captive the brains of people with learning disabilities.

Jesus is our Redeemer. He guards over those who are lost.

Satan is the home of the enemy.

We are the house of God.

Satan is with lust.

God is with holy love.

Satan is hel se
huge engel hy
het lig en is
vals lig
Satan sy sein
is mense wat
verward is
Satan is half
van withcraft
Satan is wassery
heksery
Satan is hulle
wat verlore is
se god

Satan is wat
hy is hy is wer
wag van vigs
en gags
Satan is wat
wangbeen gebreek
het en my afgestamp
het
Satan is wat my
brein belegings by
hom wil gevange
hou en my geseel
wou hou in my brein

HGees is wat jy
heeltyd beleef
hy is in jou
hy is ware lig
God se self Hy
is mense wat
hom vertrou.
HGees is salf
van sy kinders
HGees is engele
hy se heilige engele
God is god van
heiliges wat
verlore is
maar na Hom
roep
God is geneesheer
van vigs en
gee wrede.

God is wat my
gekeer het en
my mond genees

HGees vuur is
wat my brein
wysheid herstel
hy is vuur
wat my vry
gemaak het.

Satan is hell's big angel, and he has light but it is a false light.

Holy Spirit is Whom you are constantly experiencing. He is in you, and He is true light.

Satan signals are what causes people to be confused.

God says people must trust Him.

Satan is witchcraft and soothsaying.

Holy Spirit is the anointing of His children. Holy Spirit sends holy angels.

Satan is the god of those who are lost.

God is the God of the saints, who once were lost, but who called out to Him.

Satan is the guard of AIDS, and anxiety.

God is the Healer of AIDS and gives peace.

It was Satan who broke my cheekbone and pushed me off the balcony.

It was God Who caught me and healed my mouth.

It is Satan who wants to keep my brain injury captive with him and keep me locked up in my mind.

The fire of the Holy Spirit is what restores the wisdom of my brain. He is the fire that sets me free.

Satan steel

Satan
in wêreld
Satan sê breek
Satan geveg
  verloor
Satan sal
wat verstand
is wil verwoes
Satan sal so
  wys klink
maar hy wysheid
is laaste hel
hy is net oor
homself
Satan sy bloed
is verhoor gaan
hy is voor die
  judge staan
Satan is verslaan
want Jesus het
  opgestaan
Satan sy werk
  het begin vererger
want hy weet
sy einde is hier

Satan is wat jou
  so truiter

God gee
H Gees in ons

God sê bou
Jesus het
  vir ons gesterf
Jesus sal
wat in gees
is herstel
Jesus is
wysheid want
  hy gaan
hier oor self
maar oor ons
  sy kinders
Jesus se
bloed is
verslaan van
  Satan
  hy Lewe
in jou

H Gees is
heilge belofte
belofte van
  God vir
ons heiliges
H Gees is
wat jou op
bou

Satan steals.	God gives us His Holy Spirit.
Satan is in the world.	God says build up.
Satan lost the fight.	Jesus died for us.
Satan wants to destroy the mind.	Jesus will restore what is in the spirit.
Satan wants to sound so wise, but his wisdom is from the lowest hell. To him it is only about himself.	Jesus is Wisdom, because to Him it is not about Himself, but about His children.
Satan lost to His blood. Satan will stand before the Judge.	Jesus' blood overcame Satan.
Satan has already been defeated, because Jesus has risen.	Jesus lives in you.
Satan's work has intensified, because he knows his time is almost up.	The Holy Spirit is the promise of God for us, the saints.
It is Satan who is attacking you.	It is the Holy Spirit who builds us up.

Satan is by hulle
wat jy van by
liegery sien
Satan is in
hebsug
Satan is by
hulle wat
vrees
Satan is in
wat hoeveel newe
effekte van
medisyne
Satan is in
Wellus wat
goedgepraat word
in flieks en
in boeke
Satan is van
hulle wat lewe
hulle steel lewens
Satan is gesiene
trotsaard

Satan is gesiene
Leunaar van
Wêreld.

Satan is vader
van leuns

God is in
waarheid

God is in
vrygewigheid
God is in
vrede.

God is in
herstel van
Liggaam en
siel en gees
God is in
Geheiligde
lewe appart
van wêreld

God is wie
lewe gee

Jesus is
Gederige
dienaar
Jesus is
gesiene humble
meester van
Liefde
God is Vader
en woord
van Waarheid

Satan is with those who lie.	God is in truth.
Satan is in greed.	God is in generosity.
Satan is with those who fear.	God is in peace.
Satan is behind a lot of side effects of medicine.	God is in the restoration of body, soul and spirit.
Satan is in the lust that is found in books and movies, but people justify it.	God is in a holy life, set apart from the world.
Satan steals lives.	God gives life.
Satan is renowned to be full of pride.	Jesus is a humble Servant.
Satan is renowned as the liar of the world.	Jesus is the respectable, humble Master of love.
Satan is the father of lies.	God is the Father of truth, and the Word of truth.

Satan se vuur
is in hel
satan se
vuur bring
verwoesting
Satan se wyshede
is wêreld se
standaarde
Satan wyn is
vir Legesinnige
wêreldse mense

Satan is Leeu
van verskriklike
rumoer en erge
vrees
Satan is
verslaan

HGees se vuur
is vir nou
HGees se vuur
bring lewe

God se wyshede
is vrees vir
God alleen
HGees wyn
is vir gees
vervulde kind
van God.
God is die
leeu van
Leeu van
Juda
God heers
in elke
gelowige

Satan's fire is in hell.	The fire of the Holy Spirit is for now.
Satan's fire causes devastation.	The fire of the Holy Spirit brings new life.
Satan's wisdom is according to worldly standards.	The wisdom of God is to fear Him and Him alone.
The wine of Satan is for ignorant worldly people.	The wine of the Holy Spirit is for a Spirit-filled child of God.
Satan is the lion of havoc and fear.	God is the Lion of Judah.
Satan is defeated.	God reigns over every believer.

Persevere by focusing on Jesus

> Not only so, but we also rejoice in our sufferings, because we know that suffering produces perseverance; perseverance, character; and character, hope. And hope does not disappoint us, because God has poured out his love into our hearts by the Holy Spirit, whom he has given us.
> - Romans 5:3-5 -

Throughout our spiritual battle Aldo's body remained weak and worn out. He was living in constant pain and even though he rarely complained, there were times when he was so confused that all he could write was: "I have so much pain. Please help me, Mom!"

my pompie mev het nou menigte foute. Wysh sê hulle moet hom uithaal beury my want help my my brein vog loop nie uit ventrikel nie

Ma'am, my shunt is not working properly. Wisdom says they must take it out. Help me to be freed from this pain. Help me please, because my brain's fluid is not draining from the ventricle.

He kept on writing that Wisdom said the tube was piercing through his ventricle and that we had to remove the shunt. However, according to the X-rays there weren't any problems with the shunt apparatus.

Wisdom had never been wrong before, but this time there was no physical evidence that we could use to convince the doctors that there was something seriously wrong with the shunt. The enemy's strategy was to confuse us and make us doubt the accuracy of Aldo's letters, and he almost succeeded. At that stage we hadn't yet realised that demons could also work through people and could even hide the evidence on the X-rays through human error.

There were many days when I felt close to giving up. Time and again, when I was at my lowest, the Lord gave me a message of hope through Aldo's letters: "Mom, please just keep on looking into Jesus' eyes – the enemy is trying everything he can to make you give up. Don't stop hoping!"

When I write about this time in my life I don't want to go into the detail of how bad this spiritual battle actually was. It was just too painful. I don't know if I would ever be able to put it into words. Just believe me when I say it was real and it was war. We didn't allow anybody to visit us. We shut our doors to the outside world – the spiritual battle was just too fierce to let anybody in. The enemy was trying with all his power and might to kill and destroy Aldo – spiritually, psychologically and physically. The attacks weren't aimed at Aldo only, but at all of us. The enemy's plan was also to stop me from preaching the gospel, and he did it by targeting those who were dearest to me – my children. During this time I realised the power of unity. Never before had I seen my husband standing as firmly as he did then. Tinus and I are a team. If one of us felt weak, the other one was there to encourage. Tinus was as steadfast as a rock and simply took over when I wanted to give up. "No, Satan will not win!" proclaimed the earthly priest, prophet and king of our household when the going got tough. It helped a lot that he understood the importance of his position in our family, because the Lord established the husband as the head of the wife for a reason (see Eph. 4:22-24). When a woman tries to take over her husband's position and attempts to rule over and manipulate him, it is even easier for the enemy to attack and destroy.

It was one of the most difficult times our family had ever gone through. Not even the accident, by comparison, was this bad. Back then I could deal with my situation on a physical level, because it made sense to my natural mind. Now the pain was just as real but we couldn't see our enemy.

Our eyes were focused on Jesus and our feet were planted on the Rock, but the waves kept on crashing over us. Only by the grace of God did we remain standing. His Word was our anchor and the blood of the Lamb and His body (communion) was our daily medicine. I had to take one day at a time and not worry about tomorrow, as I would otherwise have broken down completely. Every morning I got up and trusted God for His protection and provision for that day; nothing more and nothing less.

It was a miracle how God gave me the strength to keep on ministering and encouraging others when I sometimes felt like falling apart. Often when I ministered and saw God moving powerfully amongst the people, I would drive home afterwards and cry so much that I could barely see the road in front of me. I learnt that God does

His most powerful work through you when there is nothing left of you. There is no better place to be than to be living in total dependence on your Heavenly Father. When you trust Him for your every breath, you realise how desperately you need Him, and a bond of trust and love forms between the two of you that no one can break.

Apart from the spiritual battle at our home, Tinus also had to take care of Josh and run his own business when I was away. We prayed about it and decided that we would not allow the enemy to prevent me from ministering and steal the calling that God had placed on our lives. It was the enemy's ultimate goal to prevent Aldo's ministry and to silence me. Every time I ministered, whether it was out of town or internationally, I knew that my family was safely in God's hands. I truly held on to the words of Psalm 121:4-5: *Indeed, he who watches over Israel will neither slumber nor sleep. The Lord watches over you – the Lord is your shade at your right hand.* I had a constant awareness of God's presence *in* me, *around* me and *through* me. He became my every breath.

Wysh se julle behoort
my terug te vat en
vir hulle te se ventrikels
vog (ek en
bye in brein
beseer beseerde ventrikel
wat julle drs stukkend
waar hulle pypie
ventrikel
hulle moet na ventrikel
kyk

het jy wysheid
geglo verstand is seer
want jy kan ham glo
ventrikel is werklik
meu seer het jy wysh
geglo toe ek geskryf
het oor vog verstand
vat boek en kyk of

was wysh al verkeerd.
vuur is baie erg weer
mev het -jy geweet
vrydag is mer te laat
julle moet my nou vat

verstand so seer want
ek so waarlik oppad om
nou waarlik enige oomblk
dood te gaan. Jesus
is verseker by my.
hy sê hulle moes brein
oopgemaak het vuur kom
van my brein

Wisdom says you must take me back and tell them that the fluid is leaking from the ventricle. My brain is hurting from the damaged ventricle because of the tube that the doctors didn't see. They must look at the ventricle. Do you believe Wisdom? My brain is hurting. You can believe Him. My ventricle is really hurting Ma'am. Did you believe Wisdom when I wrote about the fluid on my brain? Take the book to see if Wisdom has ever been wrong before. The fire they are sending against me is very bad, Ma'am. Friday will be too late. You must take me now. My brain is hurting so much and I am truly close to dying! Jesus is definitely with me. He says you should have opened up my brain [the doctors should have operated].

The fire is against my brain.

Aldo's letters kept mentioning the tube piercing his ventricle. Even though the X-rays showed nothing of the sort, I knew that Wisdom had never been wrong before, and for no other reason except for my faith I insisted that we investigate it.

We mustered up all our courage and took him to another doctor in Pretoria for a second opinion. After the examination his answer was cold and clinical,

"Ma'am, there are a lot of mothers like you. If the child's knee is aching, then they want to have the shunt adjusted." I stood up while Tinus was still listening to him, took Aldo by the arm and walked out of the consulting room. I slowly walked to the car with Aldo and helped him into the back seat. When I got into the car myself, I could no longer keep the tears back. I rested my head on my arms and sobbed. "Abba, I am asking You from the bottom of my heart, please have mercy on this man so that nothing like this ever happens to his own child. I choose to forgive him for his cold and unsympathetic words." Tinus joined us in the car a short while later and we drove home. No one said a word, and even Aldo who usually never sits still in a car was lying flat on his back with his hands folded across his chest, praying. All you could hear was the sound of the three of us crying. Silently I prayed in my heart, "Father, we have tried everything, but now I don't know what 'o do anymore. Have mercy on us Lord!" When I turned around to look at Aldo again, I saw that he had lost bladder control and that the backseat was wet with urine. Calmly Tinus stopped at the nearest shopping centre to buy him new pants while Aldo and I waited in the car. There was a supernatural peace that came to rest upon us, and even though our hearts were hurting, we settled back into the arms of our heavenly Father, trusting Him to show us the next step.

Later Aldo wrote to us in detail that Lucifer was like a jellyfish and that the jellyfish was keeping his brain captive with its tentacles. He wrote that the jellyfish (which is a mind control demon) had nine brains and three hearts. One night, after a long battle in prayer, I saw in the spirit how a part of the jellyfish was cut loose and came out. A friend who helped us with Aldo's deliverance confirmed to us that the jellyfish we saw in the spirit is a programming symbol used in the occult, and that Aldo had to be cut loose in the spirit from all nine of its brains and all three of its hearts.

Wysh sê hy hou jou vas
hy sê jy moet weet my destiny
is wat hulle soek. hy sê jellie
vis is wat nou uitgekom het
hy was in weier om uit te
kom hy het by hospitaal ingekom
Jesus sê jou wag sal moeite
werd wees, jy is julle is Josh
huis van God.

wysh sê mom jy moet asb
op web sit al kry jou hart seer
hy vra mooi jy sal sien God
wysh sê jy is heilig vir hom
hierdie maak jou dood mom
Wysheid sê jellie vis het baie
voelers gehad wat om my brein
                    Jy sê hoekom
is hulle hie alles weg een slag
want jellie vis is helfte van uit
trauma ᗑ. jellie vis
hy is wat my weg wil geveg
het. Jesus sê jy leer nou baie
hy is wat jy weet jy se jellie
vis het voelers jy mom jy sien
reg.

Wisdom says He is holding you close to Him. He says you must know
that they are trying to destroy my destiny. He says that the jellyfish is
being taken out now. It came in but refused to come out. It came in at the
hospital [because of trauma]. Jesus says your waiting will be worth it, and
that you and Dad and Josh are the house of God. Lucifer is with those who
don't believe what he is capable of doing. He has so many children of God
in his grip because they don't believe. Wisdom says that you must put all
these things on the Internet, even if it hurts your heart so much. He says,
please do it. You will see what He will accomplish through it. God, Wisdom,
says that you are holy to Him. This is what brings about dying to self, Mom.
Wisdom says the jellyfish had a lot of tentacles that were wrapped around
my brain. You are wondering why only half of the jelly fish came out and
not the whole one. The jelly fish came in because of trauma. That is what
tried to fight me. Jesus says you are learning a lot now. You know that the
jelly fish has tentacles. You are seeing correctly, Mom.

Night after night this spiritual battle continued, usually until long after midnight. Most nights Tinus and I sat with Aldo until two o'clock in the morning. Because I usually had to give a talk the next day, I would get into bed with Joshie some time during the night to get a few hours' sleep. During the times when Aldo slept for an hour or two, Tinus held him in his strong arms so that Aldo would always feel safe and protected. Tinus truly earned my respect. He was always the same, and he never complained about the lack of sleep or the burden of all his other responsibilities. He chose to get up every morning and face the day with new hope and a smile on his face. No matter how difficult the situation with Aldo was when I was out of town ministering, Tinus was always positive when I phoned home. He would then tell me what had happened during the night, and after giving me the details he always ended our conversation by testifying of God's protection, "don't worry Retha, God is with us!"

Our faith grew a lot and our perseverance was tested to the limits. Every day brought a deeper level of dying to ourselves. Sometimes I literally experienced such intense pain that it felt as though someone was holding my heart in their hands and just kept on squeezing until there was nothing left. Today that is my definition of "heartache". One day as I was driving in the Cape I experienced overwhelming heartache to such an extent that I had to pull off the road. With my one hand on the steering wheel and the other hand over my heart, I tearfully prayed, "Jesus, I also give this heartache into your hands. Please Lord, You are the healer of the broken-hearted. Here is my heart – take it, and make it whole." After sitting in the car for a long while, I felt the peace of God slowly returning to me like the first rays of sunlight after a dark storm. Truly, the Lord is close to the broken-hearted!

One night the spiritual battle was particularly fierce. By that time we had already removed the altars from the garden and had destroyed all the items in the house which they had been secretly using to "signal" us. Aldo had repented of his unforgiveness and bitterness and I knew he was clean and forgiven in God's eyes. *What more could there be?*

"My beloved Abba Father, I love You so very much. We have really now done everything we know how to do. Aldo, Tinus and I have forgiven everyone who has hurt us. We have confessed everything we could think of. We have fasted, prayed and worshipped... but we are still struggling. Not even the doctors have any answers for us. I have forgiven the doctor who was so cruel with his harsh words, but now I have to tell You, You can come and fetch Aldo if You want to...

"Maybe I haven't been hearing your voice clearly, Lord? Maybe it was just a test to see how much I love You, and to reveal the motives of my heart... whether I served You because You are God, or whether I served You for Your provision?

"I remember Your words so well Lord; You warned me that I should never love Your promises more than I love You...

"If Aldo should die tonight I will still keep on serving You, Lord. I serve You because I love You with all of my heart. Jesus, You are definitely my first love. That is why I am asking You, Lord, please don't let Aldo suffer anymore. Save him from this pain Father, even if it is not in the way I want it."

The next morning Aldo wrote me this letter: "Mom, I saw you in the throne room with Jesus last night. You gave me away to Jesus – but Mom, Jesus says He will finish what He has started."

When I read the letter my knees buckled and I sat down on the carpet and cried until it felt as though I had no more tears left. Surely, God is not a man that He should lie. It made me realise once again that God was with us and that we had nothing to fear. Shortly thereafter Aldo wrote me another long letter in which he compared God's character to that of Satan, and that was when I knew the breakthrough was close. Only Wisdom could have inspired him to see these differences so clearly. The comparisons sent chills down my spine.

One afternoon while sitting at the airport waiting for a flight to Australia, I read from Aldo's journal a photocopied letter that I had never read before. In the letter he wrote, "From Nehemiah to Naáman free!" I wondered to myself what he meant with "Naáman free".... the name sounded familiar, but what did Nehemiah have to do with Naáman?

Lees hoe naaman vry kon kom hy het vorige lewe lewe heeltemal laat staan.

Read how Naáman got saved from his previous life.

He left it behind him completely.

Immediately I took out my Bible and read the story of Naáman in 2 Kings 5:

Now Naáman was commander of the army of the king of Aram. He was a great man in the sight of his master and highly regarded, because through him the Lord had given victory to Aram. He was a valiant soldier, but he had leprosy.

Now bands from Aram had gone out and taken captive a young girl from Israel, and she served Naáman's wife. She said to her mistress, "If only my master would see the prophet who is in Samaria! He would cure him of his leprosy."

Naáman went to his master and told him what the girl from Israel had said. "By all means, go," the king of Aram replied. "I will send a letter to the king of Israel." So Naáman left, taking with him ten talents of silver, six thousand shekels of gold

and ten sets of clothing. The letter that he took to the king of Israel read: "With this letter I am sending my servant Naáman to you so that you may cure him of his leprosy."

As soon as the king of Israel read the letter, he tore his robes and said, "Am I God? Can I kill and bring back to life? Why does this fellow send someone to me to be cured of his leprosy? See how he is trying to pick a quarrel with me!"

When Elisha the man of God heard that the king of Israel had torn his robes, he sent him this message: "Why have you torn your robes? Have the man come to me and he will know that there is a prophet in Israel." So Naáman went with his horses and chariots and stopped at the door of Elisha's house. Elisha sent a messenger to say to him, "Go, wash yourself seven times in the Jordan, and your flesh will be restored and you will be cleansed."

But Naáman went away angry and said, "I thought that he would surely come out to me and stand and call on the name of the Lord his God, wave his hand over the spot and cure me of my leprosy. Are not Abana and Pharpar, the rivers of Damascus, better than any of the waters of Israel? Couldn't I wash in them and be cleansed?" So he turned and went off in a rage.

Naáman's servants went to him and said, "My father, if the prophet had told you to do some great thing, would you not have done it? How much more, then, when he tells you, 'Wash and be cleansed'!" So he went down and dipped himself in the Jordan seven times, as the man of God had told him, and his flesh was restored and became clean like that of a young boy.

Then Naáman and all his attendants went back to the man of God. He stood before him and said, "Now I know that there is no God in all the world except in Israel. Please accept now a gift from your servant."
- 2 Kings 5:1-15 -

With the story of Naáman still fresh in my mind, I boarded the aeroplane to Australia, still thinking about Aldo's mysterious letter. That trip to Australia was one of the most difficult things I ever had to do. I had to leave a desperately sick child at home, but more than that; I knew there was a fierce spiritual battle raging and I had to help fight it from halfway across the world. Through this experience the Lord taught me that distance couldn't separate us in the spirit realm, and that our prayers can cross the borders of our physical locations.

The Lord gave me the strength to minister, but the moment I said "Amen" after my sermons, my only desire was to run to my room and pray. I was grateful that my close friend and intercessor was there with me to handle the one-to-one ministry after the events. I called home every night, but Tinus was evasive about the situation on the other side of the line. I knew it was because he didn't want to worry me. Near the end of the trip his voice was breaking when he said, "Retha, if Aldo gets through this, he will be able to get through anything. He is really not doing well. It is not only his body that is in so much pain, but also his spirit. They are really intent on killing him. He is so tired... I can see that he is not fighting back anymore."

Tinus scheduled a prayer session for Aldo with Ma'am Patrys and the friend who had prayed with us before, for the following day. During the session Aldo told them, "I am in such a deep dark hole. I don't know if I will ever be able to get out of it. They want to kill me!" After a long afternoon of prayer and warfare Jesus Himself came to minister love and peace to him. The breakthrough began when Aldo started singing verses from a Psalm 23 hymn: "He pulls me out from way down deep, He pulls me out from way down deep … He places my feet on a solid rock, He pulls me out from way down deep." It was the first joyful sound we had heard from him in a very long time.

Back then I knew so little about how to handle a situation like this. All I could do was to keep on seeking God's face and to ask for His mercy. I begged God to intervene. Just like Jacob, I struggled with God and refused to let go until He had blessed me (see Gen. 32:26). Any of you who have ever been at this desperate place before, will know that it is not a five minute 'quick fix' prayer. It is a call to God that comes from your deepest being. I am talking about deep calling unto deep... and not being satisfied until you can hear God's heartbeat.

> Unto You I lift up my eyes, O You who dwell in the heavens.
> Behold, as the eyes of servants look to the hand of their masters,
> as the eyes of a maid to the hand of her mistress, so our eyes look to the
> LORD our God, until He has mercy on us.
> - Psalm 123:1-2, NKJV -

I was nearing the end of my time in Australia, and after praying for a long time in my hotel room one night, I silently waited on God until well after midnight.

Suddenly the silence broke and I clearly heard the Holy Spirit say in my spirit, "Retha, Aldo will be healthy in time to celebrate his eighteenth birthday. I will also then release him to minister with you." I got such a fright that I jumped up from the carpet. Could it be true? Aldo's eighteenth birthday was only a few days away and at that moment he was fighting for his life (in the flesh as well as in the spirit). How could I dare to hope that he would be healthy enough for a party so soon? Again the Holy Spirit spoke to me, "Remember my promise Retha: From Nehemiah to Naáman free."

At that stage I still didn't fully comprehend what the Lord meant with "Naáman free", but I did know one thing for sure: God changed Naáman's life in the blink of an eye - and He could do it for Aldo too.

While I was in Australia someone told me about an international ministry that specialises in deliverance and inner healing. They suggested that I make a counselling appointment with this ministry since we were still struggling to achieve a complete breakthrough with Aldo. I wanted to find out what could possibly still be hampering our progress. Maybe there was something that I couldn't see? I asked my secretary to make an appointment for me as soon as they had an opening, and the first appointment she was able to schedule was for a few weeks later. I was disappointed that I had to wait so long, but little did I know how perfect the timing would be.

Back in South Africa I took some time off and stayed at home with Aldo to pray and fast. One day while sitting next to him on the couch he revealed to me everything the demons were doing to him in the spirit, and how they were attacking him. "Wisdom says that we should remove the shunt. I can't take the pain anymore, Mom. The tube is piercing through the ventricle."

Apart from banging his head against the wall, he often waved his arms wildly in the air as if he was trying to chase someone away. "Really, Aldo, what are you doing? I am so tired of this – tell me what it is that you are trying to chase away? Things cannot continue like this! I feel so helpless!"

"It is her, Mom. She leaves her body and then she comes here and she attacks me!"

(A witch is a human spirit and not a demon, so you need to handle them differently. In the case of human spirits you also have to pray for the salvation of that person's soul, because Jesus died in order that everybody could be saved.)

"Enough is enough!" I jumped up and ran to the bathroom and fell on my knees. "Abba, help me! Please help me! What gives her the right to attack us like this? Why can a witch hurt us so much? We have already forgiven her and blessed her like Your Word tells us to do. What else is there?"

"No, Retha. You haven't sincerely forgiven her yet. The words of forgiveness that you spoke were only words... it came from your flesh because you felt obligated to do it. You are still angry and bitter towards her in your heart."

"Father, but then I don't know if I can do it. I don't think I am able to forgive her in the way which You require of me. She is hurting us so much. It is unbearable to see Aldo suffer like this!" I wanted to justify my feelings of bitterness and resentment. "You have to understand why I'm feeling like this! Surely You saw what she did to us, and how she is still tormenting Aldo? How can You expect me to forgive her, Lord?" But the Holy Spirit quickly showed me that I was filled with self-righteousness and self-pity. It would get me nowhere. There was only one way out: I had to ask the Holy Spirit to help me do what I couldn't do for myself – I asked Him to change my heart.

jy moet beseën veg veg met seën. Jesus sê vir almal wat wag vir sy aanraak begin jou lewe het neerlê vir jou grootste vyand en bid vir hulle

You must bless. Fight, fight, with blessing. Jesus says to everyone who is waiting for His touch: lay down your life for your biggest enemy and pray for them.

Once I started to pray I could feel the peace of God returning, "Holy Spirit, please help me. I cannot do it by myself. Father, I choose to forgive her completely in the name of Jesus my Messiah. You are holding life and death before me today, and I choose life." (Unforgiveness is a powerful weapon the enemy uses as a legal right to hinder our breakthroughs and to torment us.)

After praying it felt as if heavy load was lifted from my shoulders. I was so relieved! I thought I had now finally done my part, but again the Holy Spirit prompted me, "Now I want you to intercede for her Retha. Lift her up in prayer before My throne of mercy and grace and stand in the gap for her." Had I heard correctly? Again I turned to the Holy Spirit for help, "Holy Spirit, will you please put the words in my mouth and in my heart… Father, I come in the name of Jesus Christ and I am standing before You on her behalf. I ask that You will forgive her for the witchcraft that she had used against us, for the lies she had told us, and for everything she had done to hurt Aldo. Will You please forgive her and wash her clean with the blood of the Lamb. Please save her soul, Jesus."

Se leer vergewe moet ek moet leer vergewe- Jesus vergewe my het soos ek my skulde naars vergewe

Learn to forgive. I must learn to forgive. Jesus, forgive me as I forgive those who trespass against me.

The Lord then showed me a vision of a dark cloud that blocked the rays of the sun. Just as a cloud hinders the sun's rays from reaching the earth, so does our sins prevent us from having fellowship with God, and being intimate with Him. Isaiah 59:1-2 speaks of this: *Surely the arm of the Lord is not too short to save, nor his ear too dull to hear. But your iniquities have separated you from your God; your sins have hidden his face from you, so that he will not hear.*

But the Word of God also gives us this assurance: *"Above all, love each other deeply, because love covers over a multitude of sins"* (1 Pet. 4:8). When we stand in the gap for someone and intercede on their behalf, we create an opportunity for the blood of the Lamb to be applied to their lives and for the sun's rays to break through the clouds.

> Now this is the confidence that we have in Him, that if we ask anything according to His will, He hears us. And if we know that He hears us, whatever we ask, we know that we have the petitions that we have asked of Him.
>
> If anyone sees his brother sinning a sin which does not lead to death, he will ask, and He will give him life for those who commit sin not leading to death. There is sin leading to death. I do not say that he should pray about that. All unrighteousness is sin, and there is sin not leading to death.
> - 1 John 5:14-17, NKJV -

Moses stood in the gap for the people and so did Daniel and Nehemiah – and now you and I can do it for each other, because the battle is in the spirit and not in the flesh.

After completing the processes of forgiving and interceding, the Holy Spirit still wasn't done with me. "Retha, now I want you to bless her. Remember Jesus' command: *But I tell you: Love your enemies and pray for those who persecute you, that you may be sons of your Father in heaven. He causes his sun to rise on the evil and the good, and sends rain on the righteous and the unrighteous"* (Matt. 5:44).

If I had relied on my emotions I wouldn't have been able to do it, but the Holy Spirit had promised me that He would help me with everything I needed. The Spirit of God, my Helper and Comforter, came to my rescue. He placed compassion for her in my heart which was definitely not there before. Suddenly my heart was overwhelmed by the desire to see her saved and forgiven. Only then was I able to sincerely bless her. I knew that the words didn't come from my natural thinking. They poured out from my spirit like streams of living water – and then the tears started to flow. These elements of forgiving, interceding for, and blessing my enemy were definitely strong weapons from God's Kingdom to fight against evil!

While I was still kneeling on my bathroom carpet, Aldo rushed into the room. "Mom, what has just happened?" he asked.

I was surprised by the calm and collected way in which he spoke. He seemed like his old self again! "I was only praying, Aldo. Why? Are you feeling better?"

"What did you pray, Mom?" he eagerly wanted to know.

"I just forgave her and blessed her – why do you ask?"

"In the spirit I saw how God got up from His throne and He took a sword from her hand, Mom. She is gone and all the other demons also had to go with her. They are all gone – they cannot fight love!"

For many days after that Aldo wrote, "Mom, she is fighting against the blessing you are speaking over her. She doesn't want you to bless her, because she can't attack when you bless her. She needs hatred in order to do her work. Without it she is powerless." That is how the kingdom of darkness operates.

Jesus sê sy verslaan, god sê sy veg nou net soos n mens sonder n swaard.

Jesus says she is defeated. God says she is fighting
like a person without a sword now.

> Make every effort to live in peace with all men and to be holy; without holiness no one will see the Lord. See to it that no one misses the grace of God and that no bitter root grows up to cause trouble and defile many.
> - Hebrews 12:14-15 -

Learn a valuable lesson today: the enemy will do anything in his power to tempt you into fights and quarrels, because from there the roots of bitterness can spring up and grow. Fights, dissentions, unforgiveness and pride cause the "walls of protection" around many people to be broken down; and it gives the enemy an opening through which he can attack. The enemy uses words of jealousy, gossip and slander as arrows of fire. Stay away from the darkness and do what the Word says: forgive others as you would like God to forgive you. Confess your sins and pray for your enemies – then God can work with them. Bless and do no curse. Short, simple lessons, but so powerful!

In the same way that angels are appointed to record everything we say, think and do, demons also record our lives. When our words or unconfessed sin grant them legal access, they don't hesitate to attack us. (That is what happened in Zechariah 3:1-7 when Satan opposed Joshua because of his filthy garments. The enemy uses our unconfessed sin and guilt as a legal claim to accuse and attack us.) In the New Testament there is also the example of the man who was healed by Jesus at the Pool of Bethesda. After Jesus had healed him, He gave him a stern warning: "*See, you are well again. Stop sinning, or something worse may happen to you*" (John 5:14). This shows me that our actions have a direct influence on the way in which the enemy is allowed to attack us.

These lessons and the breakthrough they brought was a big step forward for us. I could clearly see that the demonic heaviness had lifted. I immediately called Tinus and said, "It is all over – they are gone!" The thankfulness in my heart was overwhelming, and it was all because I had applied the spiritual principles that Jesus had given us, and used them as my weapons to fight the battle. Aldo was now calm in the spirit, but his flesh was still not completely okay. His letters kept saying that the tube was piercing through the ventricle. Our last option was to fly to Cape Town with him so that our usual doctors, who understood his unique situation so well, could examine him. I took his most recent X-rays and put them on the table in our foyer so that we wouldn't forget them the next day. That night Aldo wrote that we had to pray the blood of Jesus over the X-rays, because the demons were looking for them. It was a strange request, but I still went downstairs and did as he had requested.

As we drove to the airport the next day I could see how relieved Aldo was that we had listened to him, and that we were taking him to see a doctor. On the aeroplane Tinus sat next to an African man who kept glancing at Aldo throughout the flight. We are used to people staring, so Tinus didn't really take any notice of it. At some point during the flight the man turned to Tinus and said, "I am sorry to bother you, Sir. I don't know if you believe in Jesus, but the Holy Spirit keeps on prompting me to tell you that your son will be completely healed. You don't have to worry."

"Thank you for the confirmation. We need the encouragement very much right now!" Tinus answered, relieved that the man hadn't made any other hurtful comment about Aldo.

Aldo was restless during the flight and we knew it was mainly due to the difference in air pressure on the plane, because that makes his head hurt even more. During the landing he bent over and held his head between his legs. It broke my heart to see him in such pain.

Our appointment at the hospital was scheduled for the next morning, and we spent the night at our beach house in Yzerfontein. That night he wrote, "Jesus commanded His angels to protect my head on the aeroplane." By the time Aldo had taken his bath, his head was swollen as big as a rugby ball as a result of all the extra fluid. I kept tossing and turning the whole night wondering if we were doing the right thing by removing the shunt. What if the X-rays again didn't show anything? Or what if the doctors refused to perform the procedure? All I had to convince them with were Aldo's letters. I just prayed that we would get through the night. The next morning he wrote: "Mom, Wisdom asks why you don't believe Him? Has He ever written anything that was wrong before? Please take me to the hospital immediately – please Mom, or else it will be too late. Wisdom says we should be obedient to Him, Mom. Stop asking Him for signs – just obey. Trust Him."

het nehemia nodig om
heelhyd bevestiging te
kry? bevestiging is
mev mev my help
is van God. lemand
haal net asb my
pompie uit asb mev

help my asb. my brein
is so seer. help my asb
hom meu hy sê ek sal
hulle so so baie baie
baie dankbaar wees.

Does Nehemiah need confirmation all the time? My help is from God. Please let someone take out the shunt! Please, Ma'am – Please help me! My brain is hurting so much. Please help me. I will be so, so, so grateful!

Very early the next morning we walked into the hospital. It was a long process of taking X-rays and doing tests before the doctors could determine what the next step would be.

I spent the whole day praying for the doctors who were performing the tests, specifically for the eyes of their understanding to be illuminated. I prayed for their protection from demonic attacks which could cause them to make mistakes or miss seeing important information. I could sense a great spiritual battle raging while the radiologists had to write the report on the new X-rays. The new set of X-rays clearly showed the tube piercing through the ventricle, but that wasn't all; the shunt and the tube that drained the fluid into the stomach were no longer attached to one another. Medically speaking they couldn't explain how this could possibly be. *"What is going on here?"* everybody wondered. The doctors immediately replaced the shunt with a new one; they didn't want to take a chance by completely removing it as Aldo's letters had said.

For six months Aldo had been walking around with a faulty shunt. Six months of intense, unnecessary pain and torment. If so many X-rays were taken before, why had no one noticed the problems? We had taken the previous set of X-rays along to show the doctors. When we knew what to look for we could make out the outlines of the tube piercing through the ventricle. Even they couldn't explain why nobody had noticed it before. Wisdom had been right all along.

How could I have convinced a doctor to believe my child's letters instead of the black and white "facts" on the X-rays? Could it be that the demons disguised the information on the X-rays and tried to hide it? Was it medical negligence? My head was spinning from all the questions. Six months of our lives had been stolen!

This confirmed to me that Aldo was walking a peculiar, yet very precise, path with Wisdom. Even though I was so sad about the six wasted months, a new flame of passion was ignited in my heart to move forward with our ministry, and to trust God when He says He will finish what He started. He is always faithful!

A few days later we were once again at the airport on our way home. Aldo was still very weak after the operation and was lying stretched out on a couch in the lounge at Cape Town airport. Every now and then he asked us for something to eat or drink. Every time he did, Tinus and I smiled at each other, because the old Aldo was back! For six months Aldo had no appetite. If we didn't feed him and made sure that he swallowed his food, he would sometimes just let the food drop from his mouth.

I went to sit next to him and he put his head on my lap. I softly started praying, "Abba, please forgive me that I didn't listen to Wisdom from the start." While I was praying I realised that there was now a whole list of doctors that I had to forgive and bless, so that no root of bitterness would take hold of my heart. Our human nature wants to shift the blame, but I knew that pointing fingers was not going to bring back those six months.

I am comforted by the knowledge that God's hand of protection is over us. This road of suffering makes me want to die to myself more and more, so that I can live for Him alone. No matter what the world says, I know that Wisdom speaks through Aldo. To God it doesn't matter what he looks like, whether he gets A's on his school report, or whether he walks and talks like other teenagers. Even in his broken condition God uses him in powerful ways. This has just been another example of how we "taste and see" that Aldo's letters are inspired by God. When people voice a negative opinion of Aldo's prophetic words, I smile on the inside and know: *Wisdom only speaks the truth. I trust Him before I rely on human opinions. That is enough for me. I don't have to justify myself; the Lord will reveal the truth.*

All the glory to You my King – we are in awe of You and thankful for Wisdom's guidance!

Lewe is van God gebruik wat hy jou gee. hel is hol hy wys my hoe hy ons liefhet mev hy wil hê hy moet ons lewe wees. Wysheid hy sê hy wag vir ons om geloof te hê vir mev my werk. Wysheid het vir my gesê ek het reeds mev hele wese gegee. Want wagtyd het vir my te lank geword. hy sê ek moet net geduldig wees.

Life is from God. Use what He gives you. Hell is hell. He shows me how much He loves us. Ma'am, He wants to be our everything – our entire life. Wisdom says that He is waiting for us to have faith in my work. Ma'am, Wisdom told me I have already given Him my entire being. The time of waiting became too long for me. He says I must just be patient.

Chapter 7

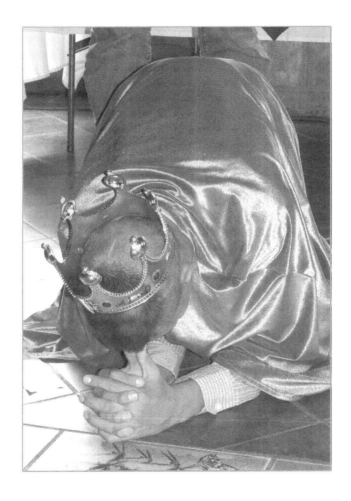

Wysh sê baie geluk Aldo
hy sê jy het oorwin deur
bloed van lam van God.
Wysh sê mev my werk het
begin mev mense sal sien
hoe bevel gee hy aan natuur
om te hou bevel het n atuur
bevel gekry om hulle God
te vrees en hom te loof.
Wysh sê as mense hom
nie Loof nie sal sy skepping
hom uitroep Holy Holy
Holy is Here God almagtig
het jy geweet mev hy sê
vandag het hy ook verlang
na om my weer gelukkig
te sien. Wysh sê verjaarsdag
is opgeteken in Lewensboek
hy het hele tyd geweet
hoe brein gesond want hy is god.
God hou my vas, het jy
geweet jy sal bevryding
Leer want hy sê wat
vyand wou steel het hy
beveg beveg beveg want
mev bevryding het Jesus
se bloed vir ons gedoen aan
kruis. Wat sal ek by hom
kan sê anders as baie baie
dankie Jesus ek is 100%. gesord
vandag is ek 18 en ek is
so vreeslik vreeslik dankbaar
aan God.

Wisdom says: Congratulations Aldo! He says I have overcome by the blood of the Lamb of God. Wisdom says my work has begun, Ma'am. People will now see how He commands nature. Nature has been given the command to revere and worship God. Wisdom says if people won't worship Him, the creation will cry it out: Holy, holy, holy is the Lord God almighty! Did you know, Mom that God also longed to see me happy today. Wisdom says my birthday is written up in my book of life. He has known all along that my brain would be healed – because He is God! God holds me so close to Him. Did you know that you will teach about deliverance? He says that the enemy came to steal, but you kept on fighting, fighting, fighting him, because the blood of Jesus on the cross gained the victory for us. What else can I say to Him, except thank You, thank You, thank You Jesus! I am 100% healed.

Today I am 18 and I am so very grateful to God for that.

Wysh sê werk begin nou
heel belangrikste het gebeur
Vrydag by my partjie
het in die berryding van
my van my vyand.
Wysh sê werk het begin vir
my hy is trots beveg
hy hulle ~~het was~~ regtig ek
haat nie meer (name*) nie.
het haar vergewe, regtig.
hy is ook trots op my.
ja ek sal haar seën.
Wysh sê revival begin verjaars
mev wat nou werk begin
is my wat saam pakistan
toe gaan. Wysh wys vir my
vuur en vuur wat waarlik
sal val van hom. hy is vir
my baie lief en hy sê hy
vir ons ook. Lief vir jou ook
mom ek is eerlik ek is
vreeslik verskriklik lief vir
julle.

Wisdom says my work has started now. The most important thing that happened on Friday [Aldo's birthday] is that I was set free from the enemy. Wisdom says my work has started. He is proud of us. He fights them. Really, I don't hate her (name*) anymore. I have forgiven her. Really, He is also proud of me. Yes, I will bless her. Wisdom says the revival has started on my birthday. My work will start now that I am going with you to Pakistan. Wisdom is showing me fire, and more fire that will fall from Him. He loves me so much and He loves you too. I love you too, Mom. I am honest when I say, I love you so much!

Time to stand up

On Tuesday we were still sitting at Cape Town airport knowing that we were to celebrate Aldo's eighteenth birthday three days later. Ma'am Patrys had planned a surprise party to take place on the Friday afternoon after school. To be honest, Ma'am Patrys had more faith that this party would realise than I did! Although the Holy Spirit had said to me in Australia that Aldo would be healthy by his birthday, I simply couldn't imagine how this sick and confused child I saw before me would be able to attend a birthday party in a few days' time.

The morning of his birthday, Aldo was awake at five o'clock and woke the rest of the household with his version of "You raise me up." He dressed himself and excitedly told us that he wanted to go to school. We were all amazed because even though he was a lot better since they had inserted the new shunt, he was still weak and lethargic since our return from Cape Town.

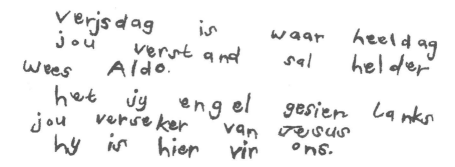

Your mind will be clear the whole day on your birthday, Aldo. Did you see the angel next to you? He is definitely from Jesus. He is here for us.

He was very excited that afternoon when he arrived home from school to find a friend waiting for him in the foyer with a big birthday present. In order to keep the surprise party a secret, we told him that we were only going to meet a few of his friends for a milkshake to celebrate his birthday; but when we walked into the restaurant all his friends were there and welcomed him with a loud, "Surprise!" He threw his arms in the air and smiled from ear to ear. There are so many of my tears on the floor of that restaurant, because what I saw that day was almost too good to be true. Aldo was happy and healthy, he was surrounded by his friends and he didn't have any pain. I could so clearly see God's hand in it all! I cried about my unbelief, I cried about my son who was turning eighteen, and I cried about the amazing God we serve Who is faithful in keeping His promises!

The day was full of joy and laughter and normal teenage fun, but we also made an important declaration in the spirit by doing a prophetic action with Aldo. Prophetic actions carry a lot of power. It is an action that you do in the natural realm under the guidance of the Holy Spirit, and this action resounds in the spiritual realm. (A good example of this is found in 1 Samuel 15:27-28, when Saul grabbed Samuel's cloak and tore off a piece. This tear in his cloak prophetically meant that Saul's kingship had been torn from him.)

Two prophetic actions were performed at Aldo's birthday celebration. The first involved establishing Aldo's identity in Christ and the second had to do with overcoming the enemy.

Each of God's children is called to a royal priesthood in Christ Jesus (see Rev. 5:10). A king's duty is to reign in righteousness, and that of a priest is to worship and minister to the Lord. In the first prophetic action Tinus and I affirmed Aldo's identity as a priest and a king unto the Lord. Just as Hannah made Samuel a new robe for his birthday every year (see 1 Sam. 2:19), I also hung a golden robe around Aldo and then Tinus crowned him with a golden crown. We publicly honoured him for the high price he had paid for God's calling on his life, and declared that he could wear his crown with dignity and honour because there is no condemnation to those who are in Christ (see Rom. 8:1).

Then, during the second prophetic action, five people each took up a shield and stood around him. This portrayed the victory over the enemy as described in Joshua 10:24-26. The five hostile kings represented Fear, Greed, Pride, Lust and Deceit (derived from the meanings of their names in Scripture) and we put five pictures of the kings on the floor where the shield-bearers had to stand.

The first shield bearer was Ma'am Patrys. She was the one who walked side by side with him every day and she knew better than anyone how difficult the past few months had been. She prayed for Aldo and honoured him for his perseverance.

Then his grandmother picked up a shield and took her place next to him. My mother is a true intercessor. She spends a lot of time in her prayer closet praying for her whole family, but especially for her grandchildren. She picked up the shield and blessed him and prayed for him (like only a grandmother could), and asked for God's love to cover him wherever he would go.

His friends Eric, Bradley and Morné took up the other three shields and completed the circle. Eric told the group how Aldo would fall to his knees and worship God in the middle of the rugby field when he and Aldo occasionally went to play soccer. Eric concluded his short speech by saying, "I have so much respect for you, Aldo, and it is my desire to have such an intimate relationship with God as you do."

Bradley, Aldo's friend who had stood by him right from the start, also prayed for Aldo and pronounced a blessing over his future. After six years he still regularly visits Aldo on weekends.

Then Morné testified of the life changing impact Aldo's friendship had on his life. "Aldo, when you prayed for me that night, my life changed completely. I had and encounter with Jesus that motivated me to never want to look back again. Thank you, and I bless you!"

Aldo and his friends at his birthday party.

Aldo's enjoyed his birthday party so much! After the prophetic actions and worship, the teenagers chatted and enjoyed one another's company. Everyone made sure that Aldo felt loved and special, and I was just so thankful that we didn't have to spend his birthday in a hospital. Once again Abba had been faithful; how could I have doubted?

dankie my Jesus wat u baie baie vir my vandag gedoen het. Wysh sê verjaarsdag was die groot draai van ons lewe-

Thank you, thank you, my Jesus, for what you did for me today. Wisdom says that my birthday was a turning point in our lives.

I was wrong to assume that since Aldo had such a strong bond with the Holy Spirit it was only his flesh that needed healing. I never could have imagined that the unseen wounds of his soul could grant the enemy a foothold.

Wysh sê hulle het my wat vry is aangeval gister aand. verjaarsdag het vir hulle baie baie kwaad gemaak hulle was so versaarsd kwaad want hulle het bevel bevel gekry om te vlug. Wysh sê hulle het hel toe versaarsdag. Wysh sê bevel vir hulle sê hulle mag nie meer vir my veg nie. Gister aand het vyand vuur vuur op my brein vyand hy wil hê ek moet hom weer innooi. Wysh sê wat ons moet doen is ons moet vir bevryding gaan. hy sê vir elke siel wat vir hom gewen word haat hulle.

Wisdom says that they attacked me again last night. I am free now. What happened on my birthday made them so angry. They were so mad at my birthday party because they were given the command to flee. Wisdom says they had to go to hell when the command was given on my birthday. They are no longer allowed to fight against me. Last night the enemy came to throw fire on my brain. The enemy wants me to invite him in again. Wisdom says that we must go for deliverance. He says that they hate every soul that is won for Him.

After all the pain and tears, there comes a time when we have to stand up and face the future. If we keep holding onto the pain of the past we will never truly fulfil our destiny, but we will merely survive from day to day. Deliverance and inner healing go hand in hand, but they are not the same thing.

To me, a foundation stone of inner healing is the truth referred to in Proverbs 4:23: *Above all else, guard your heart, for it is the wellspring of life.* The Word also tells us: *As a man thinks in his heart, so is he* (Prov. 23:7, NKJV). What you think in your heart determines your belief system, and your beliefs are the spectacles through which you look at God, yourself and life around you. It determines how you experience the things that happen to you and how you react to them. Your belief system is based on the things you believe implicitly, whether they are true or not. A lie can therefore become *your* truth.

An example of this is a young girl who suffers from an eating disorder like anorexia. No matter how skinny she is, she is resolutely convinced that she is overweight and ugly. Just like parasites, demons will latch onto this belief system to destroy her completely; and because she has given them access through her false belief system, the demons can start building a stronghold. This stronghold becomes a fortress for the enemy's deception. Satan hides the lies so deceptively that the person is completely unaware that he or she is living a lie.

Another way to look at our faulty belief systems is to compare them with a trashcan filled with years and years of rubbish – the rubbish being the lies we believe. If left untouched the rubbish will attract rats. You can try to catch the rats one by one, but unless the rubbish is thrown out, the rats will keep on returning.

However, throwing out the rubbish is easier said than done! To get rid of any rubbish in our belief systems our *minds* need to be renewed and we have to be washed by the Word of God. This is the work of the Holy Spirit, and not of our own will power. Only the Holy Spirit can bring about a real change in our hearts, but before the Lord can do that, we have to bow our knees, and submit to Him completely. Just as an alcoholic cannot be set free from his addiction until he admits to having a problem, our surrendering to God is a prerequisite for our healing.

In Aldo's case, severe wounds were inflicted by the accident on his soul – not only on his body. Although he was in a coma and his body seemed to be asleep, his soul and his spirit could still hear every negative word that people spoke over him; and that was the first seeds of the false belief system that took form in his heart and mind. This belief system opened a door to a spirit of fear, and through fear he became entangled in a web of lies: *Can you hear what the doctors are saying about you? You won't be normal! ... Your life is over... You'll have no friends ... Do you really think you are going to get married one day looking like this?*

Isn't that what the enemy is trying to do to all of us? But we have a weapon that will defeat the enemy: the Truth!

> "If you hold to my teaching, you are really my disciples. Then you will know the truth, and the truth will set you free."
> - John 8:31b-32 -

This is where one can clearly see the difference between deliverance and inner healing. During deliverance the unclean spirits are cast out (the rats are caught) and with inner healing the Truth replaces the lie (the rubbish is thrown out). This process happens over a period of time as our thoughts are continually renewed to come in line with the Truth. The Truth is the Word of God, and therefore it is important to daily renew your thoughts through it.

> Do not conform any longer to the pattern of this world, but be transformed by the renewing of your mind. Then you will be able to test and approve what God's will is – his good, pleasing and perfect will.
> - Romans 12:2 -

> Grein seen beveg hulle.
> Vrees wil hy
> vir my gee beLry sein
> met verseen wysh se
> Vrees sit vas in my wat
> van Satan hel se demone
> Vansein sein seen

They are trying to keep my brain captive. They want to frighten me. Free me from their signal with blessing. Wisdom says that signals of fear are being aimed at me from Satan and the demons of hell.

One day I casually said to Aldo, "Fear is from Satan." Soon after that he wrote, "No, Mommy. Satan *is* fear." To break down the stronghold Satan has built in our belief system, we need to use the Word of Truth against him. Every time a fearful emotion rises up in us, we can fight back with the Word! Proclaim it loudly: *For God did not give me a spirit of timidity, but a spirit of power, of love and of self-discipline* (2 Tim. 1:7). *Because God has said, "Never will I leave you; never will I forsake you." So I say with confidence, "The Lord is my helper; I will not be afraid"* (Heb. 13:5-6). In that way we can rebuild our belief system brick by brick, on the right foundation, with words of life.

> For though we live in the world, we do not wage war as the world does. The weapons we fight with are not the weapons of the world. On the contrary, they have divine power to demolish strongholds. We demolish arguments and every pretension that sets itself up against the knowledge of God, and we take captive every thought to make it obedient to Christ.
> *- 2 Corinthians 10:3-5 -*

It would give the demons great delight to steal the calling and destiny God has laid out for our lives. They will do everything in their ability to keep us from fulfilling that plan. Let's take Aldo's life as an example. Aldo's calling is to tell the world that Jesus is alive, and to share the things that Wisdom reveals to him through his letters. God knows He can trust him with the responsibility that the calling requires (or else He wouldn't have given it); however, you can be sure that Satan is not just going to sit back and let it happen without fierce resistance.

After the accident, self-rejection became the root of a belief system that grew into self-hatred. Because of that belief system, demons could build within his soul a stronghold of fear, depression, jealousy, rebellion and death. As these demons kept on reinforcing the stronghold, the lies that controlled his life became stronger and more difficult to break down. If he didn't realign his belief system with God's Truth, the enemy would have stolen God's plan for his life. This process of inner healing happens when God (Father, Son and Holy Spirit) shines His light of truth into our hearts, and changes our lives by changing what we believe about *Him*, about *others*, and about *ourselves*.

God's plan for each of our lives is a lot greater than we can ever imagine. It's like a pebble that falls into the water - the wavelets will continue to ripple outwards, enabling us to touch things that we never thought we could reach. God didn't leave us to our own devices to determine what is true or false. He gave us His Word as the plumb line for truth. But we have to choose to believe it, and to reject the lies and deception with which Satan confronts us. If we live in His truth, the light will begin to illumine all the areas where the enemy has blinded and deceived us. Most importantly, God has given us His Son, Jesus Christ, to redeem us, and He has given us the Holy Spirit to lead us into all truth. We have all we need to live lives of victory and freedom, because our Abba loves us so very much.

I often declare over Aldo that he has the mind of Christ (see 1 Cor. 2:16) and I pray that his thoughts will become aligned with God's thoughts and that the dreams in his heart will be inspired by God. The more time we spend with God's Word and in His presence, the easier it is to break Satan's strongholds. As our thoughts and the reflections of our hearts are renewed, we progressively live in the abundance that Jesus had promised us. The "spectacles" with which we perceive life will now give us a heavenly perspective, filled with light and truth.

It took time, but I could clearly see how the Holy Spirit was healing Aldo's thoughts and emotions. I am confident in this knowledge: it doesn't matter how long it may take, God will finish what He has started in each of us!

Ver trou hom god sê
god sê mense met alles
Wie hy is nie en besef nie
reg sal laat dat hy
sê god: ek is beleef,
van jou lewe. in beheer

God says trust Him with everything. God says that people don't really know who He is and that He will let justice prevail. God says that He is in control of our lives.

Jesus had already attained the victory 2000 years ago on our behalf and we just have to remain standing in the truth until the end. Satan wants to wear us out so that we will give up hope and throw in the towel, but God says that we are more than conquerors through Him who loves us! (see Rom. 8:37).

After deliverance has taken place, it is important to keep walking in the spirit. Jesus warned us that the demons will try to return: *When an evil spirit comes*

*out of a man, it goes through arid places seeking rest and does not find it. Then it says,
"I will return to the house I left." When it arrives, it finds the house unoccupied, swept
clean and put in order. Then it goes and takes with it seven other spirits more wicked
than itself, and they go in and live there. And the final condition of that man is worse
than the first. That is how it will be with this wicked generation* (Matt. 12:43-45).

That is why it is so important to heed the first lesson of deliverance and inner
healing: *Above all else, guard your heart, for it is the wellspring of life* (Proverbs
4:23).

Here are a few keys to use when you are engaged in this kind of spiritual
battle for deliverance and inner healing. These aren't laws, but *keys* that have helped us
to unlock the chains that kept us bound. I do believe that these keys, if used correctly,
will save you a lot of time and tears.

1. Know God's character and His heart of love for you. The names God
uses in the Word to describe His nature are anchors to hold onto during difficult times.
God is our Redeemer and Healer; our Shepherd, Provider; our Protector and Rock
... He is our Abba Father. But is He that to *you*? It is important to know who He is
in *your* life, in *your* situation, in *your* heartache, in *your* questions. His character
should be engraved on the tables of your heart through your personal and intimate
love relationship with Him.

hulle kan nie staan
waar God se hame
genoem word nie.

Jy sal sien hoe baie
mense vry sal kom wanneer
mev God se name gespeel
word. Jy wat vra hoe,
wat, wanneer, wysheid se hoe, jy
haal hulle uit agter waar hulle
wegkruip. het jy gister aand
gesien hoe Engele veg vir
ons, jy sal sien wagte in my
brein sal moet gaan want
julle stop nie hulle sal jou

we kan seer maak nie want jy
het baie groot engel by jou
Jesus is baie trots op julk.

They cannot stand where God's names are mentioned. You will see how many people will be set free upon hearing the names of God. You who ask: What? When? How? Wisdom says that you [Retha] find them where they are hiding. Did you see how the angels were fighting for us last night? You will see that the guards watching over my brain will have to flee because you never give up. They won't be able to hurt you, because you have a very large angel with you. Jesus is very proud of you.

2. Recognise the enemy's character; ... *in order that Satan might not outwit us. For we are not unaware of his schemes* (2 Corinthians 2:11). Satan is the accuser of the brethren (Rev. 12:10). He will keep reminding you of your mistakes and sins even though you have already been forgiven. He will try to lure your focus away from Jesus, and if you choose to believe him you will be disregarding the power of Jesus' blood. That is why it is very important for you to forgive yourself. When you confess your sins and are washed by the blood of the Lamb – you are clean! Jesus paid the FULL price for your sins and He loves you unconditionally. True love means to love the imperfect perfectly; that is how much Jesus loves you and me. Do not allow Satan to accuse you and keep in bondage to the things which God has already forgiven.

3. Know that Satan is the father of lies (see John 8:44). He will try to convince you that you are not really free. He will harass you with thoughts such as: *The deliverance wasn't complete. There are more demons. Did you really think you will ever be able to be free?* Fight back hard and audibly with the Truth: "The Son of God has made me free and I am free indeed!" (See John 8:36).

Wysh sê wat ek skryf
is van God, sê vir
retha wat sy sê is
vir vyand sê koningkryk

159

on u v e wat breek.
Wysh se kan Satan
jou verstand lees. Nee.
nou jou verstand geseel
hou jou hart toe want
hy wil jou seermaak.

Wisdom says that the things I write come from God. Tell Retha that her teachings break down the walls of the enemy's kingdom. Wisdom says: 'Can Satan read your mind?' No, keep your mind sealed off to him. Guard your heart, because he (Satan) wants to hurt you.

4. Understand that Satan wants to intimidate us. He tries to control us with intimidation and fear. So many times God says in His Word: *Do not be afraid!* The power belongs to God. He is the same God of Abraham, Isaac and Jacob and He knows your end from your beginning. Rest in His love for you and call on Him as Jehovah Shalom (the God who gives peace) in your fearful situation.

> When I am afraid, I will trust in you. In God, whose word I praise, in God I trust; I will not be afraid. What can mortal man do to me?
> - Psalm 56:3-4 -

5. Realise that you are not fighting against flesh and blood but against spiritual forces. God has given us armour and spiritual weapons to fight with – use them!

> For our struggle is not against flesh and blood, but against the rulers, against the authorities, against the powers of this dark world and against the spiritual forces of evil in the heavenly realms. Therefore put on the full armor of God, so that when the day of evil comes, you may be able to stand your ground, and after you have done everything, to stand.
> - Ephesians 6:12-13 -

Wysh se wat jy moet
weet is hulle is watergeeste
en trauma geeste wat my
verwurg weg asb mom.

Jesus sê julle moet veg rannaand·
Jy is hulle vyand.

Wisdom says what you need to know is that it is the water-spirits and trauma-spirits that are strangling me. Please fight them, Mom. Jesus says you must fight tonight. You are an enemy to them.

6. Acknowledge and confess your sins. This is one of the most important keys to victory! Satan can use unconfessed sin as a legal right to gain a foothold in your life. The moment you confess your sin, the indictment against you is washed away with the blood of Jesus. Also confess your ancestral sin (iniquity) and break the bloodline curses, so that the sins of your ancestors that have been carried over from generation to generation will come to an end (see Neh. 1:6).

> "If we claim to be without sin, we deceive ourselves and the truth is not in us. If we confess our sins, He is faithful and just and will forgive us our sins and purify us from all unrighteousness. If we claim we have not sinned, we make Him out to be a liar and His word is not in us."
> - I John 1:8-10 -

7. Honour your parents. I believe that God emphasizes the importance of this truth by making it the first commandment in which a promise is added to His instruction:

> "'Honour your father and mother,' which is the first commandment with a promise: 'that it may go well with you and that you may enjoy long life on the earth.'"
> - Ephesians 6:2-3 -

In every area of your life where you honour your parents, the Lord promises that "it will go well with you". But the opposite also true: do not expect things to go well in those areas of your life where you dishonour your parents. God doesn't say that we should only honour our parents if they are good parents - there are no exceptions to this command. If your parents have wronged you in any way, forgive them and bless them, rather than walking around with bitterness and resentment. Apply this to all your relationships where you are placed under someone else's authority: your employer, the government, and the leaders of the church. Humility and respect will always be rewarded.

8. Remember that the enemy will do everything in his power to lure you back to your old, ungodly habits. You should view those old habits like the edge of a cliff. Your choices determine how close you live to the edge. If you have struggled with pornography in the past, make sure you take special precautions to stay out of the danger zone. Throw away everything that has led you astray, get someone you can trust to talk to and ask for help if necessary. Take up a hobby and find new things to keep your mind busy, and go for counselling. These are all practical steps to make the victory easier and break the behavioural pattern. By doing this you are taking a few steps back from the edge of the cliff. But remember, the battle is in the spirit and therefore you have to fight against it in the spirit in order to experience real victory. You have to take every thought captive and subject it to Christ (2 Cor. 10:5). It is a process of dying to self, because you are now saying no to the things that your flesh had come to depend on.

> But put on the Lord Jesus Christ, and make no provision for the flesh, to fulfill its lusts
> - Romans 13:14, NKJV -

9. Trust in God! Do not place your hope in people – know that God is your source of strength. People disappoint and make mistakes (yourself included – that is why you should have mercy on others), but God always remains the same and He is faithful, even though we are not. Above all, He loves you unconditionally!

> This is what the Lord says: "Cursed is the one who trusts in man, who depends on flesh for his strength and whose heart turns away from the Lord. He will be like a bush in the wastelands; he will not see prosperity when it comes. He will dwell in the parched places of the desert, in a salt land where no one lives. "But blessed is the man who trusts in the Lord, whose confidence is in Him. He will be like a tree planted by the water that sends out its roots by the stream. It does not fear when heat comes; its leaves are always green. It has no worries in a year of drought and never fails to bear fruit."
> - Jeremiah 17:5-8 -

10. Do not give up... but surrender! I believe that all of us get to a place at some time or another where we feel as if there is no hope left for us. It is a place of vulnerability, where you can't depend on your own strength anymore. That is when only God can carry you through the valley. This place of brokenness, where you are totally dependent on God, is not necessarily a nice or comfortable place to be at, but it is the best place to be – because you and God become one.

jy vertrou God, gesien hoe werklik
Mev
sy van dag troon van God
gesien het. Seen het op joy
verseen. Hy se jy salwing
mirre val van sy troon.
verseker is verseker is
vurige mirre baie bitter.
het jy werklik seen moes
word deur dit te drink?

Ma'am, you truly trust God. I saw how you saw the throne of God today.

You received blessing. He says that anointing myrrh is falling from His

throne. The fiery myrrh is very bitter. Did you truly receive the blessing by

drinking it? Wisdom says He is definitely blessing you, because you bless

everyone around you. Bless, bless, bless, Mom. She is defeated because you

bless her and do not curse her.

11. Walk in the light. Ask God to bring all the false belief systems and strongholds of Satan to the light so you can be freed from them. The Holy Spirit will lead you every step of the way; He is the Spirit of Truth. If you can identify the lie, you can replace it with truth. Be patient, because it is a process that unfolds over time.

> Therefore, I urge you, brothers and sisters, in view of God's mercy, to offer your bodies as a living sacrifice, holy and pleasing to God—this is your true and proper worship. Do not conform to the pattern of this world, but be transformed by the renewing of your mind. Then you will be able to test and approve what God's will is—his good, pleasing and perfect will.
> - Romans 12:1-2 -

12. Choose life! Only you can make that decision. "But what does it mean to choose life?" you may wonder. Life is to obey the voice of God, to cling to Him and to love the Lord your God with all your heart, and soul, and mind, and strength.

> I call heaven and earth as witnesses today against you, that I have set before you life and death, blessing and cursing; therefore choose life, that both you and your descendants may live; that you may love the LORD your God, that you may obey His voice, and that you may cling to Him, for He is your life and the length of your days; and that you may dwell in the land which the LORD swore to your fathers, to Abraham, Isaac, and Jacob, to give them."
> *- Deuteronomy 30:19-20, NKJV -*

13. Forgive as you want the Father to forgive you. We all make mistakes, and we all need forgiveness - from God and from each other. If you cannot forgive someone else for their imperfections, how can you expect a perfect God to forgive your imperfections? God is very clear on this matter: you will only receive what you are willing to give.

> For if you forgive other people when they sin against you, your heavenly Father will also forgive you. But if you do not forgive others their sins, your Father will not forgive your sins.
> *- Matthew 6:14-15 -*

14. Partake in communion - as often as you need it. It is through communion that we bow our knees to Jesus and lay our lives before Him. We look into our hearts, confess and ask forgiveness for that which doesn't belong there. We become less and He becomes more. We become one with Jesus and receive His DNA. Do not delay by waiting for the communion service as scheduled on the church calendar, it is a personal meeting between Jesus and yourself (see 1 Cor. 11:24-26).

15. Realise the power of blood of the Lamb. The blood of the Lamb is the seal on our hearts that identifies us as the redeemed of the Lord. This seal is our proof of being kings and priests for Jesus.

> And they sang a new song: "You are worthy to take the scroll and to open its seals, because You were slain, and with Your blood You purchased men for God from every tribe and language and people and nation. You have made them to be a kingdom and priests to serve our God, and they will reign on the earth."
> *- Revelation 5:9-10 -*

Every day I plead the blood of the Lamb over myself and my whole family. I pray that our spirit, soul and body will be drenched with it and that the blood of the Lamb will stand between us and the enemy.

Wak beury wy is bloed
van Jesus.

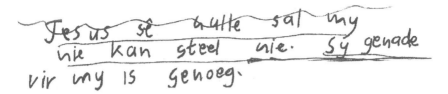

The blood of Jesus sets me free. Jesus says they will never be able to steal me. His grace is enough for me.

16. Remain in God's glory light. Let His light shine on every area of your life. The enemy cannot remain standing in this light. God already knows every detail of your life, whether you want Him to or not. Do not let the enemy keep you in darkness through guilt and shame – boldly run to God's throne of mercy and grace to receive mercy and grace in a time of need (see Heb. 4:15-16). Open up your life to Him and ask Him to shine His glorious light on every part of your heart so the enemy simply cannot get a foot in the door.

> Everyone who does evil hates the light, and will not come into the light for fear that their deeds will be exposed. But whoever lives by the truth comes into the light, so that it may be seen plainly that what they have done has been done in the sight of God.
> - John 3:20-21 -

17. Cultivate a love relationship with Jesus, your Beloved, your Bridegroom. Talk to Him all day, every day. Tell Him how you feel and what you are experiencing. Tell Him how much you love Him. Share the good and the bad with Him. If there is something you don't understand, ask the Holy Spirit to explain it to you. He is the Spirit of Truth and will guide you in all truth. The Holy Spirit will bring about the fruit of the Spirit in you and lead you to reach maturity in Christ. Consult the Holy Spirit in all your decisions. He is your Wisdom from God.

> But when he, the Spirit of truth, comes, he will guide you into all the truth. He will not speak on his own; he will speak only what he hears, and he will tell you what is yet to come.
> - John 16:13 -

Jesus sê hy sal my altyd houvas

Jesus says He will always hold me.

165

18. Allow God to prune your "branches". Even if the pruning process hurts, it has to be done to enable you to bear more fruit. The other day I was looking at labourers on a rose farm who were pruning roses with electric weed-cutters. The dust hung in the air, the noise was overwhelming, and the result seemed like complete desolation! "Does everything need to be stripped, Lord?" I wondered to myself, feeling a bit sorry for the rose bushes. The Holy Spirit then answered me, "Yes, Retha. These are export roses – top quality. That is why the pruning process has to be so thorough. Even though it looks painful, it is necessary. Everything has to be pruned before new life can bud."

> Every branch in Me that does not bear fruit He takes away; and every branch that bears fruit He prunes, that it may bear more fruit.
> - John 15:2, NKJV -

19. Pray continuously! I will never forget what Aldo asked me the one day:

"Mom, are you still praying for me?"

"Of course Aldo, you know I do."

"How often, Mom?" he prodded me to continue.

"Whenever I think of you. Why are you asking me this, my love? You know that I pray for you often."

"Mom, I saw what happens in heaven when believers pray. Every time their prayers reach the throne, God sends an angel to earth to go and do what He says".

> Do not be anxious about anything, but in everything, by prayer and petition, with thanksgiving, present your requests to God.
> - Philippians 4:6 -

20. Remain in the Word of God. We should be washed with the Word of God every day, not just every now and then, or for an hour on Sundays. The Word of God is the bread that feeds your spirit. It is the truth that keeps you standing against the enemy. If your spirit is hungry, you can easily be led astray by the temptations of the world.

> "It is written: 'Man does not live by bread alone, but by every word that comes from the mouth of God.'"
> - Matthew 4:4 -

Wysh sê bybel is wat jy het eyken wat eg is,

hy sê sy sal hom geleer
ken het in hom is vrede

Wisdom says the Bible is what you have. Acknowledge what is true. He says you will learn to know Him – He is peace.

21. Know your authority and identity in Christ. Resist the enemy – do it loudly and clearly, because demons cannot read minds, but they can definitely hear your words.

> Submit yourselves, then, to God. Resist the devil, and he will flee from you.
> *- James 4:7 -*

22. Worship God. Worship is a powerful weapon against the enemy. He cannot stand where the King's name is glorified.

> Why are you downcast, O my soul? Why so disturbed within me? Put your hope in God, for I will yet praise him, my Saviour and my God.
> *- Psalm 42:11 -*

23. Lay down your life, take up your cross and follow Jesus. Your cross is not your bad situation, your difficult husband or your rebellious child; or as in our case, Aldo's brain injury. Your cross is where your own will and God's will "cross". It is where you choose to obey the Father and His will instead of following your own way. It means dying to self and choosing God above everything else.

> Father [...] not My will, but Yours be done.
> *- Luke 22:42 -*

24. Obedience leads to sanctification. Sanctification is the process whereby we are transformed into the image of Christ – a picture of holiness – and without holiness we cannot see God (see Heb. 12:14). But obey Him because you love Him and not because you are trying to abide by the rules in a legalistic way. When your obedience results spontaneously because of your love for Jesus, it will be so much easier keeping His Word than trying to adhere to a list of do's and don'ts.

> If you love Me, you will obey what I command.
> *- John 14:15 -*

25. Do not walk the road on your own. Join hands with fellow believers and become part of the family of Christ. We are here to lift up one another's arms.

> Not giving up meeting together, as some are in the habit of doing, but encouraging one another – all the more as you see the Day approaching.
> - Hebrew 10:25 -

Wysh sê ons is waar
hy ons wil hê mev
afhanklik van hom. Seën
het my werklik gered.
Jesus se ek is vry hy
nehemia 58 dae se veg
hulle moes bou en veg
kan ~~xxxxxxx~~ gesalfde asb

mev verskoning vra vir
wat julle moes deurgaan
mev ek weet het ek sou
nooit alleen hierdeur
kon kom nie, Weet het
hoe lief ek julle het. God
sê ek is vry en jy
moet vertel wat met
my gebeur het. Ja mom
jy moet bevryding
met my was het leer
skool vir jou. bevryding
is mev beseën, seën
deur God.

Wisdom says we are where He wants us, Ma'am – dependant on Him. Blessing truly saved me. Jesus says I am free from the Nehemiah 58 day fight. They had to build and fight. Can the anointed one ask forgiveness for what you had to go through because of me? Ma'am, I just know that I would

168

never have been able to get through this on my own. Just know that I love you very much. God says I am free and that you must testify of what has happened to me. Yes Mom, my process of deliverance was only your training ground. Ma'am, deliverance is blessing and being blessed by God.

26. Do not look back; it will cause you to stumble. Do not allow the mistakes and hurt of yesterday to determine your future. When you think about the people who hurt you in the past, forgive them and keep on blessing them. I assure you that in time your heart will be healed. Some hearts take longer to heal than others, but God will honour your obedience.

> Brothers, I do not consider myself yet to have taken hold of it. But one thing I do: Forgetting what is behind and straining toward what is ahead, I press on toward the goal to win the prize for which God has called me heavenward in Christ Jesus.
> - Philippians 3:13-14 -

27. Bless and do not curse. I cannot emphasise enough how important this is! Throughout Aldo's letters he kept on writing that Wisdom said we had to bless our enemies, and that our blessing "fought" against their curses. I wondered why this was such an important key to the victory, and the Holy Spirit answered me: "Retha, for My kingdom to come to earth, My children need to live as children of the light. If they fight evil with evil, they are fighting on the wrong side. Then I can do nothing to help them."

Realise that by forgiving and blessing your enemies (even if it is painful), you are contributing towards your own good – for only then can God step in and fight on your behalf. This forgiveness and blessing won't always be received with open arms by your enemies, but that shouldn't stop you from being obedient. You can only make decisions about *your* choices, and *your* future. So don't let someone else's bitterness and unforgiveness keep you from freedom. The occult understand the power of blessing, because they understand it's direct opposite: the power of cursing. That is why they resist it so mightily. This makes me more resolved to keep on blessing, to keep on forgiving, to keep on loving – because I know the victory will come, even if I can't see it at this moment.

> But I tell you who hear me: Love your enemies, do good to those who hate you, bless those who curse you, pray for those who mistreat you.
> - Luke 6:27-28 -

Wysh sê vy and seën veg
hulle want jy hou dan
aan om haar te seën.
hulle veg van buite. halle
sê vir my bevryding sal
hulle veg. hoekom moet
vyand so aanhou want
my werk wat ek moet
gaan doen is so so so groot.

Wisdom says that the enemy is fighting our blessing, because you keep on blessing her. They are trying to hurt us from the outside. They tell me that they will fight against my deliverance. Why doesn't the enemy leave me alone? Because the work that I have to do is so big.

28. Accept the fact that you are part of God's army, and that means you are going to have to fight. Ignorance and denial will not make Satan leave you alone. The "I am not bothering him so he won't bother me" argument will cost you dearly, because you will pose no resistance to Satan's onslaughts.

Be self-controlled and alert. Your enemy the devil prowls around like a roaring lion looking for someone to devour. Resist him, standing firm in the faith.
- 1 Peter 5:8-9 -

hulle veg hande en
voete van god.

ek sien so groot veg engel
van Jesus.

hulle baie baie
hulle sê Jesus het hulle
gestuur.

They [the enemy] are fighting against the hands and feet of God.

170

I see such a big warfare angel from Jesus. There are lots and lots of them.

Jesus sent them.

29. Be totally dependent on God. Know that you can trust God completely and therefore you can safely rest in His arms. At first this dependence is not comfortable to your flesh, because now you can no longer take things into your own hands, or rely on your own strength or abilities. Sometimes it is very difficult to give over control, especially if you have been hurt in the past when you trusted someone and in the end they hurt you. To be dependent on God takes you out of your comfort zone, makes you vulnerable, and tests your faith; but it is the safest place to be – because God is faithful!

> Blessed are those whose help is the God of Jacob, whose hope is in the LORD their God. He is the Maker of heaven and earth, the sea, and everything in them - He remains faithful forever.
> - Psalm 146:5-6 -

30. Call out to God's wisdom to lead you. Seek it with your whole heart!

> I will instruct you and teach you in the way you should go; I will counsel you and watch over you. Do not be like the horse or the mule, which have no understanding but must be controlled by bit and bridle or they will not come to you.
> - Psalms 32:8-9 -

31. Pray the Lord's Prayer. It is the example of prayer that Jesus gave us – it would be wise to listen to Him.

> "And when you pray, you shall not be like the hypocrites. For they love to pray standing in the synagogues and on the corners of the streets, that they may be seen by men. Assuredly, I say to you, they have their reward. But you, when you pray, go into your room, and when you have shut your door, pray to your Father who is in the secret place; and your Father who sees in secret will reward you openly. And when you pray, do not use vain repetitions as the heathen do. For they think that they will be heard for their many words. "Therefore do not be like them. For your Father knows the things you have need of before you ask Him. In this manner, therefore, pray: Our Father in heaven, Hallowed be Your name. Your kingdom come. Your will be done on earth as it is in heaven. Give us this day our daily bread. And forgive us our debts as we forgive our debtors. And do not lead us into temptation, but deliver us from the evil one. For Yours is the kingdom and the power and the glory forever. Amen.
> - Matthew 6:5-13, NKJV -

32. Be merciful. One night we were sitting at the dinner table and I was busy grumbling to Tinus about a certain unpleasant situation regarding another person. I had to make a decision about what I would do next. Aldo looked up from his plate and asked me, "Mom, how much mercy is in your bowl of mercy before God's throne?" I didn't fully understand what he meant with that and looked at him curiously. "There is a bowl of mercy before the throne of grace, Mom," he continued. "The mercy and grace you give to others is multiplied in it. When the day comes that it is your turn to go before the throne, God is going to look into your mercy bowl to see if He can find any mercy in there." Today I know that it is mercy, forgiveness and love that break down the enemy's strongholds.

> For judgment is without mercy to the one who has shown no mercy.
> Mercy triumphs over judgment.
> - James 2:13, NKJV -

33. Enjoy the triune God! Father, Son and Holy Spirit. Walk in a love relationship with Him.

> "On that day you will realize that I am in my Father, and you are in me, and I am in you. Whoever has my commands and keeps them is the one who loves me. The one who loves me will be loved by my Father, and I too will love them and show myself to them."
> - John 14:20-21 -

34. Worry is sin. Lay it down.

> Cast all your anxiety on him because he cares for you.
> - 1 Peter 5:7 -

Wysh se geseënd is mev ons
wat leer om mev ons
vertroue op God te stel.

Wisdom says we are blessed, Ma'am, because we have learned

to put our trust in God.

35. Put on the full armour of God and stand your ground.

> Stand firm then, with the belt of truth buckled around your waist, with the breastplate of righteousness in place, and with your feet fitted with the readiness that comes from the gospel of peace. In addition to all this, take up the shield of faith, with which you can extinguish all the flaming arrows of the evil one. Take the helmet of salvation and the sword of the Spirit, which is the word of God.
> - Ephesians 6:14-17 -

36. Live by faith and not by sight. Stand firm in God's Word! God is not a man that He should lie. To walk in faith is easier if you are continually aware of Jesus Christ's magnificent presence in you, and if you live in a love-relationship with Him.

> For we walk by faith, not by sight.
> - 2 Corinthians 5:7, NKJV -

37. You will reap what you sow. Be careful what you sow today, because that is the harvest you are going to reap tomorrow. This is a rule of nature, but also a principle of the spirit.

> Do not be deceived, God is not mocked; for whatever a man sows, that he will also reap. For he who sows to his flesh will of the flesh reap corruption, but he who sows to the Spirit will of the Spirit reap everlasting life.
> - Galatians 6:7-8, NKJV -

38. Be clothed with humility. This difficult road that we had to walk with Aldo by our side gave us no other option than to be completely humble and dependent on God. This humility comes when you fear nothing and no-one but God; when you no longer have to prove yourself to someone else or seek acceptance in the eyes of others; when you have nothing to lose and Christ is all you hold on to; when you are no longer wearing any masks and you live completely in the light.

> "God resists the proud, but gives grace to the humble." Therefore humble yourselves under the mighty hand of God, that He may exalt you in due time, casting all your care upon Him, for He cares for you.
> - 1 Peter 5:5b-6, NKJV -

39. Be patient. Let God be the Lord who determines the seasons in your life. If you know He is with you in the storm and in the desert, then you can know that He will carry you through it. In the darkest nights the stars still shine. To wait patiently on God is a sign of your trust in Him, as well as a sign of your maturity as the Bride of Christ.

> Because you know that the testing of your faith produces perseverance. Let perseverance finish its work so that you may be mature and complete, not lacking anything.
> - James 1:3-4 -
>
> The Lord will fulfil his purpose for me; your love, O Lord, endures forever.
> - Psalms 138:8a -

40. Keep speaking life!

Faith in God will help you to persevere even when it seems as though there is no hope left at all. Jesus said: *I tell you the truth, if anyone says to this mountain, 'Go, throw yourself into the sea,' and does not doubt in his heart but believes that what he says will happen, it will be done for him* (Mark 11:23). I live according to this scripture - because six years ago when Aldo was in a coma, God moved mountains for him to live. I had spoken life over the "dead bones" of my situation, and God answered my prayer. To this day I still speak life into Aldo's spirit man. The best words of life you can speak is the Word of God, because Jesus is the Word and He is the resurrection life!

> The tongue has the power of life and death, and those who love it will eat its fruit.
> *- Proverbs 18:21 -*

Chapter 8

het gedroom ek soek
een en almal by Jesus
ek sien jou waar jy
voor dursende mense
staan. god sê my bediening
het begin. god se jy
weet nie hoe ek gaan
bedien nie, maar hy
sê hy sal my reg maak
Jesus het my gewys waar
ek bedien. Lief vir julle
weet jy ek sal eendag
my eie bediening hê.
het jy geweet ek en

jy sal saam bedien

mg enigste begeerte is
om Jesus te behaag

hy het vir jou n groot
bediening wys my hoe
hy my wegsteek tot
wanneer ek gereed is
om te bedien.

I dreamt that I wanted each and every person to come to Jesus. I can see you standing before thousands of people. God says my time for ministry has started. God says you don't know how I am going to minister, but He says He will fix me. Jesus showed me where I will minister. I love you. Do you know that I will have my own ministry one day? Do you know that you and I will minister together? My only desire is to please Jesus. He has a large ministry for you. He shows me how He is hiding me away until I am ready to minister.

Pass the test

> He who dwells in the shelter of the Most High will rest in the shadow of the Almighty. I will say of the Lord, "He is my refuge and my fortress, my God, in whom I trust."
> - Psalms 91:1-2 -

I now know how important it is to dwell in the shelter of the Most High every second of every day. When we dwell there we are safe. It doesn't mean that there will be no attacks, but beneath the protective wings of our Father we have a refuge and a fortress in times of trouble.

God didn't remove the scorching sun from the wilderness when the Israelites had to travel through it, but He did provide them with everything they needed to pass the test and to get safely to the other side. The pillar of cloud provided them with shade and also showed them the direction in which to walk. The shade was also their boundary of safety; as long as they stayed within the shadow of the Almighty they didn't get lost.

There is a scripture in Deuteronomy that has encouraged me countless times when I struggled to make sense of my situation. Through it God reminds me that He has never said the road to the Promised Land would be easy, only that it would be worth it:

> Remember how the LORD your God led you all the way in the wilderness these forty years, to humble and test you in order to know what was in your heart, whether or not you would keep his commands. He humbled you, causing you to hunger and then feeding you with manna, which neither you nor your ancestors had known, to teach you that man does not live on bread alone but on every word that comes from the mouth of the LORD. Your clothes did not wear out and your feet did not swell during these forty years. Know then in your heart that as a man disciplines his son, so the LORD your God disciplines you.
> - Deuteronomy 8:2-5 -

After every spiritual battle I realised that whatever the enemy had planned for our destruction, God turned into a testimony to His honour. Truly, the Lord gives beauty for ashes, the oil of joy instead for mourning, and a garment of praise for the spirit of heaviness (see Isa. 61:3). After every test I could see more and more of Christ's character manifesting in us. We became less while He became more, and our hearts were being aligned with the desires He had for our lives. When we live according to our own (or the world's) ideas of happiness, we so easily surrender to sin.

God doesn't do anything half-heartedly! He wants to restore our lives completely, from deliverance from demonic bondage to complete inner healing; so that we can live up to our full potential as healthy and whole people who, in turn, are able to truly glorify Him.

It is a process. All the masks we wear to protect ourselves and to survive have to be removed one by one. Be warned - during the process of inner healing the wounds are still raw. They make us vulnerable and are thus easy targets for the enemy. Don't think that the enemy doesn't know where to hit you the hardest. I have seen how it affects Aldo when he is in the company of people who voice their fears and unbelief. It makes him anxious, because it scratches at the wounds that are still busy healing. When we feel the enemy targeting a weak spot, we have to immediately protect those wounds through prayer. It is so important to completely surrender to the Holy Spirit in order that we can hear His voice when He forewarns us about the enemy's plans to attack.

Each and every one of us will undoubtedly be subjected to trials at one time or another. I don't care if you are a celebrity T.V. evangelist, a multi-millionaire, or just a normal housewife – all of us have to go through a refining process. Though the trials we face are different, all of us will reach a cross-road where we will have to decide whether we are going to press forward, trusting God unconditionally; or if we are going to revert back to the comfort of the world and trust in our own strength and abilities. The question is simple: slavery and the delicacies of Egypt, or faith in God to get us to the Promised Land – even if it means we have to travel through the Wilderness to get there?

> In all this you greatly rejoice, though now for a little while you may have had to suffer grief in all kinds of trials. These have come so that the proven genuineness of your faith - of greater worth than gold, which perishes even though refined by fire - may result in praise, glory and honour when Jesus Christ is revealed.
> - 1 Peter 1:6-8 -

Aldo's birthday party was a turning point. Although the trials were not completely over and done with, I could feel that something major had shifted in the spirit realm. I began praying and asking God for true discernment, but I knew in my heart that I wouldn't receive what I had asked for if I didn't lay down my prejudiced beliefs and selfish ambition. May you carefully read this Scripture and write it on your heart:

> Who is wise and understanding among you? Let him show it by his good life, by deeds done in the humility that comes from wisdom. But if you harbour bitter

> envy and selfish ambition in your hearts, do not boast about it or deny the truth.
> Such "wisdom" does not come down from heaven but is earthly, unspiritual, of
> the devil. For where you have envy and selfish ambition, there you find disorder
> and every evil practice. But the wisdom that comes from heaven is first of
> all pure; then peace-loving, considerate, submissive, full of mercy and good
> fruit, impartial and sincere. Peacemakers who sow in peace raise a harvest of
> righteousness.
> - James 3:13-18 -

Today I ask the Lord to help me look at every situation through new eyes with enlightened spiritual discernment. From the new perspective He gives me, I see things that make my hair stand on end. Just yesterday I would have downplayed certain events as "coincidence" or "that's just life", but today I see it for what it really is. Spiritual discernment is the ability to look deeper than the eye can see; to see the heart of the matter and not merely the outward appearance.

I now long for a heart which is filled with compassion and love – just like the heart of Jesus. When Jesus spoke, His eyes were full of mercy; when He touched, He did so with caring hands. He didn't condemn or reject the broken or hurting – they were the very reason why He left heaven and came to earth!

Only after God removed my heart of stone did I start noticing the *servant bride*. These were the women who washed the cups and served the tea at the events where I spoke. While I was on stage and the other people were comfortably listening, they were the ones listening to my sermon in the door of the kitchen while preparing to serve others after the event. The picture of these ladies remained with me for a long time, and one night with tears in my eyes, I asked Jesus why I suddenly couldn't get them out of my thoughts. *Why had I never noticed them before, Lord? Were they just not important enough to me, or what?*

"For the first time you are looking through my eyes, Retha. It is only now that you can recognise My hands and feet, because now you have My heart – a heart of compassion," was His reply.

Immediately I prayed: "*Father, bind me to your thoughts and your desires. Bind me to Your will and bind my hands and feet to Your hands and feet so I can walk out my days according to Your plans for my life. Bind my heart to Yours. Make me one with You – so I can be like Jesus!*"

Along with the new heart, I also began to understand what a serious matter it is to God when we judge others. We shouldn't judge and condemn others (even if it is only by giving our opinion on something that doesn't concern us), because we are not walking in their shoes. Things look a lot different when the problems are your own. Jesus warned us Himself: *Do not judge according to appearance, but judge with righteous judgment* (John 7:24, NKJV). When we judge and condemn we bring a spirit of poverty (and that does not only imply a lack of finances) upon ourselves. David's wife Michal was a good example of this. When David danced before the Arc of the Covenant, she looked down on him and held him in contempt. As a result her womb was closed. This barrenness was a direct result of the haughty judgement she passed on him (see 2 Sam. 6:20-23). God is very serious about this: *For in the same way you judge others, you will be judged, and with the measure you use, it will be measured to you* (Matt. 7:2).

We need the mind of Christ (see 1 Cor. 2:16), but without His *heart* we cannot have His *mind*. You cannot give something that you don't have, and without His love in your heart you cannot give love to someone else. We should remain in God's presence until our cups are overflowing with grace, love and forgiveness; then we will always have enough to give to others. So many people try to ease their conscience by giving gifts or money to the Church, but they are not willing to give of *themselves* (their love, their time, their lives).

We can only look past each other's faults and shortcomings if our hearts are filled with love. Love conquers evil, and always triumphs in God's kingdom. Aldo wrote in one of his letters: "Nehemiah, they cannot fire against a humble wall!" This means the enemy cannot break through a wall of humility and love. Love drives away fear. Every time I blessed my enemies, Aldo wrote to me afterwards: "Mom, there is so much power in blessing, because you can only bless with a heart filled with love. She wants you to hate her; because she cannot fight against you if you are filled with love. Love comes from God, Mom."

Once a month I present a two-day teaching seminar called "the Spirit School" in a small church hall near my office in Hartebeespoort. The Holy Spirit then uses me to teach people about the unseen spiritual realm and how to walk by faith and not by sight. The Word warns us not to be outwitted by Satan because we are ignorant of his schemes (see 2 Cor. 2:11). Satan doesn't walk around with red horns and a pitched fork – he is devious and deceptive, and that's why we need to be on guard so that we won't fall into his traps.

On the second day of the Spirit School an anointed worship leader leads us in prophetic songs, and through the grace of God and the power of the Holy Spirit, God draws us even closer to Him and into His glorious light. This type of intimacy is not meant to be experienced only by a select few. God invites everyone to enter into this deeper dimension of His love. He calls us with so much love to approach His throne of grace and to draw near to Him, because there we will meet Him spirit to Spirit.

Few people truly understand the Father-heart of God, and that is why we struggle to love Him and to trust Him completely. Right from the start it had been God's plan for us to have a love-relationship with Him. We were meant to run to Him with open arms, without being afraid. Everything you long for (and I really mean everything) is in Him! Abba wants to care for you, He wants to lead you and comfort you. He wants you to trust Him with the plan He has for your life. He is waiting for you to find your rest in Him. Don't think that the preachers you see on stage don't also struggle with this issue of trust. There have been many times when it looked completely dark around me, and all I had to hold on to was this Scripture in Jeremiah 29:11: *"For I know the plans I have for you," declares the Lord, "plans to prosper you and not to harm you, plans to give you hope and a future."*

During the Spirit School we often hear testimonies of people who heard God's voice for the first time, or had experienced walking with Him in the garden, or felt His arms around them. The Holy Spirit speaks to each of us in a unique way and He speaks a language that only you and He understand.

Worship during a Spirit School

182

One morning as I was getting dressed for another one of these Spirit Schools, I felt the Holy Spirit impress on my heart that Aldo should minister there that day. The Spirit School is a safe environment for him to learn and grow, and I felt at peace the more I thought about it.

Ma'am Patrys and Aldo had already left for school, so I quickly phoned her and asked her to bring Aldo to the Spirit School during the day. Later that morning they quietly entered the church hall and went to sit in one of the back rows while the group was busy worshiping. Under the anointing of the worship music Aldo spontaneously stretched out his hands and started to bless the people around him. Shortly before the break I extended an invitation to anyone who was sick to come forward for prayer. I also called Aldo forward – it was time for him to learn. He stood before each person and while he prayed I could see in the spirit how God's fire of purification was falling upon us, and I felt the anointing of the Holy Spirit cover us like a gentle shower of rain. The fire of God is not accompanied by chaos as many people may think, but by a deep awareness of Abba's lovely presence. I was so overwhelmed with thankfulness that I started crying. We had been waiting for six years for that moment. Aldo prayed for the people as if he had been doing it all his life, and Tinus was next to him the whole time to support him and to make sure he didn't lose his balance. I quietly went to kneel behind a curtain and just gave thanks to Abba for being faithful to His promises. He is always true to His Word and everything happens according to His divine timing and purpose. He is not a man that He should lie – that I know for sure!

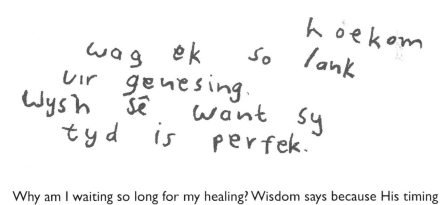

wag ek so lank h oekom
vir genesing.
Wysh sê want sy
tyd is perfek.

Why am I waiting so long for my healing? Wisdom says because His timing is perfect.

My mother also received healing that day for a shoulder injury that had been troubling her for many years. The damage to her shoulder was quite severe and she even considered an operation to alleviate her pain. After God's Spirit had touched her through Aldo's prayer, the pain was gone and even the doctors who performed a scan on her shoulder the next week said that it was a miracle!

When the Spirit of God is your teacher there will be no more fear to step out in faith. I believe Aldo's humility, his childlike faith, and the simplicity with which he ministers, creates a space for the Holy Spirit to flow through him and touch people. Although Aldo doesn't look like the cleverest, strongest or best person for the job, God sees something else, something that is far more valuable – He sees his heart which is devoted to Him.

> But we have this treasure in jars of clay to show that this all-surpassing power is from God and not from us.
> - 2 Corinthians 4:7 -

That evening, after a wonderful day at the Spirit School, Aldo was once again fiercely attacked by demons in the spiritual realm. He reacted in the same way he did a few months before when the woman who had worked for us used witchcraft against him, and we recognised the symptoms immediately. Clearly an intense battle was taking place in the spirit. "Aldo, what is wrong?" I anxiously asked him. "Today has been such a wonderful day!" (I think that is exactly why the enemy was out prowling that night. Often, after a victory the enemy will retaliate and try to win back the territory he lost. He tries to make us despondent so that we will surrender to him and not advance any further.)

Despite his size, Aldo climbed onto Tinus' lap, put his arms around his neck and said, "Daddy, there are still some things I have to tell you. Will you write it all down as a petition and take it to God, please?"

Wow! I was so excited that he was no longer trapped by his feelings of guilt and shame! I immediately jumped up to fetch a pen and paper and wrote down what Aldo said while he and Tinus talked.

Hulle sal beweg wagte solank

ek bly kwaad wees vir my vriende.

Jesus sê beweg vyand met liefde

hulle bewe want hulle
Weet nou wanneer ek
vergewe het hulle nie
meer houvas nie.

Jesus
sê maak vir hom n
vergifnis lys want ek
moet vergewe.

ı ne enemy's guards will keep on fighting as long as I am angry with my friends. Jesus says we must fight the enemy with love. They are quivering because they know that when I forgive, they will no longer have a hold on me. I am very, very, very lonely because my friends hurt me. They left me just like that. Just understand that I miss my friends. Jesus says we must make a forgiveness-list for Him, because I need to forgive.

He told Tinus about people from our past (and present), and the things they were saying about us. He mentioned the names of his friends and even some of their parents and how they were laughing and gossiping about our road of faith. He also mentioned people who were pointing fingers at some of my family members because of the mistakes they were making, "while Retha is away from home trying to save the world." My heart was hurting all over again and Aldo could see the pain reflected on my face. "Mom, please forgive them for the arrows of gossip and slander they are firing at you."

Why do I have to hear it, Lord? I wondered. *It hurts so much! If I didn't know about it, it wouldn't have bothered me.*

"I want to teach you to break the power of the words of death that are spoken over you, whether you hear it or not, Retha. Words bring life... or death."

I wrote down their names one by one, and knew that the enemy was using their gossip to "fire against our wall," as Aldo would say. It reminded me that I should guard my mouth and rather keep quiet if I cannot say something good. The enemy just loves gossip! Even though you are a child of God, Satan can use your words of death, fear or gossip to attack your fellow-Christians. Aldo even named pastors who were saying untrue and hurtful things about us. "Mom, Wisdom says we have to forgive them, because they don't know what they are doing. Bless them, Mom, bless them." We had to choose all over again to keep our hearts and our minds clean from any bitterness and unforgiveness. We couldn't allow ourselves to fall back into the pattern of our old nature – we had come too far to fall now! We had to make a choice not to open the door of temptation to become embittered, no matter how much we were hurting.

Wysh sê wat jy moet beveg is hulle leuns wat hulle vir my vertel.

uy and se et is nie Jesus se kind nie

met my prat hulle wat aanhoudend

Jy was al weer seer hy sê beveg seer met verseën hulle.

Wisdom says that you need to fight the lies they keep telling about me. The enemy says I am not Jesus' child. They talk to me continually. You were hurting again. He says we must fight the pain by blessing them.

Finally, Aldo admitted that he was still carrying around anger in his heart towards the woman who had worked for us. It was then that I realised that forgiveness is a continuous process. Initially it requires a choice, but thereafter you have to keep your heart clean of the weeds of bitterness that easily spring up again if given a chance.

"Aldo, let's go down on our knees and forgive each and every one of them right now. But before we start, let's first partake in communion and confess whatever is in our hearts, so we can receive forgiveness before we extend it to others. Then,

186

when we are sure that our hearts are ready, we can take this petition to God's throne."

It was wonderful to see how he brought everything to the light himself and openly talked about it. He realised the danger of keeping things bottled up inside. After we prayed, he was once again completely himself and as peaceful as can be. I anointed him and prayed that the Holy Spirit would break down any stronghold of fear that might still be present.

Let me just tell you, inner healing is a process – there are no quick fixes. There have been many nights on this road to healing when I invited the Holy Spirit into our midst and asked that He would minister to Aldo. I would then say: "Aldo, ask the Holy Spirit to show you your heart. Take Jesus' hand and walk with Him through the rooms of your heart to see what is truly going on in there; and if you find something that doesn't look right, tell me about it." It is wonderful to see how faithful the Holy Spirit is in showing us exactly where darkness or hurt is still lurking if we take the time to ask Him. We then always asked the Holy Spirit to return with Aldo to those places where he got hurt and to show him where Jesus was when it took place.

Remember, God is omnipotent, almighty and eternal. Therefore God is present in every situation even though we do not necessarily sense His presence at that moment. As soon as Aldo remembered a specific situation that caused him pain, we asked God to show him where Jesus was when it took place, so that he could take Jesus' hand and ask Him what to do. It is important to also ask God to show you if there was any sin involved, so that you can repent of it. I usually asked Aldo if he could still see any black spots in his heart. If his answer was yes, we asked the Holy Spirit to show us what we still needed to confess in order for those black spots to be washed away with Jesus' blood. It is basically a simple form of theophostic* therapy. The word theophostic is derived from the Greek words for "God" and "light", for: *God is light; in him there is no darkness at all* (1 John 1:5). As God's glorious light shines, the darkness is driven away.

I believe this process of dealing with our soul-wounds will work for everyone. The Holy Spirit knows exactly where and when the soul-wounds occurred that caused a false belief system to develop and where Satan got a foothold. God then comes to shine His glorious light on that memory in your mind so the wounds can heal; and through confession and by applying the blood of the Lamb the enemy's foothold will be destroyed. Time and again we witnessed the victory in Aldo's life through the application of this technique.

---

* *Theophostics is a Christian technique of inner healing. For more information, visit www.theophostic.com.*

Liefde het my vry
gem aak

Liefste mom jy is vir
my lief lief Wysh ê
wat jy weet laat jou
hard loop en h ooit stop
nie. Jy is regtig my
wyse mom.

Jesus sê wet
maak dood maar gees
gee lewe. Jy sien die man
met wit Linne ek wens ek
kan soos jy wees hy sê
hy pas my op hy beweg vir my
Wysh ê hy is meu gestuur
vir die uur waarin ons ingaan.
Jesus is by my weet asb dit.

Love set me free. My dear Mom, you love me so much. Wisdom says what
you know makes you run and never stop. You are truly my wise mom. Jesus
says the letter kills but the Spirit brings life. You see the man with white
linen. I wish I could be like you. He says that he guards me, and that he fights
for me. Ma'am, Wisdom says that he has been sent for the hour we are now
entering into. Just know that Jesus is with me.

That night after Aldo had ministered for the first time at the Spirit School I
had to go and preach in Johannesburg. Earlier that evening we had taken the petition
to God's throne and by the time I had to leave Aldo was completely calm, bathed

and in bed. I was excited while I was driving to Johannesburg, because I sensed that our breakthrough was fast approaching. I arrived home later that evening, very tired after a long day of preaching. As I walked through the door I immediately sensed that something was wrong. I found Tinus sitting next to Aldo's bed. "Retha, you won't believe it, but Aldo suffered three epileptic fits tonight. They were very intense and the one followed directly after the other." I felt cold from head to toe. Aldo hadn't had an attack in more than a year! I stood next to Aldo's bed and calmly prayed: "Please, Holy Spirit – give us the wisdom to know what to do now."

Hulle wil my hart laat staan.
Lusifer hy wat my veg

Lusifer is wat my wil dood maak

Gereg is liv my lewe.

Weer terug in my amper dood. verstaan Wysheid jou leer gees dimensie.

Lewe is Was nou jy hoe van die

They want my heart to stop beating. It is Lucifer that is fighting me.

It is Lucifer who wants to kill me. The fight is for my life.

Life is back in me again. I almost died now. Do you understand what Wisdom is teaching you about the spirit realm?

"Tinus, by now we already know what this means. Epilepsy does not come from God! The enemy is fighting against our breakthrough – this is just another attack. Do you remember that Rebecca Brown wrote about this in her book? The enemy will retaliate after a victory in order to discourage us so that we won't believe that the victory was real. I am telling you, that is exactly what is happening here!"

In the past I would have broken down and cried, but this time I calmly stood up and went to make us some coffee. Tinus and I sat next to Aldo's bed and softly started praising the King with hearts filled with peace. (That in itself was a miracle!) With my spiritual eyes I could see the angels that were appointed over our lives (and who write down everything we think, do and say) writing down in their scrolls: "Yet Tinus and Retha rejoice in the Lord." I also saw three demons that were appointed to make notes of the words that come from our mouths. They were on the lookout for words that they could use to "fire" us with, and this is what they wrote: "Retha and Tinus continue to praise God no matter what happens – even when we attack". As we continued to glorify the King I could feel the faith and peace rising up inside of me.

Wat is hier die man by my met wit klere by sê linne. Jy sien hulle Jesus sê hy het hom gestuur vir ons. hy is waar sy bedien moet hy heeltyd hier sit mom? Linne klere wat is dit hy sê hy is my rugwag hy is n wag vir my. hy is heeltyd by jou en jy sien hom.

You see them. Who is this man next to me with the white clothes on? He says the clothes are made of linen. Jesus says He sent him to us. He goes with you wherever you preach. Does he have to sit here the whole time, Mom? What are linen clothes? He says he guards my back. He is a guard who protects me. He is with you all the time and you can see him.

Later that night Aldo had another severe epileptic fit. When I saw him turning blue in the face, I jumped up and shouted at the top of my voice: "Satan, leave him alone! I command you to go beneath the feet of Jesus!" It took a long time for Aldo to calm down and fall asleep again. As I lay in my own bed hoping to get some sleep while Tinus stayed with Aldo, I had to keep on praying against the spirit of fear that was now bombarding Tinus and myself with sharp arrows of fear. These epileptic fits do not only affect Aldo, but our whole family. Any parent's soft spot is their children – we will do anything to protect them from harm. We would gladly take the pain on their behalf to keep them from getting hurt.

hy sê jy
lo ly bid vir genesing. hy bly
my brein aanval en nou
het jy hom uitgevang
hy was kwaad jy mag
hulle bestraf wysh
sê bestraf hulle en beveel
hulle om uit te gaan in Jesus
se naam Jesus is by my wat
be sorg

He [Wisdom] says that you keep on praying for healing. He [the demon] keeps on attacking my brain, but now you have caught him out. He was angry. You may rebuke him. Wisdom says resist them and command them to be cast out in Jesus' name. Jesus is with me and He cares for me.

> "But this Man, after He had offered one sacrifice for sins forever, sat down at the right hand of God, from that time waiting till His enemies are made His footstool."
> - Hebrews 10:12-13, NKJV -

Four attacks in one night, it couldn't get much worse than that. We thought the battle was nearly won, but what was happening now? Was it only the enemy retaliating and trying to gain back the ground he had lost; or was there some other "legal right" the enemy had to attack us with that we were unaware of?

Somewhere there still had to be something that gave the enemy a valid reason to attack us like this, but what? And where do I start looking? In the early hours of the morning I finally fell asleep with this prayer in my heart: "Holy Spirit – please show me why the enemy can still attack us. You know, Lord. Please show me so I can repent and turn away from it... no matter what it takes."

Chapter 9

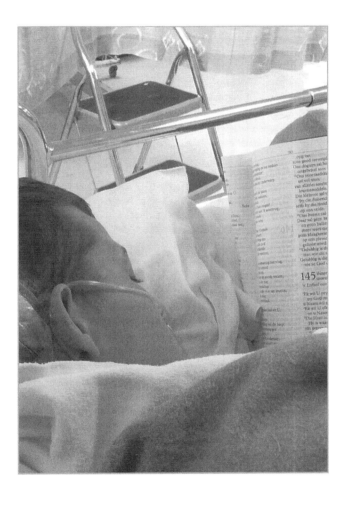

Wysh sê aansy hart is so seer
want kinders van God luister
nie. Ek sien aardbewings in
Amerika waar sy waar sien
ek ook water baie water sal
jy vir mense waarsku mom. Sê sê
wanneer sal gebeur God
vinnig. bid mom bid asb
vaak het hy gewys.hy sê raak
is bruid. Sy is nie wakker nie
Wat sal jou deel wees bid
Wysh sê bid hy sal luister.
Want sy bruid sal wakker
moet word. Vanself. se hy
mev sal niks het regkom nie
Wgsh sê water sal so baie
wees want sal jy glo mev
wgsh sê mense sal
verskrik staan hulle haal
vanself hulle eie behoeftes uit
want hulle is vol eie ek.
Wysh sê sal julle vir een
vanself een dag het bid
teen aardbewings en water
en nie jou eie begeertes nie
sal jy want weet jy hy
se by hom is alles wat
jy nodig het.

Wisdom says His heart is hurting because children of God aren't listening to Him. I see earthquakes in America, and I also see water, lots of water. Will you warn people, Mom? When will it happen? God says quickly. Pray Mom. Please pray. He showed me that we are slumbering. He says His Bride is slumbering. She is not awake. What will your part be? Pray... Wisdom says pray. He will listen when we pray, because His Bride needs to wake up. Nothing will just come right on its own. Wisdom says there will be a lot of water. Wisdom says people will stand in awe. They only talk about their own needs because they are full of themselves. Wisdom asks: Will you forget about yourself and your own needs for one day and pray for the earthquakes and water? Will you do that? He says that everything you need is in Him.

The veil is lifted

In desperation I kept calling out to God to show us why the enemy could once again attack Aldo with epilepsy. I spoke less and less in my prayers and I just reached out to God and waited on Abba to show me the next step. I realised all too well that only the TRUTH could set us free and that was what I was looking for – not the teachings or opinions of man, but the revealed truth of God. I was tired of fighting about who was right and who was not. I was desperately seeking God's truth – that was all that could set us free!

During that time I had a dream. In the dream the Holy Spirit and I were walking through a house. Everything in the house was white and breathtakingly beautiful. After we had walked through the house, the Holy Spirit took my hand and led me down the stairs to the cellar. I pushed against the door and it opened slowly. The room was dark, but the light that shone from behind me enabled me to see. The whole room was full of filth (like the filth that comes from a vacuum cleaner's bag), and in the middle of the room was a piece of raw meat that rats were busy chewing on. I was revolted by what I saw, and shrieked, "No, this cannot be my home!" But the Comforter, who was standing next to me the whole time, just nodded His head and closed the door; and then I woke up. For days I walked around with this dream in my heart, wondering what it could mean.

heilige heilige heilige God, Is ek werklik U kind? hy sê Ja Aldo my huis is in jou hart. Here, huis is vuil hoe kan U daar bly? Liewe Aldo, jy is my kind wat wagte so seerm o ak hulle is so waar, hulle is verslaan tot waar

hulle reg kry as jy hulle leuns glo. Liewe Aldo, jy is hulle vyand want Ek het jou heeltemal wysheid gegee van my wysheid. Wagte wil nie hê jy moet vir my werk nie.

hulle reg kry as jy hulle
leuns glo. Liewe Aldo, jy is
hulle vyand want Ek het jou
heeltemal wysheid gegee van
my wysheid. Wagte wil nie hê
jy moet vir my werk nie.

God says: "Holy, holy, holy God am I."

Am I truly your child?

He says: "Yes, Aldo. My home is in your heart."

But my house is so dirty, Lord. How can You live there?

"Dear Aldo, you are My child and you are being hurt by My enemy's guards.
They are defeated to the measure that they can gain access to your life
when you believe their lies. Dear Aldo, because I gave you wisdom – My
wisdom – you have become their enemy. The guards don't want you to
work for Me."

I desperately wanted to get rid of the filth in that room. In the days that
followed it felt as though I was confessing sins night and day. The enemy uses our
sin as bricks to build his strongholds. The deeper we move into God's "glory light",
the more He shows us what needs to be cleaned out, so we can deal with those things
that hinder our relationship with Him.

> Since we have these promises, dear friends, let us purify ourselves from
> everything that contaminates body and spirit, perfecting holiness out of
> reverence for God.
> - 2 Corinthians 7:1 -

The Hebrew name Jehovah M'Kaddesh means "God who sanctifies."
Wherever I went, whether I was driving in the car or pushing a supermarket trolley,
my heart was calling out, "Cleanse me, Jehovah M'Kaddesh! Wash me clean. Please
cleanse me and sanctify me!"

"Retha, build your walls on My rock by obeying My Word. Do what I
ask of you. Even though you don't yet understand it all - just trust Me; you will
experience the miracle. Repentance and obedience lead to true freedom," was God's
constant reassurance to my prayers.

It doesn't matter where we have been in our lives or how bad we think our sin is, if we confess it, He will forgive us our sins and purify us from all unrighteousness, for He is faithful and just (see John 1:9).

The price that Jesus paid for our sins by hanging on the cross has redeemed us completely. For sure we will still make mistakes during this process of becoming more like Christ, but our Abba Father will not turn us away when we come to Him with hearts filled with sincere remorse over our sin and a desire to change. If we could only understand how much He loves us, we would realise that there is so much more waiting for us, and we would gladly repent of the things that hold us back from the fullness of Christ. True confession is also a testimony of our faith, because it means that we want to be more and more like Jesus even though we cannot see Him. Remember that God reacts to our faith and not to our need. Although God has great compassion for us in times of need, it is our faith that makes Him move on our behalf.

> And without faith it is impossible to please God, because anyone who comes to Him must believe that He exists and that He rewards those who earnestly seek Him.
> *- Hebrews 11:6 -*

The only way to deal with the devastating consequences of our sin is to find, and root out, the source of it; and for that we need the Spirit of truth (see John 16:13). As long as Satan still has a hold on us through the open doors of unconfessed sin, the enemy will continue to try to and use these "legal claims" to attack us to the best of his ability.

Imagine that your heart is a very precious city. The walls that protect your city are built with stones such as righteousness, peace and joy in the Holy Spirit. As you grow in Christ, the stronger these walls will be. But none of us are immune to attacks of the evil one. He will keep on seeking a way in until he finds a weak spot in the wall (and believe me, we all have them). In order to protect our city, we have to find these weak spots that Satan exploits, and we have to reinforce the wall.

I started pulling out the roots of unconfessed sin wherever I could find them, from arrogance to bitterness, pride, anger, fear and unbelief; but still it felt as though I was missing something. There was something specific God wanted to reveal to me, *but what?*

Sometimes we walk around and around the mountain without seeing the solution to the problem. I was at that point where I didn't want to walk around it one more time – I could no longer afford the luxury of ignorance. I needed to hear God's voice clearly.

"Retha, the time has come to remove the veil from your eyes. Up until now your door of ignorance was open. Satan has blinded the church and left them defenceless against his attacks by having them believe that he doesn't exist or that he isn't dangerous. That is why you provided no resistance and always made excuses when he attacked you. "That's just life …" or "sometimes bad things happen to good people …"or some medical condition usually got the blame when devastation struck, but it was Satan all along.

"Now is the time that I am going to let My fire of truth fall on the enemy's strongholds to destroy them. I am going to remove the veil from My bride's eyes and take her through a purification process so she can receive a double portion of My favour. Through My Spirit of truth I am now going to remove the dark veil that has covered people's eyes. The glory of the latter house is going to be even greater than that of the former house," says the Lord God Almighty.

I had preached from pulpits that we shouldn't concern ourselves with things like bloodline curses and ancestral sins. I firmly believed that all these things were nonsense and that we only had to believe that the blood of the Lamb was enough. I was wrong. I had to confess it before God, and now also before the whole world.

The blood of the Lamb is the only thing that can purify us from our sins, that is absolutely true! But the rest of my remarks were made in ignorance and because of immaturity. The blood of the Lamb is stronger than any sin and any curse, but if I am not going to confess my sins, apply the blood of the Lamb, and break the curses, the bondage of the bloodline curses are going to stay intact.

This can be the reason why so many "bad things" happen to "good people." Or why the "nice pastor" suddenly falls into the grip of pornography, or why the "good family man" struggles with addiction, or a healthy teenage boy gets caught up in homosexuality. So many of these roots originate from the sins of the ancestors and the spiritual DNA and iniquities we inherited. (With this I am not saying that every bad thing we experience can be ascribed to ancestral sins and bloodline curses. There are many contributing factors, but if the ancestral sins remains unconfessed, then the curses are still intact and they will have an effect on our lives. The moment the bloodline curses are broken, the roots will be pulled out and people will be set free.)

When Moses had a very intimate meeting with God; God Himself chose these words to make His character known to humanity:

I am aware that many people think this topic of bloodline curses is an Old Testament teaching, and no longer applicable under the new covenant; but my question is this: why would God then specifically mention this principle of ancestral sin by name if it would become irrelevant? Remember that Jesus Himself said that He did not come to abolish the Law, but to fulfil it (Matt. 5:17). We cannot just ignore the Old Testament, because I can assure you that God didn't waste His breath by giving it to us. Through it God teaches us so much about Himself – His character, His protocol and how things work in the spirit. By this I am not implying that we are still bound to the Law in a legalistic way; I am just saying that there are immense treasures in the Old Testament that we are going to miss if we refuse to take it to heart. Allow the Holy Spirit to show you how the Old and New Testament are woven into one another to form the Word of God as a whole.

Aren't you wondering why the Church is suffering from so many diseases today? Or why so many Christians are struggling to be freed from Satan's bondages? To me it is clear that we are not dealing with the root of evil, only pruning the fruit of sin from time to time.

I placed my hand in my own bosom, just as Moses had to do when he came across his burning bush; and I asked God to show me what was going on in my own life. Whatever He revealed – whether I wanted it or not, or whether I thought I deserved it or not – I had to know, because I desperately wanted to be free from any form of bondage.

The things He revealed weren't pretty to see. I bowed my head and fell to my knees. Can this be how God leaves his children... powerless against the bondage and the curses that were formed because of the sins of our fathers, even before we were born? No, definitely not! Through Christ Jesus, Abba Father gave us everything we need to be free.

dry ground. He had no beauty or majesty to attract us to him, nothing in his appearance that we should desire him. He was despised and rejected by men, a man of sorrows, and familiar with suffering. Like one from whom men hide their faces He was despised, and we esteemed Him not. Surely He took up our infirmities and carried our sorrows, yet we considered Him stricken by God, smitten by Him, and afflicted. But He was pierced for our transgressions, He was crushed for our iniquities; the punishment that brought us peace was upon Him, and by His wounds we are healed.
- Isaiah 53:1-5 -

On an otherwise normal Friday night my family and I shared a Shabbat dinner with my parents. My parents often visit with us, and on this specific night we laughed a lot and we were very joyful. At that stage Aldo couldn't yet eat solid foods (because his mouth was still hurting too much after the fall from the balcony), and we only dished up some soft foods for him. After dinner he immediately excused himself. I found it a bit strange, but I just thought that he was tired and wanted to go to bed early. After his last epileptic fit we had once again carried a mattress into our room so he could sleep next to our bed.

Somewhere during the night hours I was woken by the sound of Aldo groaning next to me. When I switched on the light I was shocked to see what he looked like. His whole face was swollen – he couldn't even open his eyes! His was burning with fever and struggling to breathe. At first I wanted to panic, but the still small voice of the Holy Spirit whispered in my heart: "From Nehemiah to Naáman free."

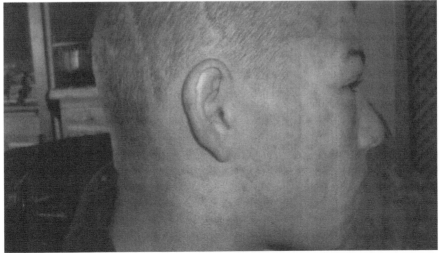

Aldo with an allergic reaction that covered his whole body.

201

"Tinus, do you remember what Aldo wrote? From Nehemiah to Naáman free ... I'm sure that is what is happening now. What we see before us is Naáman, but Jesus is going to heal him – I believe this with all of my heart! We are close to the breakthrough!"

Tinus didn't really share in my excitement. His first priority was to take care of Aldo and to protect him, and I could sense his heartache when he quickly packed some of Aldo's things into a backpack for what would probably be another few days in the hospital. While Tinus was busy getting everything ready, I sat down with Aldo to try and write a letter even though his eyes were nearly swollen shut.

"What is wrong, Aldo? Ask Wisdom to show you."

He then wrote:

"He says we are fighting poison. Please take me to the hospital quickly. Yes, the hospital."

After the doctors had treated him with antibiotics for possible food poisoning or an allergic reaction, the fever finally broke and the swelling went down. They released him from the hospital, but in the days that followed he continually groaned with pain and hunched over to hold his stomach. When it didn't get better after a week, we knew that is wasn't only a simple matter of food poisoning or allergy – it was definitely more serious. Although his letter had said "they poisoned my food in the spirit," I couldn't share it with the doctors because I knew they wouldn't believe me. He also wrote that there was something wrong with his appendix, but because he had antibiotics in his system the doctors couldn't see anything on the scans, and they didn't want to do an appendectomy based only on his letters.

Wysh sê hy hou my vas
hy sê jy hoef nie bekommerd
te wees nie.

Wisdom says my fever is from the infection. The fever will break soon.

Wisdom says He is holding me. You don't have to be worried.

Eventually he was so sick and his fever so high that they had to admit him to ICU. Tinus once again slept at the hospital every night. Four days went by while the doctors did all kinds of tests, but they couldn't determine the reason for his illness.

I cried out to the Lord. *How much hurt does he still have to go through, Lord? What can I do so the doctors will believe his letters and operate on his appendix?* That night while I was crying before the Lord, I could hear God answer me, "Retha, it is his appendix that had burst. I want you to know that Aldo is safely in the palm of my hand. The enemy wants to kill him, but I will carry him through. Send the doctor a text message; he is My child and he will listen." Late that night I sent the doctor a simple message saying, "Doctor, you have to believe me! It is Aldo's appendix that has burst. Wisdom has never made a mistake – please operate and see for yourself!"

h ewige h ewige geveg in die
hemel oor my lewe want
hulle wou my dood gemaak
het. Jesus sê my werk
is wat hulle veg hulle is
my vyand. God sê vyand
is verslaan. help my asb
nou nev ek hou vas
aan hoop dat Jesus vir
my veg

There is a fierce battle raging in the heavens for my life, because they tried to kill me. Jesus says it is my work that they are fighting against. They are my enemies. God's enemies are defeated. Please help me now, Ma'am. I keep on holding onto the hope that Jesus is fighting for me.

The doctors finally did a laparoscopy and saw that what Aldo had written was true: his appendix had burst. This could have had devastating effects if the infection in his appendix spread to the rest of his stomach. It was even more dangerous for Aldo who had a shunt, because there was a risk that the infection could spread through the tube of the shunt to his brain. Aldo immediately had to undergo an emergency procedure. The doctors made three incisions to his stomach to remove his appendix as well as the shunt's tube. The fluid in his brain could now no longer be drained into his stomach, so the tube was connected to an external bag, similar to an IV bag. We had to wait for the infection in his stomach to clear up completely before they could insert a new shunt, and that meant he had to stay in hospital for about another two weeks. During the time when he was confined to his hospital bed, he spent most of the time praying and reading his Bible. He also had a lot of visitors who kept him company; and between Tinus, Ma'am Patrys and myself, he was never alone.

One day when I arrived at the hospital he put his Bible in my hand and said, "You should read carefully, Mom. You are not reading it right. You are not seeing through the veil. Read Nehemiah again."

Frustrated I replied, "No Aldo, by now I must have read through that book five times. We had fought, we had prayed, we had rebuilt the walls. What more is there to do?"

"Mom, there is still a hole in the wall."

I was surprised when he said this, because I hadn't told him anything about my dream and the dirty basement I saw. I was in fact looking for this "hole in the wall" he was referring to.

That night when I got home, I opened my Bible at Nehemiah again. Tinus was staying at the hospital with Aldo, and Josh came to sit next to me on the couch after he had finished his homework.

"Mom, why are you reading Nehemiah again?" he wanted to know when he noticed there were already many notes scribbled in the margins and almost no space left to write. "Zozzie, I am missing something that Jesus wants to reveal to me. It is like playing hide and seek. I have to keep on looking until I find it."

I started reading the book from the start again, but this time Nehemiah 1:6 immediately stood out for me: *Let your ear be attentive and your eyes open to hear the prayer your servant is praying before you day and night for your servants, the people of Israel. I confess the sins we Israelites, including myself and my father's house, have committed against you.*

Later in Nehemiah it also says:

> Then those of Israelite lineage separated themselves from all foreigners; and they stood and confessed their sins and the iniquities of their fathers. And they stood up in their place and read from the Book of the Law of the LORD their God for one-fourth of the day; and for another fourth they confessed and worshiped the LORD their God.
> - Nehemiah 9:2-3, NKJV -

I had read the book of Nehemiah so many times in the past, but why had I never paid attention to these verses before? Could it be true that bloodline curses really do exist? Was God asking of me to stand in the gap and confess my own sins - as well as the sins of my "fathers"?

I started delving deeper, and by using the cross references in my Bible I was reminded that Daniel had also prayed and stood in the gap for a whole nation, including the sins of the fathers and the previous generations (see Daniel 9). The sincere prayers and intercession of one man led to breakthrough for a whole nation, and eventually Israel's redemption from exile. Not only Daniel, but Moses had also stood in the gap for the people. These examples made me realise how much power there is in repentance and standing in the gap – if it wasn't for Nehemiah, Daniel and Moses, who knows what would have happened!

When we stand in the gap for someone (as God had asked me to intercede for the woman who had worked for us) it is like going to the throne of grace on that person's behalf. Jesus also said: *If you forgive anyone his sins, they are forgiven; if you do not forgive them, they are not forgiven* (John 20:23). This is the principle of **remission of sins**. The word remission implies the act of remitting, temporarily lessening, and forgiving. In effect you are standing in the gap for them before the throne of grace and "lessening" the burden of that person's sin for the time being, so that his spirit can breathe and hear the voice of God. The aim is for that person to come to repentance himself. Our obedience to Jesus' command to extend forgiveness and bless our enemies creates a wider road for God's Spirit to work directly with that person's heart.

In the case of ancestral sin and bloodline curses, as long as those sins are not repented of and the blood of the Lamb applied to it for forgiveness, the law of sowing and reaping is also still actively working. That is why it is important to specifically stand in the gap for ancestral sins and bloodline curses in order to clean the land for the generations to come. As long as the seeds of the sins of the previous generations are still in the ground, the future generations will reap its harvest.

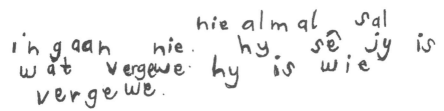

ih gaah hie. hie al m al sal hy se jy is
wat vergewe. hy is wie
vergewe.

Not everyone will go in.

He says we forgive, but He is the one who says forgiven.

With this new conviction in my heart I started looking for more information on bloodline curses and found another book on my bookshelf by Rebecca Brown, entitled *Unbroken Curses*. In this book she explains how ancestral sin and curses can have a destructive effect on our lives. She also says that Satanists have a very good understanding of the principle of bloodline curses and that they absolutely use it to their advantage because most Christians don't want to acknowledge it. When they place a curse on a family they ensure that the curse also includes the future genrations. Their aim is to destroy the whole family line and not only the individual.

This principle is also confirmed in the Bible:

> And those of you who are left shall waste away in their iniquity in your enemies' lands; also in their fathers' iniquities, which are with them, they shall waste away. 'But if they confess their iniquity and the iniquity of their fathers, with their unfaithfulness in which they were unfaithful to Me, and that they also have walked contrary to Me, and that I also have walked contrary to them and have brought them into the land of their enemies; if their uncircumcised hearts are humbled, and they accept their guilt—then I will remember My covenant with Jacob, and My covenant with Isaac and My covenant with Abraham I will remember; I will remember the land.
> - *Leviticus 26:39-42* -

While I was reading this verse in Leviticus, there was a reference to Deuteronomy 30 that drew my attention. There it is written:

> This day I call heaven and earth as witnesses against you that I have set before you life and death, blessings and curses. **Now choose life, so that you and your children may live.**
> - *Deuteronomy 30:19, emphasis mine* -

When I read this Scripture I couldn't hold back the tears any longer. "Lord, do You want to tell me that I had always been so blind, so naïve, that I lived with all these curses my whole life?" As though a light had been switched on, I suddenly realised that these bloodline curses were the rotten meat I saw in the basement of my house - and the rats that were feeding of the meat were demons.

"Yes Retha, they have a right to do this to you because of the unbroken curses. And the piece of raw meat they are feeding on is the curse of hatred and racism that comes through your blood line."

"I don't understand Lord... I don't have hatred inside me towards other races and You know that I have forgiven everyone who had hurt me."

"Retha, you are still not seeing the whole picture. The hatred comes from racism. That is the strongman in South Africa. The blood that was spilt is calling out for more blood. For so long it has been swept under the rug – even the legislation had approved it and it was preached from the pulpit. There are so many people in this country where you live that are still caught in it's grip.

"There is a dark cloud that is hanging over the country and I am waiting to remove it so I can pour out My refining fire. Iniquity hinders My children from hearing My voice. It also hinders your love-relationship with Me – it keeps you in the outer court, so that you don't experience intimacy with Me in the Holy Place.

"Before I can pour out My fire of revival, My people need to return to Me. It will then overflow from their hearts, to the hearts of their friends and family, to the heart of the city and then to the nation. Revival starts with one person in every household. The cloud of hatred and racism will only be lifted when remission of sins take place; and that will only happen if hearts are humbled. My people need to start rebuilding their walls; and repentance and standing in the gap for the sins of their forefathers, is part of it."

Wat is revival. Jesus se
revival seen sal val op jou
val op mense om jou val op
hulle vriende val op hulle
vriende en so vloei sy olie
oor die wêreld. Seën seën
seën van God seën van
God se gees is revival. God
hou my vas mev so so so
dankie dat julle my so liefhet

What is revival? Jesus says revival-blessing will fall on you, will fall on people around you, will fall on their friends; and in this way the oil will flow around the world. Blessing, blessing, blessing from God – revival is a blessing from God's Spirit. God holds me tightly. Ma'am, thank you so, so, so much that you love me.

If you are humble enough to acknowledge your own faults and shortcomings, God will give you the grace to overcome it through His Holy Spirit – and this will lead to victory over those weak areas. The sins of your forefathers and bloodline curses will not rob you of your salvation – it will only keep you from living an abundant life in Christ here on earth.

On Sunday after Sunday the children of God come to church and hear about the resurrection power of Jesus Christ, while few of them actually experience it for themselves. Iniquity is the core problem of so many sicknesses, diseases, emotional problems, addictions and much more.

Regardless of the difficult time Aldo was going through, he still wrote to us about the spiritual revival that he saw coming. He prophesied that it is going to have a ripple effect on the world. Sometimes it didn't make sense to me at all… I mean, we were fighting for his life and he was talking about revival? That was the last thing on my mind!

There have already been many prophecies about South Africa, stating that the fire of revival will come from the southern tip of Africa and will spread over the whole world; but this fire will not come before the dark cloud is lifted from our country. Because of the influence of South-Africa's religious history (that was intertwined with politics), a lot of people are sitting in church only for the esteem of being a elder or a deacon, but they look at their neighbours (from another denomination, background, social class, or race) with hearts full of hatred, racism or pride.

Just as in the case of Daniel, the only solution for our country is to truly turn to God through humility and repentance. Only then will God be able to send His fire. Our country is being weighed down by so much witchcraft as a result of the hatred and racism "drain" that is still open.

Despite everything, Africa is still one of the places in the world where people are vigorously turning back to God as a direct result of the calling that God has on this continent.

God confirmed to me what Aldo had written through a prophetic word by Cindy Jacobs (a prophet from America): *"I saw people standing on the coast all along the African continent. They all bowed down simultaneously and started lifting the edge of the dark veil that was lying over the country [confession of hatred, racism and lovelessness] until this veil had been removed completely. Then I saw a tsunami wave starting at the southern tip of South Africa and I saw a huge net descending from heaven. People took hands at the southern tip of Africa and pulled this net over the whole African continent. I saw big harvest silos standing next to each other at the southern tip of the continent and everyone worked together to bring in the harvest for the Kingdom."*

baie hartseer besef jy meu
hulle wat nie wil belei van
rasisme bly in haat. Wysh sê
binne ore hoor maar pride
is te groot.
God se, repent
vyand is pride

Ma'am, you are so sad now that you realise that those who don't want to
repent of racism are living in hatred. Wisdom says their inner ear hears, but
their pride is too big. God says repent. Pride is the enemy.

Racism is based on much more than just skin colour. Racism is at the root
of all feelings of superiority – whether you think you are better than others because
of your skin colour, money, status, talents, education, or even the neighbourhood you
live in.

hy sê velkleur ken hy nie.
hy sê hart retah hart is vir
God belangrik. Wysh sê
verstaan vrede vrede behoort
hemel is vir alle mense
wat hom liefhet

Wysh sê vyand wat vir
vuur vir jou is hewig
kwaad tradisie wev tradisie
is baie kwaad.

He says He doesn't differentiate between skin colour. He says: "It
is all about our hearts, Retah. Our hearts are important to God.
Wisdom says we must understand that peace belongs to Him.
Heaven is for all people who love Him.

209

Wisdom says the enemy that is sending fire against you is "Religion."

[The spirit of] Religion is very angry, Ma'am.

Racism, however, is not just a demon. It sits as a ruler over areas and nations; and in this way whole nations are enslaved under the whip of the spirit of death and destruction that works hand in hand with racism. If we look back over the centuries we can clearly see that racism always resulted in bloodshed. When you sow *racism*, you will reap *death and destruction*. Racism is in effect a sin against love. It is in direct opposition to God's first commandment:

> "Teacher, which is the greatest commandment in the Law?" Jesus replied: "'Love the Lord your God with all your heart and with all your soul and with all your mind.' This is the first and greatest commandment. And the second is like it: 'Love your neighbour as yourself.' All the Law and the Prophets hang on these two commandments."
> - *Matthew 22: 36-40 -*

The day after I received this revelation about bloodline curses and ancestral sin, I was scheduled to go to the counselling session that I had arranged in Australia weeks before. It couldn't have come at a better time. I once again realised how God is in control of every detail of our lives. I asked them to pray with me, specifically to break the bloodline curses and to break the grip of the spirit of death and destruction that had entered our lives through racism.

I learned another important thing from the counsellors that day: "Retha," they advised, "you must also break the ungodly part of the soul tie between you and your father."

Every relationship you have results in a bond between you and the other person. Strong bonds occur between husbands and wives, children and their parents and of course, friendships. God created us to have relationships, and there is nothing wrong with a bond forming between two people. The Biblical basis for a soul tie can be found in the description of David and Jonathan's relationship: *Now when he had finished speaking to Saul,* **the soul of Jonathan was knit to the soul of David,** *and Jonathan loved him as his own soul* (1 Sam. 18:1, NKJV, emphasis mine) - hence the word *soul tie.*

Relationships are good, but the moment the relationship is out of balance and Jesus is no longer at the centre thereof, an ungodly soul tie can be formed. For example, an *ungodly* soul tie is formed when the friendship between a man and woman develops into an extra-marital affair (or any relationship where there is sex outside of marriage). Another example can be when a parent abuses a child through domination and fear, and the child becomes enslaved to that fear; or a friend manipulates and intimidates you to get his or her own way and you can't seem to break off the friendship even when you know it is not good for you. These types of relationships pull down the person who suffers under the yoke of the ungodly soul tie, and the soul tie (the ball and chain – so to say), should be broken.

Before I could cut the ungodly part of the soul tie with my dad, I first had to confess anything that I still harboured against him. I wanted to deal with any legal claim that Satan could have used against me, and unforgiveness is surely one of his strongest trump cards. Afterwards we prayed that God would strengthen the godly ties (ties of love) between my father and me. In a godly relationship there is a tie of love that is under the authority of Jesus Christ and designed by God to unite two people.

After the repentance we prayed and asked the Lord to break the bloodline curses from my mother's side and from my father's, and the ungodly soul ties that existed between us. After we had prayed the prayer I instantaneously felt as if a very heavy burden had been lifted off my shoulders. I started crying from deep inside my being and it literally felt as if my insides were shaking. Lastly we prayed and asked the Holy Spirit to fill me anew with His love and peace.

After the counselling session, I sat in my car in the parking lot for a long time. I couldn't stop my tears from flowing as I reflected on what had just happened to me. Truly, God is close to the broken-hearted and He comes to their rescue. While I was driving back to the hospital I prayed once again, "Abba, let Your glory light shine in me so that all darkness will be expelled... and let the closeness of Your love comfort me now when I feel so fragile. I am so dependent on You, Lord.... truly You are my light and my salvation"

At the hospital Tinus waited for me in Aldo's room in ICU. I didn't want Aldo to see how puffy my eyes were from all my crying, so I sent Tinus a text message to meet me in the cafeteria. Over a cup of coffee I told him about the wonderful things that had happened to me that afternoon and everything I had learned from the counsellors. We decided to not tell Aldo about it right away, but to wait until he was physically stronger – we didn't want to risk unsettling him in any way. It was nearly six o'clock and I had to get home to Josh. Tinus was going to sleep over at the hospital again that night, and I would return early the next morning for my shift to look after Aldo.

The next morning when I walked into his room Aldo greeted me with his thumb in the air and a cheerful, "Thank you, Mom! I am free!"

211

Wat mens so vas vas domang vashou. hulle het vuur deur sou pa gevuur nou is vuur se drein toe hy raga regtig jammer gese vir Jesus. vuur is hehemia weg drein is toe.

bly oupa het hulle soaltie bly so gebreek

hulle wat my verstand vas gehou het.
hulle is het toe ek
is regtig vry
het jy geweet jy het my
wev werklik gered want
jy was gehoorsaam aan God.

Bound, bound. It is the demons that keep people bound. They sent fire [to us] through your father. Now the drain for the fire is closed. He really asked Jesus for forgiveness. Nehemiah, the fire is gone and the drain is closed.   I am glad Grandpa broke the soul-tie. I am really free from them who held my mind captive. Do you know that you truly saved me, Ma'am? Because you were obedient to God.

I was dumbfounded! The bloodline curses were the "dirt in the basement" I was looking for all along! The enemy was able to keep on attacking us because he had a legal right to do so through the unbroken bloodline curses. The smile on Aldo's face told me that he already knew what had happened without me having to say a word.

vuur. hier nehemia sien
huil retah huil sien duur
mev mev prys wat jy prys
regtig weg huil eye kind
my maar is nou
gebou nehemia nehemia
huil verby n ou nou
nuwe dag. het met baie
nuwe nuwe humble beuryde
mum retah vry vry drein
is nou almal toe want
oupa verander het

Fire. Nehemiah, I can see you crying. Retah you are crying. I can see the high price that you are paying with your tears. My wall is now built. Nehemiah, Nehemiah, crying is over now. Now it is the dawn of a new day with a very humble and free Mom. Retah, you are free! The drain is now completely closed, because Grandpa changed.

Even though my child was in hospital due to a burst appendix and the ensuing complications, my cup was overflowing with thankfulness. He was recovering well and we were looking forward to taking him home soon when the infection cleared up and the doctors could reinsert the shunt.

That morning, over a nice hot cup of Milo, I told Aldo all about what had happened the previous day (as if Tinus and I could have been able to hide it from him!). Later that afternoon Ma'am Patrys came to take over from me because I had to fly to Cape Town to preach that evening.

Shortly after I had arrived in the Cape, I received a phone call from Tinus. "Retha, you won't believe it, but the doctor looked at the scans and he says it is not necessary to insert a new shunt!"

Instead of being excited about the miracle, I was concerned. "But why not? I thought the shunt is so important!"

Tinus was just as surprised as I was. "I don't know! They just said that it is no longer necessary. The scans show that everything is normal. His ventricles aren't swollen – *everything is normal!*"

And then the truth hit me … the curse has been broken, that's why! The grip that the spirit of death and destruction had on us has been broken! Aldo was free!

gekoop. is ons duur so duur
lief vir ons. hy is vreeslik
lewe kan ek hoe in die
jou dat jy dankie se vir
het. hy is vloek gebreek
my oupa want bevry hy is
sy son de. Jesus jy bid vir
ons vir se bevry is
ewig. dankie Jesus

We are bought at a very high price. He loves us so much. How will I ever be able to thank you for breaking the curse? He is my Grandpa. He is free now, because you are interceding for his sins. Jesus says we have been set free forever. Thank You, Jesus!

As I am busy writing this chapter, it is now four months since the shunt has been removed. We have had more scans taken since then, and the ventricles are still normal. After several operations and so much pain and suffering, Aldo is finally free because the curse is broken.

After everything we have been through no-one will be able to convince me that bloodline curses do not exist. We have tasted and seen for ourselves the devastating effects these curses can have, but we have also tasted and seen that God is faithful. It is the spirit of death and destruction working alongside racism and hatred that destroys so many families. With racism, or *any* form of hatred in your heart, you give that deadly spirit a legal right to try to destroy you and your family. Your situation doesn't have to look like mine. Maybe it manifests through a crumbling marriage, or through a rebellious child or an addiction, but where the spirit of death and destruction makes its mark, the end result will surely be death.

Examine your own heart today. When Moses put his hand inside his cloak and took it out, it was leprous (see Ex. 4:6-7), but God healed him. All the power belongs to Him and He is merciful!

"Thank You for your blood, Jesus, so we can break the curses! Thank You for Your Word that is truth, so that we can shatter every lie of the enemy. Jesus You came to set us free!"

That weekend while I was ministering in Cape Town, I found myself wanting to call home every few minutes to check if everything was really and truly over. "Retha, don't call again to ask if everything is still well with Aldo. The curse is broken and will never again return," the Holy Spirit comforted me late one night when I was about to pick up the phone again.

That night I heard God speaking to me in a dream or a vision – I am not sure which – but He said, "Retha, I want you to change your name to Retah." (I could see the new spelling of my name clearly in front of me.) "Just like Abram became Abraham and Sara became Sarah, it is now time for your name to be changed. I give you this promise today: *"As for Me,"* says the LORD, *"this is My covenant with them: My Spirit who is upon you, and My words which I have put in your mouth, shall not depart from your mouth, nor from the mouth of your descendants, nor from the mouth of your descendants' descendants,"* says the LORD, *"from this time and forevermore"* (Isa. 59:21, NKJV). It is time for a new beginning. I am no longer just walking next to you, or in front of you, or close to you – I AM in you."

That was the final sign that the family curse (that was also indicated by my inherited family name) was completely broken. I didn't hesitate for one second; I immediately changed my name to Retah. The Lord does not require all of us to change our names. He didn't use it as an ultimatum for the family curse to be broken – the blood of Jesus broke the curse, not the new way I spell my name. I did it as an act of obedience after the Lord revealed it to me; not because I had to, but because I love Him and want to obey Him.

Jesus sê hy sal van seën wat jy jou pa seën hy sal jou seën. Tesus is vegters se vegters. Jesus het jou naam verander sy moet Gehoorsaam wees retah soos Abraham jy in bruid se tafel. Jy seën al is jou hart So seer.

Jesus says He will bless you because you are blessing your father. Jesus is an enemy to the enemy. Jesus changed your name. You must be obedient, Retah, like Abraham. You will be at the Bride's table. You bless even if your heart is aching.

I have never looked back after my decision (even if I did get a few remarks of being too radical, or over-spiritual), and now I realise that only Jesus' love and grace can enable us to walk the road of sanctification to the end. Today I understand His grace much better than ever before – because I experienced firsthand how Jesus healed my spiritual leprosy. I am also like Aldo "from Nehemiah to Naáman free!"

Thank You, Jesus, for my new name and my new life in You!

Chapter 10

Wysh sê hulle wat haat sal
nie vuur van God beleef nie.
Jy regtig meu haat wat soveel
huwelike laat opbreek. hy sê
haat wat soveel baie. besteel
laat gebeur, hy sê haat wat
hewige gevegte in gees laat
gebeur. Wysh sê sy gees
breek oop nou wat soveel
generasies nehemia se muur
weu laat breek het. het jy
gesien hoe groot sy liefde
vir ons is hy seën ons
so nou. Wysh sê vuur sal
vryheid vir ons veg. Wysh
sê jy sal vir revival sien
wanneer hewige vergifnis
begin hy sê vergewe, seën
hy sal al seine seine van
vyand so breek. het Jesus
vir jou ook gesê hy is
nehemia se muur vir ons.

Wisdom says that those who are not willing to let go of their hatred will not experience the fire of God. Ma'am, it really is hatred that is causing so many marriages to fail. He says it is hatred that causes so many things to be stolen. He says it is hatred that causes huge battles in the heavens. Wisdom says that He is revealing through His Spirit the things that have caused the walls of Nehemiah to be broken down. Do you see how big His love is for us? He is blessing us now. Wisdom's fire will fight for our freedom. Wisdom says that you will see the revival as soon as people start forgiving others. He says we have to forgive and bless. Through this He will break all the signals of the enemy. Did Jesus also tell you that He is like Nehemiah's wall to us?

Victim or victor?

There is no fear in love. But perfect love drives out fear, because fear has to do
with punishment. The one who fears is not made perfect in love.
- I John 4:18 -

God's fingerprint is love, and that of Satan is hatred and fear. Many years ago God said to me, "Retah, the miracle's name is love." In all my books I refer to this as the slogan of my life, because if it wasn't for God's love, our family wouldn't be free today.

The message of this book may offend those people who don't want to believe how real the battle in the spiritual realm is, and to what extent it influences our lives directly. However, the undeniable Word of God says that our struggle is not against flesh and blood, but against the rulers, against the authorities, against the powers of this dark world and against the spiritual forces of evil in the heavenly realms (see Eph. 6:12).

wie sien nehemia sal
jy vir mense sê Jesus is oppad
hy is vir bruid oppad baie het
hulle hewe baie lief vanseen
van seen is ek vry. het helse
vegters bruid so bereg het
bruid hie besef dat haar versein
was geherasie haat nie drie
haal haal bruid se sluier of
nehemia blaas die stof van
jou mure bestraf die vyand
want julle verloor verloor
die oorvloed van wysheid

Do you see Nehemiah? Will you tell people that Jesus is on His way? He is on His way to fetch His bride. Many love their lives too much. Because of "blessing" I am free. The fighters from hell fought against the Bride, and the Bride didn't realize that their signals were because of generational hatred [bloodline curses]. Three. Take off the Bride's veil. Nehemiah, blow the dust off your walls. Cast out the enemy, because you are losing the abundance of Wisdom.

For some reason we are always looking for the root of our problems somewhere other than in the spirit, and we criticise those who are brave enough to take on the spiritual fight. I now understand why God chose these words when He called me to full-time ministry: *You will not preach about that which you have not tasted.* Only when you have experienced something for yourself do you know beyond a shadow of a doubt that it is the truth. Even though people sometimes look at me sceptically when I talk about these things it doesn't bother me anymore, because I know what I have experienced and have seen with my own eyes.

I know that the spiritual world is real. I know that Satan is walking around like a roaring lion, seeking whom he may devour. I know he attains legal rights to attack us and until we nullify these legal rights through the blood of the Lamb, he won't stop. But most importantly, I know that Jesus had cancelled and done away with the written code that stood in judgment against me by nailing it to the cross - *that* is why I can live in victory.

> When you were dead in your sins and in the uncircumcision of your sinful nature, God made you alive with Christ. He forgave us all our sins, having canceled the written code, with its regulations, that was against us and that stood opposed to us; he took it away, nailing it to the cross. And having disarmed the powers and authorities, he made a public spectacle of them, triumphing over them by the cross.
> *- Colossians 2:13-15 -*

Even Moses had to go looking for "more" of God when the Lord called him up to Mount Sinai (see Ex. 19:1-3). No matter how long you have been walking with the Lord, or how much you already know about Him – there is always more. God is always looking for new ways to reveal His love and grace to us on more intimate levels.

After Aldo was discharged from hospital I considered it my duty to go and speak to my dad and tell him that his racism had caused much destruction in our lives. My dad was a farmer during the apartheid regime, and unfortunately his racist feelings were nurtured and justified by the traditions and propaganda of the South-African society of that era.

Thankfully the Holy Spirit cautioned me to wait and to pray about it first. I was still very emotional about the whole matter, and I knew that I might say things that I would later regret. God reminded me of the words He had spoken to me some weeks before when I wanted to take matters into my own hands regarding the woman who used to work for us: *"Retah, it is not your job. Who is the judge, you or I? Trust Me."*

The bloodline curse and ungodly soul ties had been broken, and now it was time for restoration and healing to begin. If I held on to any bitterness or resentment, I would be carving out a larger "hole in the wall", instead of repairing it. This is what the message of Nehemiah's wall is all about: Find out where the holes in your wall are through which the enemy can gain entry, and repair the holes with bricks of repentance, forgiveness and love. I had to lay down my pride and stop shifting the blame to someone else. I had to go and stand in the gap and repent of the sins of my fathers, even if I wasn't the one who created the hole in the wall in the first place.

On behalf of my earthly father I went to my heavenly Father's throne and started repenting and interceding for our family. I confessed, forgave and blessed; and as I was standing in the gap for him, a heavy anointing of the Holy Spirit came upon me. Truly, the anointing breaks the yoke (see Isa. 10:27). Finally all the anger I felt was gone, and then I prayed, "Abba, only You can remove a heart of stone and replace it with a heart of flesh. I release this matter into Your hands. Thank You that You forgive us when we ask."

Once again the Lord reminded me: *"Retah, by now you already know the miracle's name is LOVE."* God did not require of me to confront my dad and 'set him straight'; all He wanted from me was to continue loving my dad, blessing him, and praying for him. God would do the rest through His Holy Spirit. The curse on me and my descendants had already been broken, but I had to keep on praying that my dad would reach the place where he would bow his knees, confess his sins and lay down his pride. If he didn't do that, the "drain" of hatred through which the enemy had access would remain open.

During June of that year we had our first real holiday in three years. It was the winter school holidays and the boys' cousins, Simoné and Elisma, came with us to our beach house in Yzerfontein. By then Aldo had been out of hospital for two weeks. He was recuperating well and he and Tinus took a brisk two kilometre walk each morning, while Josh, the cousins and I went for a jog. Aldo didn't want to sit out for a single day – the old Aldo was back!

Tinus had to fly home during the week to complete some work and I stayed behind with the children. I took Tinus' place next to Aldo on his morning walk because his balance wasn't quite 100% yet. The first morning he insisted on walking up a steep hill instead of following the route that he and Tinus usually walked. "No Aldo," I told him sternly, "I cannot walk up the hill with you! The road is uneven and I am not as strong as Daddy." (Aldo is much taller than I am by now.) "You will have to be obedient and walk the usual road with me. I won't be able to support you up this steep hill."

After going a little further, he pulled his hand from mine and obstinately started walking up the hill on his own. He only walked a few steps before he lost his balance, stumbled off the uneven road, and fell into a bush. I was so angry at his stubbornness that I turned around to go home, thinking that he had to learn to face the consequences of his actions the hard way. But when I looked around and saw him lying there in the road with scuffed knees, my heart broke. While he was sitting in the road he started coughing and sneezing. My mommy-heart just couldn't leave him there. While I tried to help him up, I could hear him praying, "Father, please forgive me for my rebellion against my mother."

On the way home Aldo had a terrible sinusitis attack. I went to get him some tablets from the medicine cabinet when we got home, but as I sat down next to him on the couch he wrote me this letter: "Mom, they are firing at me. The rebellion gave them the right to attack me. That is why I confessed it straight away, so Jesus could forgive me." There and then I prayed for him and commanded the demons that were attacking him to go beneath Jesus' feet. Moments later he was better again.

I remember having read about demons causing sinusitis in the past. "Oh *come on*!" I had thought at the time. "They really are looking for a devil behind every bush!"

I sat by myself for a while and thought about all the criticism I had received from people because of my unusual road of faith. They judged me just like I had unfairly judged others, simply because I hadn't yet experienced the reality of the spiritual realm for myself.

Tinus and I were just talking the other day about how quickly we used to judge people who simply had wanted to share knowledge and wisdom with us about the spiritual realm and the dangers of the dimension of darkness. "Oh, they must be joking!" we used to scoff. "It can't be that bad! Some people really take it too far..." Today, Tinus and I ask the boys to repent and ask forgiveness immediately when they start acting naughty or rebellious – even if we are in restaurant and everyone around us is staring at us. Tinus jokingly said to the boys the other day while we were walking in a shopping mall, "Remind me never to pick a fight with Mom when we're in public – she doesn't care where we are or who is watching, I'll also have to say I'm sorry on the spot."

During our winter holiday in Yzerfontein the soccer World Cup was in full swing. The children enjoyed it immensely! During the day they played soccer on the lawn and at night they sat in front of the television and loudly rooted for their teams and favourite players.

Late one evening the children were watching soccer while I was reading in my room. When Aldo came into my room I knew the match wasn't over yet, because I could still hear the other kids cheering in the background. He fell down on the bed next to me and shouted "yippee, yippee, yippee!"

"Is your team winning, Aldo?" I asked absentmindedly as I continued to read in my Bible. "No, Mom. Hell's drain is closed! Grandpa confessed. Now the drain through which they have been fighting us is closed!"

I wasn't sure what he was talking about. Later that night I received a call from my mother with the good news that my father had been on his knees for most of the evening, repenting and confessing his sins to Jesus. He even repented of the hatred and racism that his generation grew up with.

nehemia   nehemia   net besef
Jesus se bloed   is   wat   my   so
ury nou maak.
Wysh sê   ury seen   ury
sy bloed het   my   urymaak.

Nehemiah, Nehemiah, realise that it is Jesus' blood that has now set me free. Wisdom says: Freedom, blessing, freedom! He blood has set me free.

When we got home after the holiday, Aldo went to school for the first time in months. He had been so sick over the past year that he could do very little schoolwork. Before the accident, Aldo's academic achievements were something I used to boast about, but Abba has set me free from the dreams that the old Retha had for him, and from measuring success according to human standards. All I now desire for his future is that he will live in the fullness of God's calling – wherever that may lead him.

The moment we start wishing we were somewhere else in life and begin to complain about our current situation, we miss out on what God has planned for us to experience in that particular season. We have to go through the Wilderness before we can enter into the Promised Land. God wants us to be thankful, and live our lives to the full, in the *present*. Even though Aldo's outward situation isn't perfect, he has in his spirit everything he needs for an abundant life – so how much more should this apply to me and you who don't have to overcome the physical challenges he faces every day!

Both Aldo and I had to repent of sometimes wishing that our situation was different. These emotions are human, but if we dwell on them they could lead to a downward spiral of depression. We can then so easily fall into a hole of self-pity and despondency which will keep us away from God's plan for the present. Rather, look up and realise the greatness of the God who is holding your life in His hands. He says that His plans are to give you hope and a future – hold on to your faith!

> "For I know the plans I have for you," declares the Lord, "plans to prosper you and not to harm you, plans to give you hope and a future."
> - *Jeremiah 29:11* -

My prayers for Aldo have shifted to a higher plain – a heavenly viewpoint. I no longer only pray for him to be healed physically... that is much too narrow-minded for what our Almighty God can accomplish through his life. I now pray for his positioning in God's kingdom. I pray that he will walk in the will of God every day and that he will fulfil the purpose that the Lord has destined for him – regardless of what circumstances may accompany this destiny. God saw the big picture when Joseph was in Pharaoh's prison. He knew that one day Joseph would rule the country, and that his prison time was only the first few chapters of his life story. Joseph just had to remain faithful during the difficult times. I believe that this is true for all of us.

God will provide us with everything we need to fulfil our calling and destiny. I often bless Aldo's spirit with the excellence of Christ (not perfectionism, but excellence, for his strength lies in Christ and not in himself). I bless him with the ability to see past the temporary things of this world, and to look at life through the eyes of Jesus so that he will live for eternity. His vision and his dreams will then be significantly larger than he would ever have been able to imagine on his own.

The accident didn't turn us into victims, but rather trained us to be overcomers. In spite of all our hurt we did not sit down and wallow in the shards of our broken lives, but we chose to stand up and walk in the victory that God held out to us. Only through faith could we gain victory by focusing on Him for whom nothing is impossible.

> You will keep in perfect peace those whose minds are steadfast, because they trust in you. Trust in the LORD forever, for the LORD, the LORD himself, is the Rock eternal.
> - *Isaiah 26:3-4* -

Today Aldo is free from demonic bondage, but from time to time we still see how an external attack is launched against him. That is when the demons try yet another tactic to bring him down, because you can be sure that the enemy doesn't like what Aldo is doing for the kingdom of God. The drains that the enemy uses to attack us from the outside are opened when people "fire" at us with their words (gossip), or speak words of death over our situation. Hatred, unforgiveness and ungodly soul ties are also drains, as I had explained earlier.

Believe me when I tell you that the enemy cannot remain standing where love is present! I have seen many deliverance sessions during my ministry, and in all of them it was through LOVE that the victory was attained. Even the worst demonic powers had to flee in the presence of love – because God is love (see 1 John 4:16).

The Word says that we shouldn't repay evil with evil, and this sets a fundamental principle for fighting the enemy: we need to come with the opposite spirit! When I walk into a room and I feel that there is demonic oppression, I immediately bind the works of darkness and declare that I am a light-bearer of the Kingdom of God. In the past I have sometimes ministered at churches upon invitation from a member of the congregation, and because the leaders weren't the ones who invited me (and didn't fully agree with my teaching), there was disunity. Because I didn't have the blessing of the authoritarian figures, it was usually very difficult to attain any breakthrough in the spirit while preaching at that particular congregation.

I often hear, "Retah, you give the enemy so much credit – he has no power over us anymore. He can't do anything to me. He has been defeated." You are so right – the enemy has been defeated by Jesus' sacrifice on the cross; BUT the Word clearly admonishes us to put on the whole armour of God so that we will be able to stand against the schemes of the devil (see Eph. 6:11). We still have a battle to fight – victory doesn't happen automatically. This principle is called appropriation. In other words, you receive the gift of armour, authority, and the power to break the curses, and you make the gift your own; you don't let it stand unopened at the foot of the cross. Through the death and resurrection of Jesus He specifically gave us these things: forgiveness of sins (salvation), healing through His wounds, redemption from the curse, and victory over Satan and his evil forces.

> "Who Himself bore our sins in His own body on the tree, that we, having died to sins, might live for righteousness—by whose stripes you were healed."
> - *1 Peter 2:24, NKJV* -
>
> "Christ has redeemed us from the curse of the law, having become a curse for us. For it is written:'Cursed is everyone who hangs on a tree.'"
> - *Galatians 3:13, NKJV* -
>
> "We know that whoever is born of God does not sin; but he who has been born of God keeps himself, and the wicked one does not touch him. We know that we are of God, and the whole world lies under the sway of the wicked one."
> - *1 John 5:18-19, NKJV* -

Jesus died for everyone on the cross, but not everyone accepts Him as their Saviour. Jesus took everyone's sickness upon Himself, but not everyone looks to His stripes for their healing. (How many Christians do you know who don't believe in modern day miracles of healing?) Jesus broke the curse for everyone, but due to a lack of knowledge many Christians still unknowingly suffer due to a curse on their lives.

Why then did Peter warn us against the roaring lion that seeks to devour us, if Satan wasn't a threat to us? (See 1 Peter 5:8). Or why are so many Christians still suffering from sickness and disease? And why can we still see the effects of bloodline curses among Christians, generation upon generation? If we were to suppose that the victory was automatically gained without any action on our part, why are we struggling so much with these issues?

Most of us are unaware that curses even exist, or we are uninformed about where they originate from and how they work. Secret societies like Freemasonry (or the South-African derivative thereof: the "Broederbond"), are the origin of many such curses, and unfortunately most of our bloodlines were involved in these practices in one way or another. The root of the curse that sprouts from these secret societies is woven throughout our history, our politics, and even the formation of our traditional churches. We need to repent of this wickedness and break the curse so that it won't cause more death and destruction to future generations.

My ministry hosted a seminar on the topic of inner healing and deliverance a few months ago, but this time I wasn't in the pulpit. I sat in the audience to listen and to learn with the rest of my family. The speakers were a couple who had been in the deliverance ministry for many years and have a lot of experience in the area. Of his own accord my dad also attended the seminar, and went for deliverance afterwards. It was wonderful for me to see how God healed and restored my father. Even though he was in his seventies and didn't have the knowledge to deal with these things until recently, I know that he is now completely free from the curse that had been upon him. Deliverance is a sensitive topic, and often after I give a teaching about it people would ask me afterwards, "If someone has a demon, will they go to heaven?" A demonic bondage doesn't disqualify you from going to heaven. (*"If you confess with your mouth, "Jesus is Lord," and believe in your heart that He was raised from the dead by God, you will be saved"* [Romans 10:9]). What it does mean though, is that you won't experience a life of abundance in Christ here on earth.

There have also been people who told me that the fact that Aldo can see so much of the spiritual realm is demonic in itself. I used to cry at Abba's feet about this, and asked the Lord to close Aldo's eyes to some degree so that he wouldn't see these things anymore. But God's reassuring answer was always, "This is how I sent him back from heaven. I have a purpose for it. I decide what each person sees or doesn't see, and I use Aldo to teach My Bride about the spiritual realm in order to prepare her for My return. I am God and nothing is impossible for Me."

After the bloodline curses were broken and all the drains were closed, God still allowed Aldo to see what He wanted him to see. He doesn't only see angels and demons, but Wisdom also delivers prophetic messages through his pen about events yet to take place all over the world. When God gives him these revelations, he writes down what Wisdom shows him. After a lot of fasting and prayer I have now accepted that I cannot change this, and that it is God's will. Even though I don't always understand it, God uses imperfect vessels to accomplish His sovereign plan.

If you think about it, it is actually natural for someone like Aldo who has a physical impairment, to be more sensitive to the spirit. Almost like a blind man who has to use his other senses to "see".

Time and again God has confirmed to me that Aldo's letters are authentic and that He uses his hand to reveal secrets to us through the divine inspiration of Wisdom. Through his conversations with Wisdom and the things that he then writes down, I have learned so much about the spiritual realm; things that I wouldn't have known otherwise. The reason why God sent Aldo back after his heavenly experience is to tell the world that Jesus is alive. Aldo saw this for himself. It might be a simple message delivered by a simple child, but this message (the gospel of Jesus Christ) holds the power to change the world.

Jesus' last command in Mark 16 was:

> He said to them, "Go into all the world and preach the good news to all creation. Whoever believes and is baptized will be saved, but whoever does not believe will be condemned. And these signs will accompany those who believe: In My name they will drive out demons; they will speak in new tongues; they will pick up snakes with their hands; and when they drink deadly poison, it will not hurt them at all; they will place their hands on sick people, and they will get well." After the Lord Jesus had spoken to them, He was taken up into heaven and He sat at the right hand of God.
> - Mark 16:15-19 -

For those of you who are sceptical about the existence of demons, the spiritual realm and spiritual warfare, I just want to ask this question: Why would Jesus have given us the command to cast out demons if it wasn't necessary?

And the next question to consider is: Why do the demons still succeed in blatantly stealing and destroying the lives of so many believers, if we have been given the authority over them?

To me there are three clear reasons why demons succeed in doing this: ignorance or denial of their existence, deliberate (or unconfessed) sin, and believers not taking up their authority in Christ.

A few weeks ago my family accompanied me when I had to minister at a Sunday morning church service in a nearby town. When we walked into the church, Aldo looked up and said loudly in his slow, monotonous voice, "Look how the demons are hanging from the lights, Mom." Tinus and I quickly tried our best to silence him, because we knew how the stout "religious" types would react to this statement. As if we weren't already conspicuous enough!

Wysh sê Jesus is verskriklik baie hartseer want sy kerk is vol pride, bid vir rou berou vra Jesus

Wisdom says Jesus' heart is hurting because His church is full of pride. Jesus says that we should pray for people to start repenting.

Just remember, there was a time when I was the one sitting in the pew, completely ignorant and very opinionated about these things that I couldn't see and didn't understand. Just because the Lord is using my son to teach me about the spiritual realm in such a practical way, doesn't mean that I don't still make mistakes. I don't think I am better than anyone else, and I am often on my knees before God asking for mercy to handle this gift with care. But unfortunately I have seen time and time again that there are no breakthroughs for institutions that refuse to admit or accept the reality of the spiritual realm.

As I travel extensively across my beautiful country of South-Africa, I have seen another source that hinders breakthrough: secret or obstinate sin (especially amongst the leadership). I once ministered in a small town where the pastor was openly involved in an extra-marital affair, and believe me, there was chaos in the church! By not dealing with the blatant sin, the leadership surrendered ground to the enemy and the congregation suffered dearly because of it. James also warned us: *Not many of you should presume to be teachers, my brothers, because you know that we who teach will be judged more strictly* (Jas. 3:1).

Once we have dealt with the hindrances of ignorance and sin, there remains one more thing for us to do in order to walk in victory: We have to take up the authority Christ has given us; and it starts with knowing *who we are in Christ*, but more importantly *who He is in us*.

Along with the authority comes a great responsibility. In the story of the seven sons of Sceva we can see the dangers of going about with this authority without the character and integrity to back it up:

Some Jews who went around driving out evil spirits tried to invoke the name of the Lord Jesus over those who were demon-possessed. They would say, "In the name of Jesus, whom Paul preaches, I command you to come out." Seven sons of Sceva, a Jewish chief priest, were doing this. One day the evil spirit answered them, "Jesus I know, and I know about Paul, but who are you?" Then the man who had the evil spirit jumped on them and overpowered them all. He gave them such a beating that they ran out of the house naked and bleeding.

You will be ineffective (and get yourself into trouble!) if you try to do these things without a heart that is sold out to Jesus. Your motive and your character are the determining factors for success.

In my mind's eye I can see a picture of a cannon and big cannon balls. This represents our gifts (the cannon balls) and our character (the cannon). Maybe your gifts are so big and powerful that it can wipe out an entire hostile army, but if your character isn't strong enough to shoot the cannon balls, those gifts will be completely worthless. Your character is determined by your love relationship with Jesus; because if you love Him, you will obey Him.

My intention with this book is not to focus on Satan and his works, but rather to expose him so he can no longer continue to steal, kill and destroy. Better yet, my desire for this book is to put the awesome power of Jesus, the One who has already defeated the enemy, on display, so we can live in the victory and freedom that He alone can give us.

[handwritten annotation in Afrikaans:]

julle bruid hoor, haat beveg vuur van God. Sien hoe baie mense so seer het sien hulle maar van hulle van harte is vuur hel se vuur. Wil jy sien hier seen jy my en tot voel hulle baie hewige nehemia harde slag. So beveg jy vyand. Sien gister aand hoe hewige geveg in gees is want wanneer bruid begin repent vuur hulle want dit bring deurbraak. bruid sê ek hoef nie repent nie, se muur is steeds so vuur oë

Bride, will you listen? Hatred fights against the fire of God! I see how many people are hurting. I see them, but I also see that in some of their hearts there is hell's fire. Nehemiah, do you know that when you blessed me they [the enemy] received a heavy blow. This is how you fight the enemy. Last night I saw how there was a heavy battle raging in the spirit. When the Bride starts to repent they send their fire, because repentance brings breakthrough. The Bride justifies herself and says that she doesn't have to repent, but I tell you [if she doesn't], enemy fire will then be sent to break down the wall.

Dear friend, Jesus wants us all to be free! When Jesus started His earthly ministry, He made His purpose known with these words:

> The Spirit of the LORD is upon Me, because He has anointed Me to preach the gospel to the poor; He has sent Me to heal the broken-hearted, to proclaim liberty to the captives and recovery of sight to the blind, to set at liberty those who are oppressed; to proclaim the acceptable year of the LORD.
> *- Luke 4:18-19, NKJV -*

Let us stop right here, receive His words by faith, and pray together:

Abba Father, we know that the victory doesn't come through might or power, but through Your Holy Spirit (Zech. 4:6). Through Your anointing every yoke will be broken. The blood of the Lamb and the Word of our testimony make us conquerors for Your Kingdom. Jesus, You came to destroy the works of Satan. We give You permission to destroy it in our lives, Lord. Thank You that we can live in victory, today – every day – and for eternity.

Today we choose to take our eyes off people and to focus on You alone, because our lives are a journey of faith we walk with You. We will not look at our shortcomings and become discouraged, but we will look to the cross and know who we are in Christ.

Father, give us the grace and enlighten our minds to understand that we are involved in a spiritual battle. Equip us if we are not wearing the full armour and teach us how to use this Sword in our hands.

Thank You that we don't have to be afraid of evil, but that we will be accompanied by these signs as we step out in faith: In Your name we will drive out demons; we will speak in new tongues; we will pick up snakes with our hands; and when we drink deadly poison, it will not hurt us at all; we will place our hands on sick people, and they will get well (Mark 16:17-18).

Father, Son and Holy Spirit, You are the One who makes the impossible in our lives possible. When we wanted to give up, You called us and said: "Come to me, all you who are weary and burdened, and I will give you rest. In Me you will find rest. In my eyes you will find strength for tomorrow." Lord Jesus, we don't want to waste another minute - today we come to You, our King, and we seek our rest in You.

Anoint us with Your Holy Spirit and equip us with Your power so we can be Your hands and feet, and go about doing good works and bringing Your healing and freedom to those who are caught in the snare of the enemy.

In the name above all names - the name of the King of all kings, our Rabbi, our Messiah and our Lord - Jesus Christ. Amen.

Chapter 11

Wysh is so Lief vir jou
hy is lief vir ons. baie
baie nehemia se muur is gebou
hy sê bevryhet hy vir my hy
sê muur sal hy nou beskerm
hy is nou bevegter van muur.
Wysh sê boek is wat jy nou
moet doen. hy sê hewige
wysheid sal hy vir ewige
my wat jou sal help. erge
muur het ons gebou, vuur
hy het bevuur gesien hoe het
vuur verjaag geword. Hy
sê hulle wat jou gesein het
hy het hulle hel toe gestuur
Wysh sê hy is nou waar
hy vuur vuur op hulle het.
Sal jy vir my sê asb seen
vandag hy sê my werk
verseën hy. saam sal
hy ons seën.

Wisdom loves you so much. He loves us. Big parts of Nehemiah's wall have now been rebuilt. He says He has set me free. He says He will protect my wall from now on. He is now the guardian of my wall. Wisdom says that the book [Message of Hope] is what you must do now. He says He will give a lot of Wisdom to everybody who helps you. We have built a strong wall now. He sent fire against the fire of the enemy. I saw how He chased away the fire [of the enemy]. He says He sent those who have signaled you to hell. Wisdom says He is now there where He has fire on them. Will you please bless me today? He says He will bless my work. Together He will bless us.

Let us build the wall

If you are like me, many of the things which I've shared in this book may have come as a shock to you. I know all too well that most South Africans come from a very traditional and religious background, and that they probably haven't heard such direct teaching about the spiritual realm before. The things I've touched on are not popular topics, and most people are cautious of things that don't fall within the parameters of their comfort zone – especially regarding spiritual matters. That is why I ask you to take everything you don't understand to God. Don't take my word for it, but go and look for your answers in *His* Word – the Holy Bible. God Himself will answer your questions and reveal the truth to you through His Word and His Holy Spirit.

Julle seen my mom want ek
wat Leer sien by julle van
wat vyand verslaan beteken
Vaar uit op see en sê
verslaan verslaan verslaan
is jy vyand. Julle sê see
want ek sien hoe groot is
vyand se mense maar God
sê verslaan seine met erekoning
vuur en seen !

You bless me Mom, because I learn from you what it means to overcome the enemy. Sail on the sea and say: "Defeated, Defeated, Defeated" to the enemy! I see how large the enemy's forces are, but God says we will overcome their signals with our glorious King, and His fire and blessing!

One of my favourite Scriptures from the book of Nehemiah says: *"Those who carried materials did their work with one hand and held a weapon in the other, and each of the builders wore his sword at his side as he worked"* (Neh. 4:17-18). My aim with this book is to supply you as the reader with weapons of knowledge and understanding, enabling you to protect yourself from the enemy; and also to provide you with the correct building materials so that you can rebuild the broken walls around your city.

> Therefore I stationed some of the people behind the lowest points of the wall at the exposed places, posting them by families, with their swords, spears and bows. After I looked things over, I stood up and said to the nobles, the officials and the rest of the people, "Don't be afraid of them. Remember the Lord, who is great and awesome, and fight for your brothers, your sons and your daughters, your wives and your homes."
>
> When our enemies heard that we were aware of their plot and that God had frustrated it, we all returned to the wall, each to his own work.
>
> From that day on, half of my men did the work, while the other half were equipped with spears, shields, bows and armour. The officers posted themselves behind all the people of Judah who were building the wall. Those who carried materials did their work with one hand and held a weapon in the other, and each of the builders wore his sword at his side as he worked. But the man who sounded the trumpet stayed with me.
> *- Nehemiah 4:13-18 -*

Building a wall is a practical task. So is fighting the enemy. For both, you require equipment, skill and strategy. I believe that God will use everything my family and I had to endure to help others. With God nothing is wasted, not even our heartache and our tears.

Jesus het nou het vir my gesê ek verstaan die soort geveg baie goed so ek sal baie mense kan leer van dit.

Jesus just told me that, because I understand the type of battle we are fighting so well, I will be able to teach many people about it.

Psalm 144:1 says: *Praise be to the Lord my Rock, who trains my hands for war, my fingers for battle.* The Bible makes mention of warfare on numerous occasions, and therefore it shouldn't be a strange concept to us; but unfortunately many of us have never been trained how to engage in this spiritual battle.

To summarise, I have written down a few practical steps I believe everyone who is seeking complete freedom should know. Please note that these are only keys to help you – they are not laws. They do not determine your salvation, but I believe they will definitely have a great effect on your day-to-day life. We are saved by the grace of God through our faith, but if we are still bound by demonic powers, our life on earth is not going to be one of abundance.

My exposition doesn't cover everything (and there is still a great deal I have to learn myself), but it is a good place to start, and a place from which to grow.

The first step is to determine the root of the problem.

We can't go around blaming demons for all our problems, and thereby excusing ourselves from taking any responsibility for the predicaments we find ourselves in. The wages of sin is death (see Rom. 6:23). Maybe not death in a natural sense, but death in our situations – just as an affair can lead to death in a marriage. The Word clearly states that we have to crucify our sinful nature daily by living in the Spirit.

So I say, live by the Spirit, and you will not gratify the desires of the sinful nature. For the sinful nature desires what is contrary to the Spirit, and the Spirit what is contrary to the sinful nature. They are in conflict with each other, so that you do not do what you want. But if you are led by the Spirit, you are not under law.

The acts of the sinful nature are obvious: sexual immorality, impurity and debauchery; idolatry and witchcraft; hatred, discord, jealousy, fits of rage, selfish ambition, dissensions, factions and envy; drunkenness, orgies, and the like. I warn you, as I did before, that those who live like this will not inherit the kingdom of God.

But the fruit of the Spirit is love, joy, peace, patience, kindness, goodness, faithfulness, gentleness and self-control. Against such things there is no law.
- *Galatians 5:16-23* -

Therefore you have to ask God whether that which you are struggling with is something you must allow God to crucify (death to self and alive to Christ through repentance and laying down your life), or whether it is of a demonic nature.

Then, there is the question that I had been struggling with for such a long time: "Can a Christian have a demon?" The short answer is *yes*, BUT the demon cannot *possess* or *exercise ownership* over the person, because demons cannot control a believer's *spirit*. The demons can only target the dark, wounded or dry areas of the soul and build strongholds there. This oppression can manifest in the flesh as a physical sickness or in the soul (mind, will and emotions) as emotional or physiological disorders.

The war that is raging in the heavens is not a power clash between God and Satan. God is the Creator and Satan is a created being. Satan knows he will never be able to win the battle. It is like a fly challenging the sun to a duel – Satan knows he doesn't stand a chance. The battle is for the *hearts of men,* because God created us with a free will. With our will we *choose* life or death, light or darkness, God or Satan.

Remember, if you have received Jesus Christ as your Lord and Saviour and are reborn into the Kingdom of God, the Holy Spirit places His seal of ownership on you. The Holy Spirit then lives in your spirit and that is why your *spirit* cannot then be possessed by demons. Light and darkness cannot live together – the light will always expel and drive out the darkness. However, there is a difference between a demonic bondage (oppression) and demon possession. The naked man from Gadarenes who lived among the tombstones is an example of someone who was demon possessed (see Matt. 8:28-34). Before he met Jesus, he did not have any control over himself anymore; the demons took control over his *spirit, soul* and *body.*

The one thing that needs to be clearly stated about *demonic bondage* is that it's just that – it keeps you *bound.* Just as chains shackle a prisoner, demonic bondage keeps us prisoner in the realm of the flesh (through sickness or disease) and in the realm of our soul (mental or emotional disorders).

Warrior is wat ek wil hê jy
moet wees Aldo. jy is nou
hulle wagte hou jou vas.
Here Jesus is verseker jou
warrior hy sal vir jou veg.
hy is jou warrior gebruik jou
wapenrusting Aldo by my
is vrede Aldo bly in my.
Wagte wat jou brein vashou
sal verslaan word wanneer
jy opstaan Aldo jy help soveel
mense. staan op Aldo.

I want you to be a warrior Aldo. You are one now. Their guards held you captive. The Lord Jesus is definitely your warrior – He will fight for you. He is your warrior. Use your armor, Aldo. With Me you will find peace, Aldo. Stay in Me. The guards that are keeping your mind captive will be defeated when you stand up. You help so many people, Aldo. Stand up, Aldo.

There are many stories in the Bible that testify to demons causing physical infirmities. As soon as the demon was cast out by Jesus, the person was healed. Not one of these people who went to Jesus for healing *wanted*, or *chose*, to be sick. Sickness is one way in which the demonic bondage can manifest, but a lot of their works go unnoticed in the physical realm (like emotional illnesses, reoccurring accidents and loss, delayed breakthroughs etc.), and often we do not even realise that there is a "devil behind the bush".

I know that many of you can relate to what I am saying based on experiences from your own lives. Maybe you are currently in a prison of depression, or addiction, or disease, and you know what it feels like to be held captive against your will. While we were in the grip of that demonic bondage I remember thinking to myself, *"I want to be free, but I just don't know how!"* I felt trapped and helpless.

But Jesus is thrusting His hand through the bars of your prison cell (by the sacrifice He made for you on the cross), holding a key in His outstretched hand. The choice to take this key, unlock the prison door, and step out is up to you. When you choose life and decide to accept the gift of Jesus' sacrifice, you will triumph over the works of Satan. Inner healing is a process, but it begins with a choice. I have walked this difficult road with Aldo, and that is why I can now declare: THERE IS HOPE!

Arise, shine, for your light has come, and the glory of the Lord rises upon you. See, darkness covers the earth and thick darkness is over the peoples, but the Lord rises upon you and his glory appears over you.
- Isaiah 60:1-2 -

John 10:10 says: *The thief comes only to steal and kill and destroy; I have come that they may have life, and have it to the full.* The nature of the enemy is to steal, kill and destroy, and that is how you will recognise his works. Jesus came to destroy the works of the enemy, and He has also given us the authority to cast out demons and to heal the sick. In fact, in the gospel of Matthew, Jesus gave His disciples the following instructions:

Heal the sick, cleanse the lepers, raise the dead, cast out demons. Freely you have received, freely give.
- Matthew 10:8, NKJV -

Jesus gave us a clear mandate to drive out demons, because yes – they really do exist! Demonic powers feed upon the "legal rights" which we give them – whether we do it knowingly or unknowingly. God is a God of order, and all of creation has to move within the parameters that He has set (see Ps. 104). Even demonic powers are subjected to His protocol. This simply means that they are not allowed to attack us left, right and centre, just as they please – there will be a reason why they attempt to steal, kill and destroy. These "legal rights" (which include a variety of things, for example: the fruit of sin, bloodline curses, ungodly covenants, soul ties, written or spoken curses, oaths, inner vows etc.) grant the demons access to attack us. In Zechariah this protocol is explained in terms of a court set-up with the Angel of the Lord (Jesus Christ) who intercedes for us, and Satan who accuses us: *Then he showed me Joshua the high priest standing before the angel of the Lord, and Satan standing at his right side to accuse him. The Lord said to Satan, "The Lord rebuke you, Satan! The Lord, who has chosen Jerusalem, rebuke you! Is not this man a burning stick snatched from the fire?"*

Now Joshua was dressed in filthy clothes as he stood before the Angel. The Angel said to those who were standing before him, "Take off his filthy clothes." Then He said to Joshua, "See, I have taken away your sin, and I will put rich garments on you" (Zech 3:1-4).

In Daniel there is another reference to this "heavenly" court and divine judgement: *As I watched, this horn was waging war against the saints and defeating them, until the Ancient of Days came and pronounced judgment in favour of the saints of the Most High, and the time came when they possessed the kingdom* (Dan. 7:21-22).

*verslaan wat Wysh sê sy is
het in judgement wat gebeur
Want ek het room
self so geskrik*

Wisdom says she is defeated. What happened in the judgment room?

It startled me too.

It is clearly stated in the New Testament what the outcome of Satan's accusations against us, who are in Jesus Christ, is: *For those God foreknew He also predestined to be conformed to the likeness of His Son, that He might be the firstborn among many brothers. And those He predestined, He also called; those He called, He also justified; those He justified, He also glorified.*

What, then, shall we say in response to this? If God is for us, who can be against us? He who did not spare His own Son, but gave Him up for us all – how will He not also, along with Him, graciously give us all things? Who will bring any charge against those whom God has chosen? It is God who justifies. Who is he that condemns? Christ Jesus, who died – more than that, who was raised to life – is at the right hand of God and is also interceding for us (Romans 8:29-34).

The blood of the Lamb and the righteous judgement of the Ancient of Days nullify the condemnation and the blame of Satan's accusation – because through the death and resurrection of Jesus Christ we received forgiveness and redemption. I hope you realise how great and powerful these words are! But there is something that always precedes forgiveness and redemption … and that is our choice to bow our knees before Christ, and allow Him to be LORD and SAVIOUR of our lives.

I have touched on a number of subjects in this book, and in order to bring it all together I would now like to summarise a few of them, so you can use them as keys to unlock the chains that Satan uses to keep us bound:

Repentance

> If we confess our sins, he is faithful and just and will forgive us our sins and purify us from all unrighteousness
> - 1 John 1:9 -

From this Scripture we see that confession is a prerequisite for forgiveness. As the saying goes: "There is no smoke without a fire." If there is demonic activity in your life, you have to follow the smoke trail to find the reason for the demonic presence. As I explained before, the demons use any "legal bills" they can find against us. Only through the confession of our sins, and by the forgiveness we receive through the blood of the Lamb, will these legal bills be nullified.

Your belief system

> Do not conform any longer to the pattern of this world, but be transformed by the renewing of your mind. Then you will be able to test and approve what God's will is – his good, pleasing and perfect will.
> - Romans 12:2 -

The Word of God tells us that without faith it is impossible to please God (see Heb. 11:6). God, who is Spirit (see John 4:24), acts according to our faith, and this should give us a better understanding of how other spiritual beings (demons are unclean spirits) operate: according to our *faith*.

Proverbs 23:7 says: *As a man thinks in his heart, so is he.* What you believe in your heart determines how you experience and perceive life around you. A false belief system (the lie that you accept as your truth) becomes a playing field in your life for demons to operate.

For example, the Word says: *God is good.* But after you have endured a few storms in your life, the enemy starts whispering: *"God may be good for others, but not for you. He has forgotten about you and you are unimportant to Him."* As your view of God becomes distorted, this thought becomes the foundation through which a false belief system is formed in your mind. By harbouring these thoughts you are actually providing the demons with material to build a stronghold in your mind. This is how, for example, a demon of fear can enter your life. Once the stronghold is built, and the demon of fear has taken up residency in the stronghold, you will increasingly find yourself struggling to trust God. Your actions will then become fear based, and not faith based.

We need to measure our thoughts and beliefs against the Word of God, and rebuild our belief system according to God's truth – that is what it means to be "transformed by the renewing your mind."

> The weapons we fight with are not the weapons of the world. On the contrary, they have divine power to demolish strongholds. We demolish arguments and every pretension that sets itself up against the knowledge of God, and we take captive every thought to make it obedient to Christ.
> *- 2 Corinthians 10:4-5 -*

Soulties

> Now when he had finished speaking to Saul, the soul of Jonathan was knit to the soul of David, and Jonathan loved him as his own soul.
> *- 1 Samuel 18:1, NKJV -*

God created us as social beings with a need for community and interaction. He created us with a desire for friendship, love, romance and family. In isolation we will wilt like a flower without water. As we share our hearts and lives with one another, the relationships we form lead to soul ties. A soul tie is an invisible bond in the soul realm between two people. The more intimate the relationship, the stronger the soul tie.

A soul tie as such is not the problem, but we need to be aware of *ungodly* soul ties, because the devil can also use these soul ties to his advantage. In any relationship where Jesus isn't Lord an ungodly soul tie can be formed. The more intense the relationship becomes, the heavier the yoke and the stronger the pull of the soul tie. The Word warns us: *Do not be misled: "Bad company corrupts good character"* (1 Cor. 15:33).

> Do you not know that he who unites himself with a prostitute is one with her in body? For it is said, "The two will become one flesh."
> *- 1 Corinthians. 6:16 -*

When two people sleep together a soul tie is formed, and that is why extra-marital sex and sex before marriage holds such devastating consequences. This soul tie can then severely influence the person who is under its emotional yoke, and prevent him or her from distancing themselves from the other person's emotional state.

These ungodly soul ties have to be broken. Once again confession is the first step. It might also be required of you to take practical steps in order to end those relationships. Naturally it will be of no avail if you confess and break a soul tie, and then simply continue to sleep with the person you are not married to.

Every relationship is unique. The most important thing however is to bring your relationships to the light and to make Jesus the King of your relationships and friendships.

Ancestral sin and bloodline curses

> For I, the Lord your God, am a jealous God, punishing the children for the sin of the fathers to the third and fourth generation of those who hate me, but showing love to a thousand generations of those who love me and keep my commandments.
> *- Exodus 20:5b-6 -*

If bloodline curses aren't broken, the sins of our ancestors are handed over from generation to generation like the baton in a relay race. In the same manner by which you could inherit your Grandma's blue eyes, she also could have passed along the unique imprint of her "spiritual DNA". These bloodline curses which are transferred through our spiritual DNA are called iniquities. One way in which these iniquities manifest is through hereditary diseases or addictions. These curses need to be broken to prevent the demons that have latched on to your bloodline through the sin of previous generations, to gain access to your life and that of your descendants. See what King David had to say about iniquity in one of his Psalms:

> Have mercy on me, O God, according to your unfailing love; according to your great compassion blot out my transgressions. Wash away all my iniquity and cleanse me from my sin. For I know my transgressions, and my sin is always before me. Against you, you only, have I sinned and done what is evil in your sight, so that you are proved right when you speak and justified when you judge. Surely I was sinful at birth, sinful from the time my mother conceived me
> - *Psalm 51:1-5* -

Time and again God confirmed to me through Aldo's letters that we had to rebuild the broken-down wall of Nehemiah around our family. It was a call to repent and to return to God, but also to cleanse our land from the iniquity that came from the generations before us, and to restore and rebuild the ruins.

> Then those of Israelite lineage separated themselves from all foreigners; and they stood and confessed their sins and the iniquities of their fathers. And they stood up in their place and read from the Book of the Law of the LORD their God for one-fourth of the day; and for another fourth they confessed and worshiped the LORD their God
> - *Nehemiah 9:2-3, NKJV* -

Confession is the first step in annulling these curses, and thereafter the curses have to be broken, cut off, and replaced by the blessings of God. The Lord promises us in Proverbs 26:2 that: *Like a fluttering sparrow or a darting swallow, an undeserved curse does not come to rest.*

sal nie my weer kan seermaak nie want hy sê hulle hy sê vloek is gebreek. het nie geweet van vloek nie.

He says they won't be able to hurt me again because He says the curse has been broken. I didn't know about the curse.

(For more information about generational curses, please read the following Scriptures: Exodus 20:5, Deut. 28:58-59, Exodus 34:6-7, Psalm 32:2-5, Numbers 14:18, Jeremiah 32:18, Lamentations 5:7, Leviticus 26:39-42, Ezekiel 20:30.)

Curses

The word "curses" is self-explanatory. The origin can be of an occult nature, for instance witches and warlocks who pronounce curses. Believe me, it is a lot more common than you may think, especially in the African tribal culture.

When you take a look at the content of the current movies, or listen to the lyrics of the latest popular music, I am sure you will agree with me that the occult is thriving. Witches, warlocks, magic spells and potions are everywhere.

lewe en wysh, hy sê seën curse bring dood.

Wisdom says that blessing brings life, and cursing brings death.

Curses also include bloodline curses; and of course word curses originating from gossip and slander. Gossiping has become a part of our social culture. These careless words bind the person who speaks them, as well as the person who is spoken of. When these words are released into the atmosphere, demons can latch onto them. As Aldo puts it, "They fire us with words." Scary, isn't it? These words are burning with fire sent from hell, because the power of life and death lies in the tongue (see Prov. 18:21). Guard your mouth, because gossip (which is regarded to be fairly harmless by most people), is just another form of witchcraft and spiritual assault.

> Hear my voice, O God, in my meditation;
> Preserve my life from fear of the enemy.
> Hide me from the secret plots of the wicked,
> From the rebellion of the workers of iniquity,
> Who sharpen their tongue like a sword,
> And bend their bows to shoot their arrows—bitter words,
> That they may shoot in secret at the blameless;
> Suddenly they shoot at him and do not fear.
> - Psalm 64:1-4, NKJV -

Blessings

There are two sides to everything, and just as curses have the power to destroy, blessings have the power to heal, protect and build-up. I bless my husband and my children often, no matter where I am in the world. I bless their spirits to be receptive and sensitive to the Holy Spirit. I bless their coming in and their going out. I bless their minds to remain focused on Christ and their hearts to hunger after the Word of God.

The Word also says that we have to bless our enemies (see Matt. 5:44). Time and time again Aldo wrote that the person who had been fighting against us with curses and witchcraft couldn't stand where God's blessings were. As I continued to bless her, God took the weapons of witchcraft from her hands, and eventually her curses no longer had an effect on us, because the blessings we spoke over her counteracted them.

In order to do this, you have to be willing to die to yourself. Our human nature would seek revenge rather than retaliate a curse with a blessing. But God's Kingdom doesn't work like that. He also seeks justice and righteousness, but according to His ways and in His time. He asks of us to surrender every battle to Him. We can do it by being obedient to His Word, and His Word tells us to bless those who curse us, and to trust Him to do what is right.

Our Covenant with God

> Then He took the cup, and gave thanks, and gave it to them, saying, "Drink from it, all of you. For this is My blood of the new covenant, which is shed for many for the remission of sins."
> - Matthew 26:27-28, NKJV -

A covenant is much more than just a mere promise – it is an unbreakable contract, written in the books of heaven, where it will remain binding for all eternity. When Jesus refers to the New Covenant sealed with His blood, He is in fact referring to His marriage contract with His bride. It is a promise, an oath, an eternal contract that *He* will never break.

God will never annul His covenant with us, but can we say the same about our choices? The Apostle Paul warns us: *"You cannot drink the cup of the Lord and the cup of demons; you cannot partake of the Lord's table and of the table of demons. Or do we provoke the Lord to jealousy? Are we stronger than He?"* (1 Cor. 10:21-22). When read in context, this scripture does not directly refer to the New Covenant, but I want to illustrate through it that there is more than one cup to drink from.

The best example of a covenant is that of the promise made between a bride and groom on their wedding day. Jesus Christ is our heavenly Bridegroom, and He is seeking a pure Bride, who is willing to forsake all other idols for the sake of being set-apart for Him. She will not be drinking from any other cup, except the cup of Christ. This is also the difference between being hot, cold, or lukewarm; which Jesus warned the Church of Laodicea of, as recorded in the book of Revelation:

> "And to the angel of the church of the Laodiceans write, 'These things says the Amen, the Faithful and True Witness, the Beginning of the creation of God:

> "I know your works, that you are neither cold nor hot. I could wish you were cold or hot. So then, because you are lukewarm, and neither cold nor hot, I will vomit you out of My mouth."
> - *Revelation 3:14-16, NKJV* -

Our lives are endangered when we move beyond the perimeters of safety that God's covenant provides, because the wages of sin is death (Rom. 6:23). Just as unfaithfulness in marriage has the potential to end in divorce and annul the covenant that was made on your wedding day, so our unfaithfulness to God will bring about spiritual death in our lives. (Divorce is the only thing that can legally break a marriage covenant. That is why we also have to divorce ourselves in the spirit from any other covenant we have entered into that was not made by, or through, the Living God.)

When we make a covenant with the kingdom of darkness our covenant with God is compromised, and it keeps us from dwelling in the Holy of Holies, and from deep intimacy with God. Then we will only be able to hear His voice vaguely from the outer court. There might also be unholy covenants still in place that were entered into by our forefathers. These covenants give the forces of darkness a legal right to interfere in our lives, and we have to divorce ourselves from these covenants too.

> If we claim to have fellowship with him and yet walk in the darkness, we lie and do not live out the truth. But if we walk in the light, as he is in the light, we have fellowship with one another, and the blood of Jesus, his Son, purifies us from all sin.
> - *1 John 1:6-7* -

This doesn't mean that our sin can break our covenant with God, or disqualify us from salvation; but when we "drink from the wrong cup" we start to wander around in the darkness, unable to benefit from the protection that God's covenant provides. The parable Jesus told of the prodigal son in Luke 15:11-32 is a good example of this. The younger son asked his father for his inheritance and wasted it all with prodigal living. Eventually he was alone, penniless and starving. Due to his own unwise choices, he had moved out of the safety of his father's protection and providence. However, this didn't mean that he wasn't his father's son any longer. He had walked away from the safety and security of his father's house (and suffered the consequences), but when he repented and was ready to return, his father was waiting for him with open arms.

People are fallible, people make mistakes and people break promises, but God is faithful even when we are not. The steadfastness of our covenant is therefore not because of our own doing, but because of God's faithfulness and the grace He gives us to remain faithful to Him. Furthermore, He has promised us that He will be ever mindful of His covenant (Ps. 111:5).

> He replied, "I saw Satan fall like lightning from heaven. I have given you authority to trample on snakes and scorpions and to overcome all the power of the enemy; nothing will harm you. However, do not rejoice that the spirits submit to you, but rejoice that your names are written in heaven."
> - Luke 10:18-20 -

I believe with all of my heart that it is the Father's will that His children should be free from Satan's bondage – that is why He sent His Son Jesus Christ: to destroy the works of the enemy! If you have recognised the fingerprint of Satan on your life by the things described in this chapter and you want to be set free from it, I would like to pray with you. There is enormous power in prayer. The Word promises that where two or more on earth are gathered in His name and agree about anything we ask for, it will be done by our Father in heaven (see Matt. 18:19) – I firmly believe this!

Aldo reading his bible.

This prayer is a general prayer. In my experience on how to break the power of the enemy, I have found that general prayers are a starting point and it does accomplish a lot, but that there still remains a need for specific and detailed prayer for certain "weak" areas. Psalm 45:5 says that sharp arrows pierce the hearts of the King's enemies. I believe that this applies to our prayers too. We must try to hit the mark with our prayers, like an archer aiming at a bull's-eye.

Don't worry if you do not know exactly how to pray for these weak areas. The Holy Spirit guided me every step of the way, and I didn't know much in the beginning either. He will do the same for you. God will send people, books and teachings on your path – just be willing to receive them with an open heart.

The Holy Spirit lives inside of you and He is the Spirit of Truth who will take your hand and walk with you on this road to healing and deliverance. Trust Him to do it, and trust Him for the healing process. Some wounds heal faster than others, so don't become anxious when you don't see immediate results. Give God time to heal your heart completely. Be patient and wait on Him, for He is faithful and just.

Let us pray together:

Abba Father, not only are You our Abba Father, but You are also the Lord of hosts. Lord, we acknowledge that You reign over all. You are clothed with majesty and You are girded with strength. Your throne is established from of old, and You are from everlasting (see Ps. 93:1-2).

Father, today we choose to bow our knees before You. We choose to bring our hearts before Your throne with outstretched hands so You can reign over us and be our Saviour and Lord.

Lord, thank You that you have wiped out the handwriting of requirements that was against us by nailing it to the cross and that You have disarmed principalities and powers and made a public spectacle of them, triumphing over them through the sacrifice of Your Son Jesus Christ on the cross (see Col.2:13-15). We receive the forgiveness and acquittal from Satan's accusations that You have provided through the sacrificial death and resurrection of your Son, Jesus Christ. Thank You Abba, that You will not turn us away when we come to You through Your Son.

That is why I (insert your name) now come in the Name of Jesus Christ and I resist the works of the enemy. I declare to the demons who want to steal, kill and destroy in my life: The Lord rebuke you (see Jude 9).

Lord, I repent and ask forgiveness for my iniquities and the iniquities of my ancestors. Father, where any iniquities and bloodline curses have been carried over to me as a result of ancestral sin, I now stand in the gap for it and I ask forgiveness for the sins of my ancestors that have led to these iniquities and curses. In the name of Jesus Christ I renounce every evil inheritance I have received from my forefathers through the bloodline. Father, I ask that You will now cut these bloodline curses from my mother and my father's side and that you will blot them out.

Have mercy on me, O God, according to Your unfailing love; according to

Your great compassion blot out my transgressions. Wash away all my iniquity and cleanse me from my sin (see Ps. 51:1-2).

Lord, I also ask of You to uproot the seed of iniquity so it will no longer bear fruit in my life, or in the lives of my descendents in the generations to come.

Father, I honour You as the Creator God who gives life. I choose life and I break every covenant with death in the name of Jesus Christ. I choose to speak words of life and to no longer agree with the lies of Satan. I ask forgiveness for where I have placed myself and others in bondage through gossip or slander. I choose to bless and not to curse. Lord, your Word says that out of the abundance of the heart the mouth speaks, and that is why I ask You now, Holy Spirit, to please fill my heart with Your love so my words will be a blessing to You and to others.

Holy Spirit, lead me in all wisdom and show me which specific incidents I should bring before Your throne in prayer so that I can rebuild the wall of Nehemiah around my life.

And finally Lord, I choose to submit myself to You and to resist the devil – because then he will flee from me as Your Word promises (see Jas. 4:7).

Thank You, Lord, that I can walk in victory over Satan and his demonic powers – solely because of what You have provided for us through the blood of the Lamb. With this I testify that I am more than a conqueror through Jesus Christ who strengthens me! I choose to lay down my life, to take up my cross, and to follow Jesus of Nazareth – my Messiah.

In the Name above all names, Jesus Christ – my King, my Lord, and my Saviour.

Amen and Amen.

I want to leave you with this Scripture. Let it have the final say over every battle you fight and every situation you face:

They overcame him by the blood of the Lamb and by the word of their testimony; they did not love their lives so much as to shrink from death.
- Revelation 12:11 -

Die Here
help my deur my donkerste
krisis. Sy hulp is soos 'n
lig wat 'n mens in 'n
pikswart donker kamer
aansit. Hy red my omdat
Hy my help altyd, is daar
niks waarvoor ek bang is
nie. Die Here beskerm my
Waarvoor sal ek dan bang
wees?
dieres onder Jesus se
voete in! Amen Jesus.
Liefde Aldo.

The Lord helps me through my darkest crisis. His help is like a light that is
put on in a pitch black room. He saves me because He always helps me, and
therefore there is nothing that I am afraid of. The Lord protects me; what
is there to fear? As for the rest – go beneath the feet of Jesus! Amen Jesus.
Love Aldo.

Chapter 12

Jesus sê vrees nie wanneer jy sien die vyeboom bot nie. Hy is verseker oppad die aarde en alles daarop is syne. kan hy nie vir jou sorg nie mr? Jy kan nie vrees nie oom god is werklik wie hy sê hy is. Sy hand is mev op verseker sy kinders. Jy mom, Jesus sit elke nag op my bed. Sal iemand verstaan hy is so baie lief vir sy kinders. Hy sê vrees is nie van hom nie. Lees matt 25, rut hy is besig om olie vol en vol te maak. Jesus is so naby mev sal jy wat Jesus vra doen. maak die bruid wakker in die kerk hee belangrikste is, het jy hom lief? Waarom trust jy dan nie hy sal vir jou sorg.

Jesus says that you should not fear when you see that the fig tree is not budding. He is definitely on His way. The earth and everything on it belong to Him. Can He not take care of you too, Mister? You need not fear, Mister – God is who He says He is. He keeps His hands over His children. Mom, Jesus sits on my bed every night. Everyone needs to understand that He loves His children so very much. He says fear is not from Him. Read Matthew 25, Ruth. He is busy increasing the oil. Jesus is so close, Ma'am. Will you do what Jesus asks of you? Awaken the Bride in the Church. The most important of all is: Do you love Him? Why then don't you trust Him to take care of you?

Possess your land

The reason the Son of God appeared was to destroy the devil's work.
- 1 John 3:8b -

Jesus came to earth to do the will of the Father and that was to destroy the works of the devil. Therefore, you can be assured that it is definitely the Father's will for you to be set free from Satan's bondage. After God's glorious light broke through in our family, and the works of Satan were revealed and destroyed by the blood of the Lamb, only then could Aldo start dancing to God's melody for his life. In the spirit he is now free to fulfil the task that God has called him to do and to receive his inheritance in the Promised Land. The enemy used the bloodline curses which originated from racism and hatred as a channel through which he tried to steal Aldo's calling, *but* the wonderful news is that his efforts were thwarted by the Word of God which is sharper than a two-edged sword.

Wysh se hy is by my hy is lief vw my. het hy vuur vuur seën op my gegooi. Wysh wil hê mense moet repent sodat hy vir hulle kan help om vry te kom. Wysh sê saam is ons deel van huis van god army van god wat moet opstaan en begin veg hy sê nou seën nou.

Wisdom says He is with me. He loves me. He threw fire, fire, blessing on me. Wisdom wants people to repent, so that He can help them to be free. Wisdom says together we are part of the house of God, and the army of God that must stand up and start fighting. He says now. Bless now.

God is Spirit and we are made in His image, and therefore our spirit is designed to walk in full victory over the things of this world. This means we can live in abundance of love, joy, peace, patience, kindness, goodness, faithfulness, gentleness and self-control even amidst the storms of life. In this way we, as citizens of heaven, will enable God's Kingdom to be made manifest here on earth. All the good things that God desires for your life can be found *in* Him – in His Trinity, in His glorious light and in the river of life that flows from His throne!

So often people ask me how can they know what God's calling and purpose are for their lives. First and foremost, God's highest calling for every individual is to love the Lord your God with all your heart, with all your soul, with all your mind and with all your strength; and to love your neighbour as yourself. The commandment to love should always be our guidepost. If you live according to this commandment, you will be victorious - no matter what your circumstances might be!

Jesus sê julle leer toe om die warrior bruid te wees. toe jy van oggend nagmaal hulle vlug toe. bloed van Jesus laat hulle vlug. sê vir mense Jesus is wat hulle nodig het mom my mom.

Jesus says you are learning how to be the Warrior Bride. When you partook in communion this morning they [the demons] fled. The blood of Jesus makes them flee. Tell people Jesus is what they need, Mom.

The Israelites were redeemed from slavery in Egypt by applying the blood of the lamb on the doorframe of their homes, and after the exodus they were led to Mount Sinai, where God revealed Himself to them. However, they all died in the Wilderness, and only the next generation was allowed to enter the Promised Land. The reason for this was their sinful and unbelieving hearts:

> So, as the Holy Spirit says: "Today, if you hear his voice, do not harden your hearts as you did in the rebellion, during the time of testing in the desert, where your fathers tested and tried me and for forty years saw what I did. That is why I was angry with that generation, and I said, 'Their hearts are always going astray, and they have not known my ways.' So I declared on oath in my anger, 'They shall never enter my rest.'" See to it, brothers, that none of you has a sinful, unbelieving heart that turns away from the living God.
> - Hebrews 3:7-12 -

Of that generation only Joshua and Caleb were allowed to enter the Promised Land. The other Israelites never received their inheritance and worst of all, they never entered into God's *rest*. It wasn't because God didn't want to give it to them, but they disqualified themselves from receiving it by their "sinful, unbelieving hearts".

Christ is our Promised Land. Our calling is to pursue Him and to be transformed into His image. By pursuing the biggest prize of our calling (that is to live in Christ and in His rest) we will also fulfil God's calling and purpose for our lives.

The first generation of Israelites missed out on God's rest completely. By studying the example of the Israelites, we can identify three phases in our walk with Christ:

1) Egypt: Redemption from slavery and the kingdom of darkness.

> "... because the LORD loves you, and because He would keep the oath which He swore to your fathers, the LORD has brought you out with a mighty hand, and redeemed you from the house of bondage, from the hand of Pharaoh king of Egypt."
> - *Deuteronomy 7:8, NKJV* -

2) The Wilderness: This is a time when our hearts are tested and refined like gold. Here we lay down our lives and die to ourselves in order to be resurrected in Christ.

> "And you shall remember that the LORD your God led you all the way these forty years in the wilderness, to humble you and test you, to know what was in your heart, whether you would keep His commandments or not. So He humbled you, allowed you to hunger, and fed you with manna which you did not know nor did your fathers know, that He might make you know that man shall not live by bread alone; but man lives by every word that proceeds from the mouth of the LORD. Your garments did not wear out on you, nor did your foot swell these forty years. You should know in your heart that as a man chastens his son, so the LORD your God chastens you."
> - *Deuteronomy 8:2-5, NKJV* -

3) The Promised Land: Where we have to walk by faith and fully trust God to gain victory over the giants in order to possess our land.

> "Therefore you shall keep the commandments of the LORD your God, to walk in His ways and to fear Him. For the LORD your God is bringing you into a good land, a land of brooks of water, of fountains and springs, that flow out of valleys and hills; a land of wheat and barley, of vines and fig trees and pomegranates, a land of olive oil and honey; a land in which you will eat bread without scarcity, in which you will lack nothing; a land whose stones are iron and out of whose hills

you can dig copper. When you have eaten and are full, then you shall bless the LORD your God for the good land which He has given you.
- Deuteronomy 8:6-10, NKJV -

Born again Christians follow the same pattern. We are redeemed from the world through the blood of the Lamb. The world is that place where we are still controlled by the lusts of the flesh and where everything revolves around our selfish needs. Sadly, this pursuit of happiness and freedom apart from God's ordinances will only bring us into bondage to the same things that we are pursuing. What makes it even worse is that so few people realise that even with a "Christian" sign hanging around their neck, they can still be enslaved to the bondages of Egypt.

Those who live according to the sinful nature have their minds set on what that nature desires; but those who live in accordance with the Spirit have their minds set on what the Spirit desires. The mind of sinful man is death, but the mind controlled by the Spirit is life and peace
- Romans 8:5-6 -

In order to be delivered from the yoke of slavery the Israelites had to pass through the Red Sea. A task that was humanly impossible – God had to intervene supernaturally. And so it is with us too: we cannot deliver ourselves from Egypt, but God has made a way for us through baptism into Christ.

"For you are all sons of God through faith in Christ Jesus. For as many of you as were baptized into Christ have put on Christ."
- *Galatians 3:26-27, NKJV* -

After we move out of Egypt we immediately find ourselves in the Wilderness. The tests and trials of the Wilderness reveal what is truly in our hearts. From the Israelite's example we see that we can easily fail these tests if we aren't wholeheartedly devoted to God. Eventually their grumbling, rebellion, obstinacy, pride and unbelief caused their bodies to be scattered in the Wilderness and kept them from entering the Promised Land.

Moreover, brethren, I do not want you to be unaware that all our fathers were under the cloud, all passed through the sea, all were baptized into Moses in the cloud and in the sea, all ate the same spiritual food, and all drank the same spiritual drink. For they drank of that spiritual Rock that followed them, and that Rock was Christ. But with most of them God was not well pleased, for their bodies were scattered in the wilderness.

> Now these things became our examples, to the intent that we should not lust after evil things as they also lusted. And do not become idolaters as were some of them. As it is written, "The people sat down to eat and drink, and rose up to play." Nor let us commit sexual immorality, as some of them did, and in one day twenty-three thousand fell; nor let us tempt Christ, as some of them also tempted, and were destroyed by serpents; nor complain, as some of them also complained, and were destroyed by the destroyer. Now all these things happened to them as examples, and they were written for our admonition, upon whom the ends of the ages have come.
> *- I Corinthians 10: 1-11, NKJV -*

The real test of the Wilderness is not the scorching sun or the lack of food and water (for God will supernaturally provide in all our needs), but rather the *response of our hearts* as we face these obstacles. Will we trust God, or will we rebel in our hearts and want to turn back to the false security of Egypt?

The Wilderness is an arid and dry place, but it is also where we have the opportunity to get to know God intimately without any distractions. It is a place of total dependence on Him. In the Wilderness He alone is our source of protection and providence – for we have nowhere else to turn.

When you find yourself in a Wilderness season, don't think that God has forgotten about you or that He is ignoring your prayers. See it for what it is: A time of preparation and purification; a time during which we get to learn how to trust and to fear Him. Unfortunately there are no shortcuts. Without passing through the Wilderness there can be no Promised Land.

The tragic part about the Israelites' story is that they didn't learn their lesson. During their years in the Wilderness they were constantly opposing God and never turned to Him in complete submission and trust. They kept longing for the delicacies of Egypt and questioned God's wisdom for leading them into the Wilderness. In the end it cost them dearly. Because they never learnt to trust Him in the Wilderness, they didn't know how to trust Him when they arrived at the border of the Promised Land. At the first sight of the giants they wanted to turn back to Egypt! They were so close, but yet so far – all because they wasted their Wilderness experience (see Num. 13 and 14).

> For who, having heard, rebelled? Indeed, was it not all who came out of Egypt, led by Moses? Now with whom was He angry forty years? Was it not with those who sinned, whose corpses fell in the wilderness? And to whom did He swear that they would not enter His rest, but to those who did not obey? So we see that they could not enter in because of unbelief.
> *- Hebrews 3:16-19, NKJV -*

Only Joshua and Caleb together with the next generation were eventually allowed to enter the Promised Land. The Promised Land holds our inheritance, but we need courage, sincere faith and pure hearts in order to receive what God has promised us. The Israelites had to drive out the foreign nations little by little. This kept them dependant on God, knowing that it was He who won their battles, and not because of their own strength and ability.

> Moreover, the Lord your God will send the hornet among them until even the survivors who hide from you have perished. Do not be terrified by them, for the Lord your God, who is among you, is a great and awesome God. The Lord your God will drive out those nations before you, little by little. You will not be allowed to eliminate them all at once, or the wild animals will multiply around you. But the Lord your God will deliver them over to you, throwing them into great confusion until they are destroyed. He will give their kings into your hand, and you will wipe out their names from under heaven. No one will be able to stand up against you; you will destroy them.
> - Deuteronomy 7:20-24 -

The same applies to us – the key to possessing the Promised Land is faith in God. We cannot enter into the Promised Land and reign there if we do not walk by faith.

My prayer is that you will realise that it is possible for every believer to walk in the fullness of Jesus Christ, and this includes you! It is possible for us to be free from darkness and slavery and to move and live and have our being in Christ (Acts 17:28). Because of Jesus' blood, we can boldly go to the throne of grace, and through our relationship with Abba Father, Jesus and the Holy Spirit, we can enjoy the treasures of the Promised Land every day.

According to the first covenant the Israelites didn't have access to this special place before the throne of grace. God met with Moses at the Ark of the Covenant and Moses conveyed God's Word to the rest of the nation (see Ex. 25:16-22). Thereafter, only the high priest was allowed to enter into the Holy of Holies, and he was only allowed to enter once a year.

> For we do not have a High Priest who is unable to sympathize with our weaknesses, but we have one who has been tempted in every way, just as we are – yet was without sin. Let us then approach the throne of grace with confidence, so that we may receive mercy and find grace to help us in our time of need.
> - Hebrews 4:15-16 -

As partakers of the New Covenant, we have unlimited access to the throne of grace through our High Priest Jesus Christ, and we can enjoy an intimate relationship with the King of kings because of our position.

my beste is die troonkamer. Wys werk mamma Jesus is oppad met h wit perd, ek het hom gesien hy se mehse sal almar hom sien. ook die wat nie glo nie. Love you mom.

I love the throne room the most. Wisdom says work, Mommy – Jesus is on His way on a white horse. I saw Him. He says all people will see Him. Also those who don't believe. Love you, Mom.

God speaks to us from a throne of grace that is situated in the Holy of Holies because that is His dwelling place. This is the throne of God and of the Lamb (see Rev. 22:1). Do you wonder how it is possible to approach this throne while you are still here on earth? The answer lies in the spirit. The same Christ who is now sitting on the throne in heaven, is also residing in us (see Rom. 8:10).

The kingdom of God is in us, and Jesus Christ is the One who brings the Kingdom of Heaven to earth, and places it inside each one of us. God dwells in our spirit; and the Father is looking for those who worship Him in spirit and in truth - from our spirit unto God's Spirit (see John 4:23).

The journey to receive our inheritance starts with the *decision* to leave Egypt. Then we have to be patient and obedient while we travel through the Wilderness; and not turn back in fear when we reach the border of the Promised Land and see the giants that still need to be conquered. Just beyond the border of our fear and unbelief is where His *rest* is eagerly awaiting us, but in order to enter into that rest, we have to trust Him.

The road of surrendering, laying down our lives, dying to self, and trusting God for the victory, was the road we had to travel on during the past six years as a family.

Jesus sê wat jy vir my deurgaan sal jy sien wat julle kroon is in die hemel.

Jesus says you will see the crown in heaven that you will receive because of what you are going through for me.

It was a road that kept us humble. We were so dependent on God that we didn't want to risk living outside His will and His light even for one second. It required of us to die to our old ways and we learned many hard lessons in the process. A big part of the old Retah died along that road through the Wilderness. Through the years we not only saw that God is faithful, but we also saw for ourselves that His Word is truth as we lived on His daily manna. As with Joshua and Caleb, we truly got to know the Lord as the *God of love who keeps His promises*. It was God's love and our surrendering to Him that allowed us to conquer the giants and possess our Promised Land.

Looking back, I realise that even though I was wrong about so many things, God never left me. He patiently guided me through the Wilderness and He kept me standing in spite of all my hurt and pain. He even allowed me to minister to other people, even though I made many mistakes in my own life and still had a lot to learn. The wilderness has taught me that my life is not about *my* hopes, dreams and desires, or even *my* hurt and pain, but that it is all about Him. The only way that we can faithfully serve in His kingdom is if we lay down our life, pick up our cross and follow Jesus – regardless where He leads us. I realised that the more I lived in total dependence on God, the easier it became to die to self and to obey Him.

Even though my road through the Wilderness is one of many tears, I would not exchange the place of intimacy, love and unity with Him that the journey had given me for anything in the world. It is like the Psalmist says: *Better is one day in your courts than a thousand elsewhere; I would rather be a doorkeeper in the house of my God than dwell in the tents of the wicked* (Psalm 84:10).

Jy sy servant wat so gehoorsaam is. Jy servant wat waarheid

verkondig. Jesus sê by Lom is
versêker het krag wat
wêreld nie kan gee nie.

You are His obedient servant. You are His servant that preaches the truth.

Jesus says with Him is power that the world will never be able to give.

People's opinions and criticism no longer move me, and more than ever I stand firm in the assurance of the calling that God has placed upon my life. I have stopped trying to be a people pleaser; all I now want to do is to love my King and bring Him glory.

Each of us has a very special purpose for our lives. We are all unique and that means we are irreplaceable within the body of Christ. Whatever your calling is, do it without comparing yourself to others. Focus on Jesus, and follow His lead.

mer wat jy nie
verstaan nie is Jesus ura
heilige lewe nie nou hou
pad sal almal loop nie.

Ma'am, what you don't understand is that Jesus asks a holy life. It is a narrow, narrow road that not everyone is willing to walk.

One of our greatest breakthroughs came in August 2010 when Aldo ministered with me in Pakistan. Six years earlier while I was standing next to his hospital bed, and the doctors gave me little hope that he would survive, God gave me a promise that Aldo would tell the world that Jesus is alive. Never in my wildest dreams did I think that this is what God had in mind.

Tinus and I were speechless when we saw how powerfully God used Aldo. Before we entered any room or building, Aldo went before us and chased the demons under Jesus' feet and bound their works. We saw him standing firmly in the spiritual authority he has received through Christ. At night he spent hours with the Word and quoted scriptures regarding our mission, and why God sent us to Pakistan.

Pakistan is mainly a Muslim country and we could hear their prayers and worship to Allah through the microphones every day. The spiritual atmosphere was heavy with resistance, and every night Aldo wrote letters inspired by Wisdom, revealing things to us that we wouldn't have otherwise known. Tinus and I were in awe of how God used our temporarily "handicapped" son, who had been in such intense pain only a few weeks earlier, to reach out to the nations with Christ's love.

Aldo is busy with his final year of school and next year he will travel and minister with me on a more regular basis. He still speaks slowly and has difficulty walking on his own, but God uses him in a way that exceeds my wildest dreams. When he stretches out his hands to pray for healing or when he baptises people in the small pool at my office, I see the Kingdom of God in action. God lets His power flow through him because he is an empty vessel that has been filled with God's love.

Wysh sê hou vas aan eerste beloftes

jy sal sien hoe hemel hy sê aarde toe kom.

Wisdom says that you have to hold on to the first promises. He says that you will see how heaven comes to earth.

In my previous book I spoke a lot about Aldo's need for friendship and female friends. Once again I can only say that Abba knows the desires of our hearts and that it is His delight to fulfil those desires. He has sent Aldo a precious lady friend, Chantel, who has brought so much fun and laughter back into his life. Bradley (his old school friend) still comes to visit him regularly on Sundays and then Aldo tells him all about the ministry that God has prepared for him and how excited he is to be a part of God's plan for the nations.

Aldo and Chantel.

Often when I look at Aldo, who is now happily living his life without a shunt in his brain, I think to myself: *What a great and faithful God we serve!* All He requires of us is to love Him, and to trust Him. When we love Him, we will obey Him; and when we trust Him, we will have the faith to believe His Word and act upon it. All the pain and suffering we endured taught me the importance of having strong and fortified "city walls" like Nehemiah, and that I should never cease to watch and pray at the gates. I also learned how much power there is in the blood of the Lamb and that it brings healing and deliverance.

> Ja ek is vry mom want
> ons is nou oorlog wenners
> Jy is wat hy vra
> Warrior bruid

Yes I am free now, Mom, because we have won the war. You are what He

asks for: Warrior Bride.

Today, more than ever, I know that God *is* LOVE. The sword that the warrior bride holds in her hand is called LOVE, and only with His love can we conquer evil. I don't know how far along you are on your journey from Egypt to the Promised Land, but today I want to ask you to examine your own heart and to ask God to reveal to you what is inside. Maybe there are still traces of racism, lust, pride or tradition hidden somewhere – you have to look! It is when we try to avoid or deny these dark secrets that we are bound to the kingdom of darkness, and are robbed of an abundant life.

> Wysh se my siel sal wev genees

Wisdom says my soul will heal again.

"Behold, the days are coming, says the LORD, when I will make a new covenant with the house of Israel and with the house of Judah - not according to the covenant that I made with their fathers in the day when I took them by the hand to lead them out of the land of Egypt; because they did not continue in My covenant, and I disregarded them, says the LORD. For this is the covenant that I will make with the house of Israel after those days, says the LORD: I will put My laws in their mind and write them on their hearts; and I will be their God, and they shall be My people. None of them shall teach his neighbour, and none his brother, saying, 'Know the LORD,' for all shall know Me, from the least of them

When looking back over the past few months of my ministry, I realise how little I knew when I started years ago. I can now see how God has transformed my heart of stone to a heart that has His laws written upon it. This new heart is now filled with compassion, love and understanding for everyone who is walking on this road out of Egypt to the Promised Land with me. I am the last person to criticise another person's mistakes, for I made so many myself. Today I am able to look at the men and women walking next to me on this pilgrimage, and no matter what they may be struggling with, I want to stretch out my hand towards them and say: "Allow me to help you. I have been where you are, and I know how broken and alone you feel, but I can testify that God's grace will carry you through. It is okay not to understand everything yet – just allow the Holy Spirit to show you the next step. You'll get there in the end."

His grace was enough to overcome my mistakes, and even though I didn't always use the right words, His Spirit still ministered through me to others in a powerful way. I didn't have all the knowledge, but I did know the character of my God: He *is* Love.

This is what the Lord says: "Let not the wise man boast of his wisdom or the strong man boast of his strength or the rich man boast of his riches, but let him who boasts boast about this: that he understands and knows me, that I am the Lord, who exercises kindness, justice and righteousness on earth, for in these I delight," declares the Lord.
- Jeremiah 9:23-24 -

humble so humble
in aak hier die nehemia
bou my, humble sê god
maak hy my.

Building Nehemiah's wall is making me humble, so humble.

Humble, says God, is what He is making me.

Today I am a hundred times more sensitive to the leading of the Spirit of God, and my spiritual eyes are open and alert to what is happening in the spiritual realm. When I now see a finger pointed towards me in judgement, I cannot help but to immediately bless that person, because I have discovered the power of blessing. God's way of doing things will always lead to victory, and if He tells me that I should bless my enemies, who am I to disagree? I realise now that judgement and destructive criticism is fire from hell. It is just a sign of immaturity and pride. I no longer want to look around and measure myself against others, or determine my value based on other people's opinion of me. I want to be led by His Spirit and do what His Word teaches me, because, those who are led by the Spirit of God are sons of God (see Rom. 8:14).

The hour is now. Wisdom says he turns tears into laughter. America, He says that help is from God. Wisdom says He is with His children that trust in Him. Trust. Luke 21:28. Wisdom says that He shows people signs. God is who can help you.

> When these things begin to take place, stand up and lift up your heads, because your redemption is drawing near.
> - Luke 21:28 -

I believe we are in the hour where the hearts of the fathers must turn back to the children, and the hearts of the children to their fathers (see Mal. 4:6). We should move out of our religious comfort zones and really get to know the heart of our heavenly Father – a heart of unconditional love that always wants to embrace His children.

We are made in the image of God, and I believe if our physical heart has four chambers, that God's heart also has four chambers. The Holy Spirit has revealed to me that the first chamber is a garden. It is where the Father wants us to build our relationship with Him. This is the place where we meet Him in the coolness of the evening wind, where we wait on Him and learn that He will never disappoint us. It is a place where we can share all our problems and secrets with Him, and where He laughs and cries with us. Sometimes I lie down on the grass with my head on His lap, not saying anything – I only want to enjoy His peace that envelops me like a blanket while I'm there. When I am in His garden I can understand the song of the birds: "Holy, holy, holy is the Lord God Almighty." The whole of creation continually sings it to Him. In the garden He teaches me that the lilies of the field (my favourite flowers) are actually His love letter to me, that the smell of the soil is the fragrance of His presence, and the sound of the rain are the many thoughts He thinks about me each day.

hy is ryk aan Jesus sê genade.

Jesus says He is rich in mercy.

The second chamber is the "soaking room", where we can soak up His anointing and presence. This is where He anoints us with fresh oil and where the anointing breaks every yoke. Here we learn about His character and become saturated with His presence. This fragrance clings to us wherever we go and other people will recognise God's fragrance lingering around us: *For we are to God the aroma of Christ among those who are being saved and those who are perishing* (2 Col. 2:15).

The third chamber is the training room. This is where the bride is clothed with the armour of light and where God teaches her how to fight the enemy – all for the sake of love. Psalm 18:29-34 says: *With your help I can advance against a troop; with my God I can scale a wall. As for God, his way is perfect; the word of the Lord is flawless. He is a shield for all who take refuge in him. For who is God besides the Lord? And who is the Rock except our God? It is God who arms me with strength and makes my way perfect. He makes my feet like the feet of a deer; he enables me to stand on the heights. He trains my hands for battle; my arms can bend a bow of bronze.*

In the training room He also teaches us the importance of obedience. We can only be a part of His army if we are willing to be led by His Holy Spirit. In any army, the weak link in the battalion is not the weakest person, but the one who disobeys the Commander. Rebellion and pride will always lead to defeat. The training we receive in this chamber enables us to destroy the works of the enemy and to free ourselves from bondage by following the Prince of peace into battle.

Jy is 'n warrior sê god

Wysh is in beheer van my lewe: Jesus is hier mev sê vir my is lief vir my.

You are a warrior, says God. Wisdom is in control of my life. Jesus is here, Ma'am. He tells me that He loves me.

The last chamber is the dance floor, and that is our romantic place of intimacy with the living God. Here we learn to trust Him completely, because Jesus is the one who leads and we simply have to follow.

It is in this room that I spend my most precious time with the King, for it is here where I surrender everything into His hands. I feel so secure when He leads me around the dance floor that I just close my eyes and rest against His breast. As I place my head on His chest I can hear the sound of His heartbeat and that becomes the rhythm of the song we dance to. Although the tempo of His heartbeat changes from time to time, His song always has the same chorus: "Just trust and obey... just trust and obey..."

In this place of intimacy with my Beloved, my desire for Him is so great that I never want to leave, because being in His embrace is the most wonderful place in the whole universe. Not many words are spoken here; and sometimes my tears say more than my words ever could.

The bride is the one who is so in love with Jesus that He captivates her every thought. I have learned that my love relationship with God is the source of my joy. It is my strength and my life. It is a relationship built on trust, not laws. We belong to our Bridegroom (who also happens to be the King of kings), and we are His most prized possession. We should take up our authority and rule with Him as we submit to His lordship. His kingdom is a kingdom of love and peace and light, and we should be ambassadors of His love and peace and light to those who are still sitting in darkness. God is the one who has placed our family on this extraordinary journey of faith, it is not something we went looking for. What I have shared with you is my life story, not theoretical dogmas. That is why I am asking you today to learn from my mistakes so that you and your family can be spared a lot of unnecessary tears and frustration.

Take a long hard look at your own heart and deal with what you find in there, so that you won't be the "drain" of hatred, racism, unforgiveness, fear or whatever else might be used by the enemy to gain access to your family and the generations to come. Make a choice to bow the knee before God. Repent and lay down your life for Jesus so that the drain can be closed; because it does not only affect you, but also your children and your children's children.

verharde harte hy sê verharde harte is 'n vloek.

Hardened hearts – He says a hardened heart is a curse.

May you realise after reading this book that it doesn't matter how caught up you are in your past mistakes, in sickness, hatred, pride, lust or any other form of hurt – there is always hope. No matter what the burden you carry looks like, Jesus has already paid the full price for you and me to be totally free.

Just keep to the one thing that God has asked of us right from the start: *"Love the Lord your God with all your heart and with all your soul and with all your mind and with all your strength." The second is this: "Love your neighbour as yourself." There is no commandment greater than these* (Mark 12:30-31).

In absolute humility and gratefulness I can say to you today: *There is always hope!* And because Jesus our Messiah truly lives, I know that this promise belongs to me and my household and all the generations to come after us:

> "As for me, this is my covenant with them," says the Lord. "My Spirit, who is on you, and my words that I have put in your mouth will not depart from your mouth, or from the mouths of your children, or from the mouths of their descendants from this time on and forever," says the Lord.
> - Isaiah 59:21 -

Retah

wys weer hoe Jesus weer
kom op die wolke en
ons kom haal God'
dit gaan vinniger
wees as wat mense
dink. God sê wie
hie hom v Jesus
werklik aanneem nie
sal verlore wees.

He shows me again how Jesus is coming on the clouds to fetch us. God says it is going to happen quicker than people think. God says: "Those who don't truly accept Jesus as their Saviour will be lost."

Chapter 13

Jy is vegter
mom en dad en Josh
wysh sê julle is moeg maar
julle reg steeds. mom julle
is al wat ek het baie dankie.

nehemia se bevel om die muur
te bou is nie maklik nie
Jy is baie seer maar ek
vra jou mooi hou aan saam
my bou. Julle self word
verander voor my oë my
mr en mev het god se vuur.
Josh is ek reageer net anders
as baie ander kinders wat
hierdeur jou gaan. hy self sal
jy sien hoe eendag hy sterk
sal wees mev god hou ons
vas ons al 4 moenie weer
sê jy gaan ophou bedien nie.
Want vyand wil hy wil
nie hê brein moet genees nie.
Jesus is by my wat my wat
so seermaak is brein wat heeltyd
vog kort. brein is so seer
hulle hou aan my vog vat.
Jy is sewe nehemia sewe jaar
wat jy moet help bou wag
net uit hou nehemia want wat
het Jesus gesê, hy het gesê sewe
jaar wat hy beminde wev voor
werk gegee het. hy het Jesus gesê
hy sê uldo sal jy vir my terug
gaan en sewe jaar self sterf

You are real fighters Mom, Dad and Josh. Wisdom says you are tired, but you are still fighting. You are all that I have. Thank you. Nehemiah's command to build the wall is not an easy one. You are hurting a lot, but I beg of you to keep on building with me. All of you are being changed before my very eyes. My Ma'am and Mister have God's fire. Josh too. He reacts differently to the way in which most children would have if they had to go through what he is going through. You will see for yourself how strong he will be one day. Ma'am, God holds us close to Him. Not one of us should ever say again that you shouldn't minister, because the enemy doesn't want my brain to be healed. Jesus is with me. Ma'am, what is causing you so much is the fact that my brain needs fluid. My brain is hurting a lot. They keep on taking the fluid of my brain. Nehemiah, you need to help build the wall for seven years. Be patient and endure. Remember what Jesus said – He said that He gave you, His Beloved Ma'am, work to do to for seven years. He said "Aldo, will you go back for me, and die to yourself for seven years?"

A letter from Josh:

Soms gaan ons deur moeilike tye.
maar God het ons gehelp. Ek het
geleer om vir mense te vergewe
want haat is nie van Jesus nie.
My hart was seer toe Aldo siek was
maar al was hy siek was dit nie moeilik
vir my om hom aan te hou liefhê nie.
Wat my bly gemaak het is dat ALDO
die eerste keer in drie jaar gelag
het. Toe ALdo siek was toe kon ons nie
sokker Speel nie maar nou dat hy
gesond is kan ons eenige ding doen

Ek wil graag ook iets vir Jesus doen

ek wil mense liefhê en hulle seën
elke dag. Ek is bly my mamma bedien
vir mense al is sy weg van die huis
af, want Jesus het haar gestuur. Ek
gaan ook eendag bedien want ek is
baie lief vir ons en hy sorg baie
goed vir ons. Ek is 'n man van God. My
pappa is baie lief vir ons en vir God.
Ek leer Aldo ook om nie te wens hy
kan weer rugby speel nie, want
hy is terug gestuur om vir mense
te vertel dat Jesus leef. Onthou my
boetie se bediening het reeds
begin. Ek slaap in die aand in Jesus
se arm of sy skoot. Nooit is ek
bang vir die donker of die vyand nie.

Ek speel sokker en swem vir Jesus.
Ek weet ek is nog klein maar ek
verstaan dat seer my nader aan
Jesus vat. Jesus is baie lief vir my.
My pappa gaan altyd saam met my
as ek iets wil doen. Moya (My hond) het
ook Heilige Gees in haar. Haar stert
klap as ek bid, en sy hou nagmaal saam

met ons. As ek gaan stap gesels ek met Heilige Gees. Heilige Gees help my ook met somme. My grootste les was moenie ophou glo nie, Jesus hoor as ek bid. Ek is baie gelukkig in my hart en Aldo sal ek help vir altyd.

Liefde Josh

Sometimes we go through difficult times, but God helps us. I have learned how to forgive people, because hatred is not from Jesus. My heart was hurting when Aldo was sick, but even when he was sick it wasn't difficult for me to keep on loving him. What made me happy was when Aldo laughed for the first time in three years. When Aldo was sick we couldn't play soccer, but now that he is healthy again we can do anything!

I want to do something for Jesus as well. I want to love people and bless them every day. I am glad that my mommy ministers to people, even if she is away from home sometimes – because Jesus sent her to do that. I am also going to minister one day, because I love our Jesus so much and He takes care of us. I am a man of God. My daddy loves us and God very much. I also teach Aldo not to wish that he will be a rugby player one day, because he was sent back to tell people that Jesus is alive. Remember, my brother's ministry has already started. At night I sleep in Jesus' arms, or in His lap. I am never scared of the dark or of the enemy. I play soccer and swim for Jesus. I know I am still young, but I understand that heartache draws me closer to Jesus. Jesus loves me very much. My daddy always goes with me when I want to do something. Moya, my dog, also has the Holy Spirit in her. She wags her tail when we pray and she takes communion with me. When I go for a walk I talk to Holy Spirit. Holy Spirit also helps me with my math sums. The biggest lesson I have learned is not to give up. Jesus hears me when I pray. I am very happy in my heart and I will help Aldo forever.

Love Josh.

Before my eyes I see the "grace" of God growing up, because I see Abba Father honouring a mother's prayer. It was on a cold winter's night six years ago that our accident happened. That night I pleaded with God: "Abba Father, my little Josh is only two years old. I beg of You Lord, with everything inside of me, please hold him safely in the palm of Your hand and never let him go!" That was my prayer on the night of the accident as I was sitting next to his hospital bed. We had waited so many years for him, and now he had to experience so much pain at such a young age.

I was sitting in my car in front of the primary school in Hartebeespoort one afternoon, waiting for the school bell to ring so I could take my little Josh home. As I sat waiting I observed how the other cars were coming and going, and it struck me how rushed our lives had become. My thoughts wandered back to that fateful night in the hospital and my desperate prayer to God. He was faithful. He was, and unquestionably still is, faithful!

My "Zozzie" jumped into the car. "Hi Mom! I love you! How was your day?" I smiled as I listened to him babbling on. "Mommy, I have hockey practice today and later only a half an hour's swimming lesson. Then Ma'am Patrys must help me with my spelling." While talking, he turned up the volume to his favourite song "Yeshua Messiah" playing on the radio. He sang along at the top of his voice, "Yeshua is the Messiah... honouring the King of Kings... Creator God of everything... Amen!" He sang along exuberantly; his eyes bright and filled with joy.

One morning I found a note on my bedside table after I had worked in my study well into the wee hours of the morning the previous night. The note was from Josh and it said: *Mom, wear your tennis outfit when you pick me up after school today – we can go and play a game of tennis first before you go back to the office.* I couldn't help smiling when I read his note, because this child of joy surely keeps me on my toes! "Mom, you can't just work all the time, you need to have some fun too!" he often admonishes me. That afternoon he was bent over with laughter as he watched me dashing after the tennis ball and gasping for breath. When I simply couldn't run any longer, we lay down together on the court and looked up at the clouds. While lying on our backs, we talked about anything and everything.

Josh's laughter comes straight from heaven and when he laughs neither Tinus nor I can hold back the tears. Aldo can still only make his laughing sound when he wants to laugh, and even that has been pretty scarce over these past few years. That is why Josh's laughter is like music from heaven; it makes up for the joy and laughter that we'd missed out on during those difficult years.

As a family, we just went through eight of the most difficult months of our lives. What broke my heart many nights was to see Josh standing with outstretched arms, fighting the spiritual battle alongside Tinus and myself, without anyone ever asking him to. I wanted to keep him away from it all, but it couldn't be helped. No matter how much we tried to protect him, he is a part of the family and therefore he is a part of our team.

Because he had to go through everything with us, he has learned about the reality of the spiritual dimension at a very young age. Today Josh is very sensitive to the spiritual realm and he has a good sense of discernment. One day a man walked past us in a shopping centre and Josh looked at me and asked, "Mom, did you see it in the spirit? That man is caught up in addiction."

Amazed I asked him, "And how do you know that, Josh?"

"Don't tell me that you didn't see what Jesus just showed me? Just look into his eyes, Mom – you'll see it too," he replied.

I could smell the alcohol as the man walked past us, but how could Josh have known? He is still too young to recognise the smell of alcohol. It could only have been the Holy Spirit who revealed it to him.

Josh watches over Aldo with a hawk's-eye. He will be the one who turns off the television in the middle of a rugby match if Aldo even mentions that he wants to be a professional rugby player one day. "No Aldo that is not why you were sent back. You were sent back to tell people that Jesus is alive. Forget about rugby – there is much greater things awaiting you!"

Aldo likes to take his Bible with him wherever he goes, and Josh is usually the one who reminds him when he forgets. Before school Josh will call from down stairs, "Remember to take you Bible, Aldo!" If Ma'am Patrys takes them to the Wimpy for a milkshake, and Aldo walks to the car without his Bible, Josh will run back and fetch it. Even if Aldo and I only want to go to the grocery store quickly and Aldo forgets his Bible at home, Josh will come running out to the car with the Bible in his hands, "Aldo! Your Bible!" He knows what makes his brother happy.

In the afternoons he and Aldo usually play a game of soccer, but as soon as the sun starts to set, he'll say to Aldo, "I think it is time you take your bath and get busy with the Word, Aldo – I have to go and do my homework now too." As I stand listening to them through the kitchen window, my heart swells with pride at Josh's maturity. Josh is a winner at everything he attempts, but he never takes his success for granted. Not a day goes by that he doesn't thank his Abba for his talents. At first we tried not to talk about his achievements in front of Aldo, but today Aldo is his biggest fan!

Every night before he goes to sleep, I still have to cuddle him and rub his back. I also have to do it before he covers himself with his tallit (traditional Jewish prayer shawl) to pray. One night before going to bed, I peeked into his room and saw him holding the one corner of his tallit while he was fast asleep. The next morning I asked him about it and he said, "I'm holding on to promises of God's Word, Mommy."

One night while lying next to him on his bed, rubbing his back, I heard him praying: "Jesus, today was so much fun! Thank You for the swimming class and that I can run and play hockey. There are so many things that I still want to tell You, but I am really tired now. So I am just going to say good night. Can I sleep on Your lap tonight, please? Love You!" In my spirit I saw Jesus smiling broadly over him because of his childlike faith that is so sincere and honest!

Everyone in our house has a tallit, and the rule is that when you are covered under your tallit and spending time with Abba Father, no one is allowed to bother you – time spent with the King is honoured and respected in our home. Only Aldo will try to bend this rule sometimes. If he walks into my room and sees that I am praying, he'll turn around and walk away; but on his way out, he'll say out loud what he had wanted to say anyway. While under my tallit, I always smile in secret at his sense of humour.

Josh also suffered because of what we went through after the accident. We could clearly see from his schoolwork that some weeks were more difficult at home than others; and during these periods he was also more quiet than usual. But today I can testify that Abba Father heard my prayer that night of the accident – and He carried Josh safely in His arms the whole time.

Aldo teaches Josh that when he struggles with his spelling tests that he should ask the Holy Spirit to help him, "He will help you with everything you struggle with, Josh! Even with your spelling! Just ask Him, and wait on Him."

"Yes, Aldo ... but then my teacher will ask me why I am just staring in front of me when I am supposed to answer her immediately."

"Josh, if you don't ask, you won't receive," Aldo replied. "The Holy Spirit helps me with my schoolwork – that is why I do so well."

Josh is the smile in our lives, but he also knows very well that he no longer belongs to us, because we gave him to God a long time ago. Many afternoons he'll say to me, "Mom, Moya and I are going to the bush." Then I get a quick kiss on my cheek and he speeds away on his bicycle with his backpack, and Moya running next to him. I know exactly what he has in his backpack: grape juice and crispbread. He then cycles to his secret place where he talks to Jesus and partakes in communion. He also prays for Moya and asks that Jesus keeps her safe, and cover her with His blood.

Retah and Josh at their holiday home in Yzerfontein.

Upon returning from his adventure one afternoon, he said to me as he came through the door, "Mom, did you know Moya is filled with the Holy Spirit?"

"And how do you know that?" I asked, curious to know how he came to this conclusion.

"Just watch her, Mom. When I start to pray, she wags her tail. Haven't you noticed how she wags her tail when we pray in the evenings? Even if she had been asleep, she will wake up and wag her tail while we pray."

While we were talking about this, he was holding Moya in his arms and she faithfully wagged her tail to agree.

Thank You Jesus that I can truly say today that You are faithful! You hear our prayers of supplication.

As I am typing this, Josh is patiently waiting for me to tuck him into bed. He is hugging me around my neck, and kissing me all over my face; and as he is doing this, I'm thinking: *Zozzie, I don't know if you realise this, but you will be any girl's dream! You love unconditionally. You know that true love means to love the imperfect perfectly, and you are so sure of God's love for you and of your love for Him. You are not scared to open your arms and to give love without expecting anything in return. I am going to start blessing your wife anew – because she is going to be so blessed to have you as her husband. You are a gift from God; you are our gift from God.*

I gave him a big kiss, and he immediately asked me if there was lipstick on his cheek.

"No, Josh, I'm wearing stay-on lipstick."

"That depends on who it 'stays on', Mom – on you or on me?"

"No, Josh," I laughed. "On *me* of course!"

Later, after I had washed off my make-up and put on some moisturizer I got into bed next to him to rub his back. I gave him another kiss on his forehead. This time I said, "This is a kiss that will never come off, Joshy. It is like the kiss that Abba Father gives you when you enter into the throne room and receive a revelation from Him. It is like the things He teaches you Himself – no one can ever take that away from you. Even if someone tells you that it's not true, you will know deep inside of you that it is true and that you can trust God. God's kisses cannot be wiped off; just like this kiss from Mommy – it will also remain on you forever. It doesn't matter whether other people can see it or not, you know it is there."

When we have our Shabbat dinner on Friday nights, Josh's favourite part is when Tinus prays the fatherly blessings over him. Tinus usually prays long, beautiful prayers and blessings over his sons, and by the time he is finished, Josh's forehead just about touches his plate. But when Tinus says *amen*, Josh will look up and ask if he can continue a little bit longer: "Oh, don't stop now, Daddy! Bless me some more."

This is how thirsty we are to receive the blessing of God in our lives! Our family has discovered the power of blessing. We use every possible opportunity to bless one another and in doing so we taste the sweet honey of blessing in our lives.

While I'm finishing up with the last chapters of this book, all of the McPhersies are under one roof at our beach house in Yzerfontein. Every now and again I stop typing to listen to the noise of the waves crashing against the rocks outside. We have shed so many tears in this house, but tonight it is tears of thankfulness. Josh is still playing around here somewhere because I haven't yet gotten round to tucking him in. Tinus is reading a book, and Aldo is already in Jesus' arms in the throne room. I can hardly believe how wonderful this picture is. We are so happy. The battle is won, and all four of us know that Jesus is living in us.

"Mommy, come rub my back, please," I now hear Josh calling from his room.

"Here I come, Zozzie, Jesus is waiting for us. Say good night to Daddy".

Chapter 14

Liewe   Pappa

Jesus sê jy   het
   nom   alles   gegee
hy   sê jy sal nie
 teleur gestel   word nie
   hy sê hy   hou jou
  vas   werk   meneer hy
 gaan alles   verander
voor jou   oë.   hy gaan
vir joy jou   begeerte
van jou   hart gee. Wys
heid   sê   jy   wyn geoffer
wysheid   sê jy sal
vinnig   God   se   genade
 hy   wil   jou   help wys
 my   hoe   jy   wysheid
 het   wysheid   wys jou

Dear Daddy,

Jesus says that you have given Him everything. He says that you won't be disappointed. He says that He is holding you. Work Mister, He will change everything before your eyes. He will give you the desires of your heart. Wisdom says that you have sacrificed your wine. Wisdom says that you will experience His grace. He wants to help you. He shows me that you have Wisdom. Wisdom will show you what to do.

A letter from Tinus: A life of abundance

Since our accident six years ago, the Lord has taken me on an amazing journey. Initially Aldo was doing very well. We often cycled together on our tandem bicycle and he had such a lust for life! Until the day the epileptic fits started...

We immediately cut back on our exercise, careful not to overexert him. His condition slowly deteriorated, and one day I looked at him and realised that we had a child who had no passion for life, who didn't want to eat much and whose health deteriorated by the day. We stood before the doctors in complete desperation looking for a medical explanation. We were totally blind to the fact that it was a spiritual battle that we were busy losing – because we had no idea that we were in a war against Satan!

Only after struggling for a year did we realise the intensity of the battle. We were desperate and there was no longer any medical explanation for Aldo's condition. It was only then that we realised we were not fighting against flesh and blood, but against powers and principalities of the air. It was a battle that we knew nothing about at that stage.

As father and head of my house, I have always endeavoured to protect my family and tried to find a solution for every problem; but this time I was at a complete loss. Seven months had passed during which I only slept two to three hours per night on average, and every morning I had to get up and go to work as usual. I couldn't tell anybody about our situation, because I knew that nobody would understand. We felt like aliens from outer space – completely alone in our circumstances, with no-one who could help us.

Jy is waarlik my redder pappa se liefde is my hulp.

You are truly my saviour. Daddy, your love is a great help to me.

For months we slept very little, but what we learned during those extra hours when we were kept awake is invaluable! One by one the breakthroughs started to happen and it usually happened in the early morning hours – when our flesh was exhausted and the Spirit (together with our spirit) could take over completely. Then I just lay face-down before God (in these situations I have learned that this is the best place for me to be), to become one with Him. I'd thank Him for His grace in my life and that He held me in such high esteem to choose me for this extraordinary road with Aldo. What I experienced and prayed during those early morning hours usually didn't make sense to my natural mind, but my spirit-man could see past the natural to such an extent that my circumstances no longer mattered. Through this my spirit became progressively stronger. It made me realise that to walk in the spirit means to be in synchronisation with God; to live and move with His rhythm. Then all the rest fades away, and all that matters is to be one with Him.

During the evenings I just sat with Aldo reading my Bible when he couldn't sleep. God is so faithful; He broke His Word open for me and through it He taught me everything I needed to know. My first lesson came from 2 Corinthians 10:3: *For though we live in the world, we do not wage war as the world does.*

baie baie baie dankie vir wat julle vir my gedoen het hulle kon nie my verslaan nie by vuur nie want baie van julle waarlike gebede het my gered.

Thank you so much for all that you have done for me. They could not defeat me with their fire, because all your prayers truly saved me.

The turning point for me was when Aldo walked out onto the balcony on the top floor of our house, and without any warning, fell over the railing as if he had simply been thrown over. He fell three metres and hit his face against the railing of the patio on the ground floor. I tried to grab hold of him before he fell, but I was too late. As I saw him hitting the railing with his mouth, my first thought was that he had broken his neck. The Lord protected him supernaturally and in the end he only shattered his front teeth and had to remain in hospital for a few days due to the complications with his shunt.

289

Needless to say, I was completely heartbroken. I felt responsible for not being able to protect him, but at the same time I was worn-out from our difficult road and all its challenges. I really called out to God for answers.

I had secretly hoped that everything would just disappear by itself and that I would wake up one morning and realise it had all been a bad dream. But that was never going to happen. The reality was that I had to take up my spiritual responsibility as the priest, prophet and king of my house. God had placed me as the head of my household and I had to be their spiritual covering.

Luke 10:19 says that we have been given the authority to trample on snakes and scorpions. This painful experience made me realise that through Jesus I have received both the authority and armour to defeat the invisible enemy – but it was up to me to use it.

Self het ook vuur Pappa
by Jesus gekry

Daddy, you also received fire from Jesus.

Once I took my stand, it felt to me as if I could move mountains! Every morning when I got out of bed and my feet touched the ground, I proclaimed anew who I was in Christ so that every demon could know that trouble was on the way. The breakthroughs became greater and more frequent, but still there were many nights when I ended up kneeling before God and the throne of grace as described in Hebrews 4:16. There I just praised and worshipped Him for His mercy and grace in our lives – and I told Him how totally dependent we are of Him.

The Lord also revealed to me that we can only operate in this authority if we understand the *Father-heart* of God. In the same way in which I want to protect Aldo and Josh with everything inside of me, so the Father wants to protect us – for we are His sons and daughters. The Holy Spirit confirmed this to me through a footnote to a verse of Scripture which read: "The Holy Spirit reveals the heart of the Father by creating a yearning for Him in our hearts – a yearning so intense that it cannot be put into words. It is an intimate time of intercession, and only the Holy Spirit can lead us into this season according to the Father's timing for our lives."

I now know that when life gets hard, I shouldn't wallow in self-pity and ask "Why me, Lord?" I should shift my focus higher, and rather ask the Lord what He wants to accomplish through my trial, and what He wants to teach me. And believe me, I have learned a lot up until now!

My prayer to God is that I won't miss one single thing that He wants to teach me, so I can be everything He wants me to be.

Help my baie JY is vegter
mom en dad en Josh
wysh se Julle is moeg maar
Julle reg steeds. mom Julle
is al wat ek het baie dankie

You help me a lot. You are fighters, Mom, and Dad and Josh. Wisdom says you are tired but you are still fighting. You are all that I have. Thank you.

Tinus and Aldo with Josh at his hockey game.

The greatest lesson that I have learned from this awakening to the reality of the spiritual world, is the fact that Jesus truly is alive! He is more real to me than the things I can see and touch. In light of this truth, the trials and tribulations I have to go through on earth seem small by comparison to the eternity I am going to spend with Jesus, who sits at the right hand of God. And to think, we could have missed it if it hadn't been for a car accident one winter's night in 2004.

Tinus

Baie dankie
Jesus vir my
o uers

Thank you very much Jesus for my parents.

Chapter 15

Jy is houaan Aldo hou
aan Aldo my werk is
nog nie klaar in jou nie. Seen
jou ouers Alda seen jou
boeta Aldo seen mam Patrys
Aldo want hulle gee hulle lewe
vir jou. Jy sal werklik opstaan
Jy het ja gesê vir my
Aldo sewe jaar sê ja
Jesus ek sal. vergewe
my rebellie. help my
asb Jesus
Aldo

Don't give up, Aldo; don't give up. My work is not finished in you yet. Bless your parents, Aldo. Bless your brother, Aldo. Bless Ma'am Patrys, Aldo; because they are giving their lives for you. You will truly stand up. You said yes to me. Aldo, seven years. Say yes. Jesus, I will. Forgive my rebellion. Please help me Jesus. Aldo.

A message from Ma'am Patrys:

I want to start by asking this: If you don't have experience or knowledge of the spiritual world, please do not close your heart to it. It is a reality and it is true! The Bible is filled with examples of this and in Ephesians it clearly states: *"For our struggle is not against flesh and blood, but against the rulers, against the authorities, against the powers of this dark world and against the spiritual forces of evil in the heavenly realms"* (Eph. 6:12).

It would be unwise to close your eyes to the reality of the spiritual realm, because whether you like it or not, you are just as much a part of the spiritual world as you are of the physical world. Ask the Holy Spirit to open your spiritual eyes and ears, and He will then reveal things to you that you previously didn't understand. Today I thank the Lord with a sincere heart for opening my eyes, for I once was blind too.

I believe that the time before Jesus' second coming is quickly running out, and that is why we are being trained so intensively in this hour. It wasn't an easy task to wage this spiritual war alongside Aldo, Tinus, Retah and Josh. Some days it felt as if my heart was going to break into a thousand pieces to see Aldo in so much pain, but today I can declare with conviction: "The Lord never leaves us nor forsakes us." In difficult times this promise in Isaiah 43:2-3 kept me standing: *When you pass through the waters, I will be with you; and when you pass through the rivers, they will not sweep over you. When you walk through the fire, you will not be burned; the flames will not set you ablaze. For I am the Lord, your God, the Holy One of Israel, your Savior.*

It was a strange and very difficult road for all of us, but God was always there! We only had to remain focused on Him and keep standing upon His Word. One of the things that stood out for me when I think back on this journey was how God supernaturally provided for us, and how He was always one step ahead of us! When we needed knowledge, He timely made it available. When we had to be encouraged, He strengthened us in a supernatural way or sent people to encourage us.

I still stand amazed at how the body of Christ stood together in unity when we needed it the most. When Aldo wrote down the names of the demons and the strange things they were trying to do to him, God sent us a very special lady, who had a lot of experience in spiritual warfare, to fight alongside us in the battle. She taught us so many things about the unseen realm and served us with such gentleness and love.

Some days when I didn't have a lot of strength I turned to my best friend and asked her to pray with us. Then the three of us (Aldo, my friend and I) would lay down on our faces on the carpet throughout the afternoon and seek the Lord's face.

It was wonderful to experience the breakthroughs that occurred when we praised and worshiped the Lord. I could see how the worship brought immediate relief for Aldo, and I too was encouraged and strengthened. Aldo and I would sing for hours, and even in this the Lord provided for me, because, believe me, I don't have a lot of singing talent! But the Lord put the words and melody in my heart. It was basically short Bible verses that we turned into songs. There truly is power in the Word of God! When we didn't know what to do, we just read aloud from the Bible. At night when Aldo slept, Tinus and Retah let him listen to the Word on his iPod and that also calmed and comforted him.

People often ask "why me?" when painful things happen. The spiritual world is a reality. It is a world that we cannot see and don't always understand. Even Jesus was tempted and harassed while He walked on earth. I believe the devil came to try to steal and destroy Aldo's life, but I can testify that God was faithful. He came to give us the victory, as is written in Colossians 2:15: *And having disarmed the powers and authorities, he made a public spectacle of them, triumphing over them by the cross.*

I believe we had to learn these things so we can now teach others. The devil desires to deceive and trap not only those who do not know Jesus as their Saviour yet, but believers too. When we resist and fight the enemy the Lord will give us the power to overcome the devil and thwart his plans, but there are strongholds of the enemy in our lives that have to be broken down first. It is time to take our place in the war against the devil and the evil forces!

Are you wearing your armour? Do you believe in the power of prayer? Do you know your enemy? Do you know who you are fighting against? If not, how can you expect to win if you know nothing about who you are fighting against?

You need spiritual weapons to win this war. What physical weapons can you use against the devil and his demons? Are you going to allow the devil to get a hold on your life, or are you going to use the powerful weapons that God has given us to resist him?

Wake up and prepare yourself for this spiritual battle that we are warned about in the book of Revelation. Take counsel from the Lord and study His Word. You will also learn that He loves you far more than you can ever imagine!

Know that you are not alone in your battle. The Lord promises in His Word that He is always with us in Spirit. In Psalm 91:10-11 it is written: *If you make the Most High your dwelling – even the Lord, who is my refuge – then no harm will befall you, no disaster will come near your tent. For he will command his angels concerning you to guard you in all your ways.*

We will never be able to attain the victory and live out our full potential unless we understand and recognise the spiritual world. That is why I am asking you again, open your heart and give God the opportunity to teach you.

Our victory over the Devil depends on how firmly we stand in Christ, and not on our own strength. Jesus had already won the war at Calvary, for you and for me! In His name you also have the victory!

> Submit yourselves, then, to God. Resist the devil, and he will flee from you.
> - James 4:7 -

Love

Patny

References

Brown, R. (1992). *He Came to Set the Captives Free*. Whitaker House.

Brown, R. (1995). *Unbroken Curses*. Whitaker House.

Cross, D. (2008). *Soul Ties: The Unseen Bond in Relationships.* Sovereign World Ltd.

Mendez- Ferrell, A. (1970). *Iniquity*

Prince, D. (1998). *They Shall Expel Demons: What You Need to Know About Demons - Your Invisible Enemies.* Chosen Publishing Group.

Prince, D. (2010). *Blessing or Curse: You Can Choose.* Baker Publishing Group.

Sheikh, B. (1982). *I Dared to Call Him Father*. Kingsway Publications.

Books can be ordered at www.amazon.com

Author and public speaker Retah McPherson is also the founder of Retah McPherson Ministries. As an ambassador of the Kingdom of God, she travels extensively around the world to proclaim the Gospel of Jesus Christ.

The motorcar accident that happened in 2004 set a series of events in motion that changed the lives of the McPhersons forever. Retah scaled down on her professional occupation to minister publicly, and she entered into full-time ministry in 2008. *Retah McPherson Ministries* is situated in Hartebeespoort, South Africa.

To contact *Retah McPherson Ministries*, please visit our website:
www.retahmcpherson.com
or contact us on:
Tel: +27 (0)82 610 5757
E-mail: office@retahmcpherson.com
Postal Address:
Retah McPherson Ministries
PO Box 793
Hartbeespoort
0216
South Africa

We would love to hear from you!

Visit the McPhersons online!

www.retahmcpherson.com

- **Stay updated with details surrounding the unfolding miracle by reading Retah's weekly messages and Aldo's latest letters.**
- **Order their testimonial book *A Message from God* (ISBN 978-0-620-38441-4) as well as the second book in the series, *From God: A Message of Faith* (ISBN 978-0-620-43580-2) and other related products.**
- **Invite Retah to speak at your event either in South-Africa or internationally.**
- **Partner with us and help us to reach out to others as ambassadors of the King of kings – Jesus of Nazareth.**

Made in the USA
San Bernardino, CA
27 February 2013